TAP–TAPS TO TRINIDAD

'The pictures on the brilliantly painted buses in Haiti are very similar to the paintings in fair grounds, and canal art, only more beautiful. The buses have wooden frames, ornately carved, and silver bells. They drive up and down the streets in a blaze of colour... they are called tap–taps.'

Zenga Longmore is an actress, singer and writer. Her column 'New Life' appears weekly in the *Spectator* and she lives in Brixton. TAP–TAPS TO TRINIDAD is her first book.

TO MUSA
THE NOBLE WISE ONE

CENTURY TRAVELLERS

TAP–TAPS TO TRINIDAD

A Caribbean Journey by
Zena Longmore

WITH DRAWINGS BY THE AUTHOR

ARROW BOOKS

AUTHOR'S NOTE

Most of the names of the people in this book are
fictitious, but all the incidents described are true. Parts of
this book have appeared in the *Spectator* and are reprinted
by kind permission of the Editor, Charles Moore. I
would also like to thank him for his kind help and
encouragement. Thanks are also due to Duncan Millar,
my sister Joma, Richard West and Diamond Jack Silver.

Century Travellers

Published by Arrow Books Limited
20 Vauxhall Bridge Road, London SW1V 2SA

An imprint of Random Century Group

London Melbourne Sydney Auckland Johannesburg
and agencies throughout the world

First published in Great Britain in 1989
by Hodder & Stoughton Ltd
Arrow edition 1990

© 1989 by Zenga Longmore

Printed and bound in Great Britain by
The Guernsey Press Co Ltd
Guernsey, C.I.

ISBN 0 09 971420 5

Contents

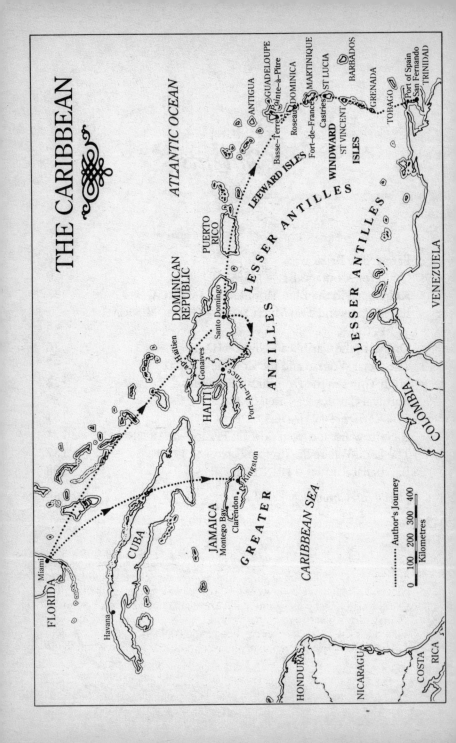

THE CARIBBEAN

ATLANTIC OCEAN

FLORIDA

Miami

Havana

CUBA

JAMAICA
Montego Bay
Clarendon
Kingston

GREATER

CARIBBEAN SEA

HONDURAS

NICARAGUA

COSTA
RICA

ANTILLES

DOMINICAN
REPUBLIC

Santo Domingo

Cap Haïtien
Gonaïves

HAITI
Port-Au-Prince

PUERTO
RICO

LESSER ANTILLES

ANTIGUA

GUADELOUPE
Basse-Terre Pointe-à-Pitre
Roseau DOMINICA
Fort-de-France MARTINIQUE
Castries ST LUCIA

LEEWARD ISLES

WINDWARD
ST VINCENT ISLES
BARBADOS

GRENADA

TOBAGO

Port of Spain
San Fernando
TRINIDAD

LESSER ANTILLES

COLOMBIA

VENEZUELA

Author's Journey

0 100 200 300 400
Kilometres

Farewell
to Brixton

J ust look at you! Lying there with a face like a sucked mango seed. Who would think that you were off to the Caribbean tomorrow? Have you thought of how you're going to manage for months with hardly any money, no knowledge of French or Spanish, and no idea what you're going to do?"

I pulled the blankets over my head and faced the wall.

Marcia had been sitting on my bed all evening, nagging and bullying me quite mercilessly. Her parents are Jamaican, and although she has never been there, she stubbornly refuses to forgive me for not rhapsodising over her parents' isle. Ever since she became my closest friend, many moons ago, her mission in life has been to compare my lifestyle unfavourably with that of the people "back home". For years I have been trying to fathom out why I put up with it.

The grey winter evening wore on into a bleak, icy night and the windows of my Brixton tower block rattled ominously. I shivered.

How could I tell Marcia how afraid I felt. Afraid of the insects, the language barriers, but most of all, the talipots.*

Maybe I should stay at home and give the whole thing up as a bad job.

"You're not listening, are you?" Marcia snorted. "Why can't you be strong like the women back home? Independent and lacking in inhibitions, free in speech and manner, hardworking and . . ."

As she lectured on, I fell into a sort of dream, and in my trance-like state I could almost smell that distinct, spicy aroma of the house where I stayed in Jamaica. That smell of rich herbs, mixed with the flowery fragrance that hangs in the Jamaican air.

Oh Jamaica . . .

---

* A quick word of explanation regarding the word "talipot". Talipot is a pseudonym for a creature of which I have so powerful a phobia that every time I write it, or see the word in print I scream. For the sake of his nerves, I was advised by my next-door neighbour to employ another term for the creature. Hence "talipot". My sincere apologies for any guesswork caused.

Quest for
Montego Bay
JAMAICA

*H*ow clearly I remembered flying from Miami to Jamaica, sitting at the back of the plane with Delson, my Jamaican brother-in-law. Boko, my sister, and her two children were seated in the front. Boko was in a foul temper because she was stuck in the non-smokers with the kids, and every time she heard either myself or her husband burst into raucous laughter, she would send her five-year-old son down the plane to tell us to shut up. For some reason, that particular airline allowed the passengers an unlimited amount of free drink, the result being that with alarming speed Delson and I were singing bawdy Jamaican ditties to the accompaniment of the clatter of airport cups. Elike, my tiny nephew, was soon running up and down the plane with urgent messages from his mother to "be quiet, or Mummy says she's flying straight back to London." I'm afraid his little legs were worn to stumps to no avail. If I remember rightly, we had begun on "Mattie Rag" (with all the rude verses left in), delivered in a discordant shout.

It felt so good to have my mind blotted out by Baileys Irish Cream, not only because of my fear of flying, but also because I had absolutely no idea of what to expect from Jamaica, and I harboured a strange apprehension. Apart from a vague feeling that I was going to be hideously murdered, I didn't really think any further. There again, it must be said that I never go on holiday without thinking someone's going to bump me off.

The plane zoomed down, and there we all were, stepping into steamy Jamaica.

Now, no matter how much people may condemn air travel, nothing can match the sensation of stepping off a plane, and feeling a new, foreign heat upon your face. Say what you like about boat journeys: more romantic they may be, but you miss out on climbing aboard a plane on an icy, drizzly day, and stepping off some hours later into a blaze of sunshine.

Jamaica's tropical humidity, however, caused me to break out into a sweaty panic. That thick, sticky air said one thing and one thing only – talipots.

"Boko," I whispered to my sister in a soft voice, so Delson couldn't hear. "There're going to be talipots here, I can sense it."

Boko was heavily pregnant at the time, and so was too tired to take in the horrifying information. Both children were asleep, one thrown over my shoulder, and one over Delson's. Walking through immigration, my eyes darted this way and that, searching for talipots. The young woman in charge of our bags looked very sour at seeing our little party. It was quite clear that she was most affronted that we had chosen to stay in Jamaica.

My youngest niece, Kuba, suddenly woke up, stared into the official's face, and began to cry. The official smiled, evidently well pleased with the effect her bitter expression was having on at least one of us.

After about an hour of questioning and searching, we waited outside the airport, surrounded by a whirl of activity. Taxi drivers touting for trade were shouting to one another, money changers and mini-bus drivers milled around in search of custom. 'How can they all be so energetic, when the air is so close and muggy?' I asked myself.

A big fat man approached us and threw himself into Delson's arms.

"This is my brother Barclay!" yelled Delson, and soon everyone was hugging, kissing and greeting Barclay in a flurry of *bonhomie*. Suitcases were thrown into a mini-bus, children placed on laps, more greetings were shouted, and off we drove into the starry night.

So this was Kingston.

Shacks made of corrugated iron and wood, lay higgledy-piggledy by the roadside, with people standing outside them, stock still, arms folded, waiting for nothing. Women dressed in ragged dresses sat on doorsteps staring ahead of them with shuttered faces, their hair tied tightly around bright yellow curlers. Men wandered slowly in and out of the shanty houses, wearing torn-off shorts, and oil-stained tee-shirts. Some of them were leaning against the box-like buildings, smoking and staring into space.

Kingston town itself seemed unbearably hideous to me that first night. Street after street of dilapidated houses, empty shops and vile refuse. Buildings that had obviously once been grand and gleaming now stood peeling and filthy. In the town centre, no one walked the streets so late at night, which produced a rather terrifying effect. An eerie ghost town where man has not walked for centuries, crumbling away to dust.

Outside of Kingston, life began again, and we were back in the shanty towns, watching tiny children covered in dirt play around the houses – or were they playing? With their expressionless faces it was impossible to glean what they were up to – maybe running errands for their parents.

Suddenly we were speeding through blackness.

"We're in the country now, Boko," said Delson, "can you smell the sugar-cane?"

Boko was still annoyed with her usually quiet husband for getting drunk and singing "Mattie Rag", so she didn't reply.

I looked around the mini-bus. A young boy was seated behind me, staring at me with round pale brown eyes.

"Hello," I said to him, feeling rather uncomfortable under the steadiness of his gaze.

"Look 'ere!" he suddenly piped in a high voice. "You-a like country-an'-western music?"

"Not much."

"Jesum Piece! Ya naw like Kenny Rogers an' Jim Reeves, dem?"

I found his patois so difficult to understand that I had to make him repeat every sentence at least seven times.

"No," I replied, after being asked for the eighth time.

"Cheeese an' bread! Ya naw like dem, nah? Mebbe dey nah 'ave dat kinda music inna Henglan', mek me put a tep pon de recorder, an' you gon 'ear sweet, sweet music nah gyal, hunerstan'?"

After a few minutes, the mini-bus was flooded with the sound of Jim Reeves Welcoming us to his World, in his soupy voice.

"Dis ya music irie," whispered the young boy in reverent tones.

"What's your name?" I asked him.

"A-wha'?"

"What's your name?"

"A-wha' ya seh?"

"What Is Your Name?"

"Is wha' she-a seh?" he asked Barclay.

"She said what's your name," said Delson in his standard English Delson accent, shooting a glance at Boko. Boko sighed meaningfully. She had been sighing meaningfully every time Delson had opened his mouth.

"Ah, me nem! Well, check now for instance, still. Me nem-a Mannie, but de people dem hall call me Middle Mannie, seen?"

"Middle Mannie, my name's Zenga."

Middle Mannie did not reply, but stared out of the window, swaying his head lightly to the Jim Reeves strains. Maybe he didn't care what my name was, but more likely he hadn't understood my accent. I had no idea at that time that throughout my visit to Jamaica I wouldn't be able to understand anyone, and no one would be able to understand me. The patois, a blend of Spanish, West African languages and English, is totally unintelligible to all but the initiated.

We swung around a corner, and found ourselves at the bungalow where we were staying, in a Clarendon town. It was so pitch black that seeing more than an inch in front of you was impossible.

Barclay was laughing about something as we picked our way through the unkempt garden. We trod warily into the house, and I saw two women in curlers sitting on a sofa, arms folded, staring blankly at us. Three children lay asleep on the floor. The room was half dark, with flickery shadows emerging from the TV. I nodded a greeting to one of the women, and then the smile froze on my lips. I had seen it! Over her head was the largest talipot I have ever seen in my life (disregarding the ones that appear every now and again on David Attenborough programmes).

For one moment the universe swooped downwards, carrying me with it in one almighty vortex.

"Boko," I rasped. "Help me. Get me out of this room." Boko put an arm under mine, and led me into the bedroom which was swathed in darkness, a tiny blue lamp swinging from the ceiling.

"What's the matter?"

"I've seen one." I could feel the sweat dripping down over my eyes, and breathing became an impossible task. I bent down double, gasping in painful puffs.

"Where is it?"

"Over that woman's head."

Brave Boko marched into the living room, looking very purposeful, while I stood shivering in the bedroom, not daring to look right or left.

"Zenga says there's a – AAAAGH."

There was a crash, a slamming of doors, and more screaming. Then the excited voice of Middle Mannie screeched, "What's de matter? She see a lizard?"

Several people laughed, especially Barclay. "Henglish girl demma 'fraid of ev'ry, ev'ry ting."

"That's it," I said to Kuba, who had wandered sleepily into the bedroom and was clinging round my legs. "I hate Jamaica. Hate, hate, hate!"

"You should like talipots. Talipots are your friends. Daddy's killed it anyway. Daddy says he hopes you're not going to carry on like this the whole time. He says you're really getting on his nerves, and the fat lady asked if you were mad. Are you mad?"

"Shhh, be quiet, Kuba."

"Are you, though?"

"Hush."

"Tell me!"

"Kuba, lie on the bed, and I'll tell you a story. Call Elike."

Elike came in and searched the room for talipots for me, and finding none, we lay on the bed, and I told soothing stories. My heart wasn't in it though. Me and Jamaica, I thought, are not going to be friends. Boko came back into the bedroom.

"It's dead. Come back and sit with the rest of us. Everyone thinks you're rude."

I tottered back into the living room, but couldn't sit down, being too scared to move. Janice, Barclay's wife, a slim dark-skinned woman, stared at me relentlessly without speaking. Everytime I caught her eye and smiled, she continued to watch me blankly until I squirmed with discomfort. There was a musty, damp smell in the house, which countless giant insects obviously found very appealing. The kitchen was aswarm with cockroaches and tiny lizards, which scuttled up and down the mouldy walls at breakneck speed.

Janice followed me into the kitchen, and watched me in silence as I made tea. "I've brought you some presents," I told her. She didn't move a muscle. "I'll show them to you tomorrow," I continued uncomfortably. Her eyes didn't leave my face, and she followed me back into the living room, and settled back to staring unblinkingly at me.

"Why does she hate me so much?" I asked Boko that night. I had insisted on sleeping with Boko and the kids after the talipot episode.

"She doesn't hate you."

"She does."

"Oh well, never mind, eh. Goodnight."

"Goodnight, Boko."

Holding Kuba's sweaty little hand in mine, I felt reassured, and soon we fell asleep.

I awoke early the next day in a bright, confident mood, the type of mood that only comes to the fore once in a while. The sort of mood when you tell yourself that yes, you can tackle anything, even a woman who stares at you without ever blinking. Roman Emperors, I believe, were very susceptible to moods such as these, when they *Veni Vidi Vici*-ed, in days of old. Before breakfast, I organised races for the eight children who were staying in the house: a difficult task as it meant trying to steer the one-year-old away from the open sewer at the back of the house into which the older kids were determined to push him at all costs. The children became completely hysterical, biting and kicking one another, as if playing with an adult were a brand-new experience for them.

As I endeavoured to eat my breakfast of fried plantain and salt fish, about seven children piled on my lap. Janice watched me with brooding eyes all the while. Trying to avoid those eyes caused a vague sinking feeling around the lower spleen. Middle Mannie, who turned out to be her brother, began to chatter brightly in completely unintelligible patois. The vague gist was that he was going to persuade some cousins of his to show me the highlife of Jamaica, Dunns River Falls, Negril,

Montego Bay, and all the other delights the discerning tourist could savour. The cousins were scheduled to arrive later on in the day, and I was not to leave the house until they all turned up.

The sun seemed determined to destroy my new-found assertiveness by lashing down great rays of fire upon my head. Boko and Delson lay in the shade of a tamarind tree, and sucked the water from a green coconut. The children insisted on more races, and party games. "Ring-a-ring-a-roses" proved a great success, as did "In and Out the Dusty Bluebells".

One little three-year-old, whom I nicknamed "Petty", left neither my side, nor my lap. He gazed up into my face with all the unnerving intensity of his mother Janice. After a few hours, I managed to plead illness, and escaped to the tamarind tree, where Boko and Delson sat sipping iced lemonade. My dress was torn and mud-stained, and traces of Petty's vomit were visible in my hair.

"The wonderful thing about this holiday," observed Boko, elegantly adjusting her sunglasses, "is that you can really relax. Just imagine if I was back in London. Elike and Kuba would be under my feet all day, but here – ah!"

If she caught the murderous glance I flung at her, she ignored it with breezy nonchalance.

The cousins did not turn up that day, nor the next, nor, for that matter, the next. Every day, for the first week, I had strict instructions to stay put and wait for these elusive cousins who obviously had much better things to do with their time than drive tourists around.

Day after day, I sat upon the concrete porch in the yard, with nothing to do save chat to Middle Mannie and play with the children, who became naughtier and naughtier. It didn't take them long to discover my fear of talipots, and after a while I was finding outsize ones in my bed, hair, and down the back of my dress. On hearing my screams, the adults would beat the offending child with a belt. The child would run whimpering like a dog to a corner, then, still sobbing, would find an even bigger talipot to pay me back for the beating. The naughtiest child was Desmond, an eight-year-old who never went to school. Not that it seemed to do him any harm. He couldn't read and write, true, but there again, nor could the children who went to school religiously. Desmond, like me in my younger years, never saw the sense in school, and would leave in the early morning dressed impeccably in grey formality, an ill-fitting school cap balanced on his head, and would swiftly pass by the school and spend the day playing truant.

"The holidays are boring," he told me once.

"But you never go to school anyway," I whispered back (it was supposed to be a trade secret).

"I know, but when it's term time, I've got something to do, like not going to school, but now there's nothing to do at all!"

However, Desmond was by far the brightest out of all the children, and spent the long hot days modelling planes, cars and motor bikes out of clay.

Jamaican nights were seemingly endless, alive with mosquitoes biting and buzzing, bats flying about in and out of the house, and every creepy-crawly that the morbid imagination can conjure up. Every now and then, a "sss! sss! sss!" could be heard in the undergrowth. We named the owner of the hisses "Hissing Sid", although we never found out who or what it was.

I would sit on the porch, drinking coconut water and white rum. In the early evening, I told the children stories, Martinique style, always beginning *"Et cric!"* and the children would reply *"Et crac!"* then the story would begin. I began by telling them cosy Little Red Riding Hood type stories, but the little darlings soon tired of such childlike banality. Very soon I learnt that the stories to make them sit up with enrapt concentration were the ones which involved stepmothers burying boys' heads under olde oak trees, and witches being torn to a thousand pieces by demons.

All the children would sit around my feet, gazing in starry wonder at the tales of death and doom.

Desmond would sit tensed, like a leopard, bristling with nervous excitement at what was coming up next. Suddenly he would realise he was being good, and so would push a child over, or throw a lump of mud at me, just to show that he *was* a bad boy after all.

The grown-ups sucked their teeth noisily whenever they caught me telling stories to the kids, and would usually call a child away to do some errand just as the story reached a dramatic climax. Playing with children, they thought, is just another symptom of English eccentricity (along with wanting to go out and enjoy yourself, and liking dogs).

Janice often came out to the porch, and sat listening to the stories, staring at me piercingly. After a few days she began to speak to me, telling me she would wash my clothes, plait my hair, and iron my dresses. Soon we became firm friends, and spent our days sitting in the shade running down everyone who lived in the house and gossiping about everyone we knew.

Going to the market with Janice was always a nightmarish experience for me. Dense crowds pushed and shoved into us, as we barged our way through, armed with shopping bags. Market women sat on the ground, arguing with shoppers over the price of yams or plantain. Janice would buy an enormous amount of groceries, which she balanced on her head, marching boldly forward.

"Janice! You haven't paid the man!" I once said in alarm when she picked up a pile of mangoes and placed them in her bag.

"Me pay 'im, y'know," came the mumbled reply, and she walked into the butchers' part of the market, where great haunches of meat lay on bloody boards, black with flies. My arms grew tired and aching with all the carrying, as we continued round and round the market, finding a stall which sold sweet potato one cent cheaper. 'I won't mention the fact that she's stolen a whole load of mangoes,' I muttered to myself, 'after all, it might embarrass her.'

Just then, she turned tail, and strode over to the mango stall.

"Seven mango me took, mas."

"Seven? That four dollar, miss."

Janice paid him, and we struggled away, in the scorching sunlight. The incident impressed me greatly. That Janice owned up to the exact number of mangoes she took, and that the man took her word for it unquestioningly, must surely prove that there is nowhere in the world as honest as Jamaica. Could that trustful event, I asked myself, have taken place in Brixton market?

Many heads turned on seeing me in the market, blank eyes gazing at me, and expressionless mouths muttering, "foreigner".

It took me a long time to realise that "foreigner" was not meant as an insult, but merely a bald statement. I was not Jamaican, so was therefore a foreigner, and it was felt that the fact had to be remarked upon. They could tell I was a foreigner by the way I walked, and the clothes I wore, long before I opened my mouth.

As I left the market place, the merciless sun beating down upon me, I must have gone into a sort of trance, because I stepped out into the middle of the road straight in front of a bicycle. The cyclist swerved, and all the vegetables that had been so carefully balanced on the front of the bike cascaded into the street and were fast being snaffled by goats and pigs.

The cyclist, who had been thrown off his bike, sprang up and glared menacingly at me, then whipped out a knife and started towards me.

A large crowd of shoppers gathered and stared blankly from me and then to the knife-toter.

"Foreigner lady gon die nah," I heard a fairly cheerful voice remark from amongst the crowd.

I instantly moved forward and, apologising profusely, picked up all the vegetables, kicking various goats out of the way, and piled them back on his bike.

The man continued to scan me with marked distaste.

"I'll pay for any loss or damage," I stuttered.

Grudgingly, the man folded up the knife, and put it back in his pocket.

"That all right, man, me nah wan tek ya money." And his lips curved into what could loosely be described as a smile.

Seeing that death was not on the cards that afternoon, a disappointed crowd dispersed, their faces as blank as ever.

"He was going to stab me, Janice!" I said, with a good deal of injured pride, during the long walk home.

"Me knooor dat."

"Well, there's no need to sound so happy about it."

"Well, it a long time since anyone see foreign lady get a licking. Normally there's not anything of interest to see at the market."

But Janice was wrong. Very often, impromptu church services would spring up in the market.

A preacher, holding a Bible, surrounded by incense and lighted candles, would begin to preach the gospel in piercing tones. Tired shoppers would gather round for the service, and gospel singing of pure beauty filled the busy market.

"Goodbye world! I am gone.
Goodbye world! I am go-o-ne.
It's the Holy Ghost and fire
Telling me to go on.
Goodbye world! I am gone."

The atmosphere was so moving, that it would be impossible not to get carried away, singing and clapping and crying.

The preacher picked out shoppers at random to stand before him and give a testimony. I stood paralysed with nerves, in case he ever chose me. All the other people, carrying heavy loads upon their heads, in worn Crimplene dresses, gave off an aura of such simplistic holiness, that I looked too obvious a brazen sinner to be able to withstand ten minutes of chastisement. Luckily, though, I was never fished out from the crowd. In any case, I wouldn't have been able to understand what was being said to me, and would have had to keep saying, "What?", "Pardon!" every time I was asked if I had cast out the devil.

All the energy in Jamaica seems to have gone into the church, a creation of slaves, a far stronger force than materialism.

Everybody goes to church on Sunday, and the ones who don't are bowed down with guilt and excuses. Only the "quashie dem" don't go ("quashie" being the *hoi polloi*, the lumpen, and "dem" being the plural; plurals and tenses are few and far between in Jamaicanese).

The service to which Delson's family took me was packed to the hilt. There were no seats available, and most of the congregation stood outside in the street, white dresses and feathered hats glistening in the sunshine.

Our little party could only obtain seats by virtue of "coming from foreign".

A woman preacher shrieked and screamed about the many guises of Satan. Amens rent the air.

It was at a church during the first Sunday of my stay in Jamaica, that my toothache began. At first, it was one of those niggly pains that you think will go away in a minute if you lay off the sky juice, but then, like Krakatoa, it erupted into an explosion of agony.

"Fancy," I said to Delson, "I've always had this tooth in my head, but have never been aware of it before. Now it seems incredible that any other part of my body exists except this tooth. It claims the very fibre of my soul, so demanding is it."

"Shhh now, and pay attention to the service," said Delson, a little too pompously for my liking.

Early Monday morning, Boko and I staggered to the dentist in town. The waiting-room presented a sad and sorry sight. Miserable people sat upon wooden benches with rags tied round their heads and held ice packs to the offending molars.

A motherly receptionist, on seeing me, ushered me straight into the surgery without any ado. Muffled curses followed in my wake as I was gently placed into the dreaded dentist's chair.

"Now, young lady, which tooth is causing your sweet face to screw up like a clenched fist?"

"That one."

"This one?"

"No, that one."

"Ah, I see," and he placed a piece of cotton wool in my mouth. "Which part of foreign are you from, miss?"

"Worng-wroulng."

"Ah! Henglan'! Me wan' go dere myself!"

During this pleasant piece of chitchat, I noticed that the man was opening a drawer, and withdrawing a pair of pliers.

"Oungh-orouhl uyoumph!!"

"Keep your mouth wide open now, miss, there's plenty of time to chat later."

The pliers gripped around my tooth. I closed my eyes in panic. The last time I had had a tooth out, I was gassed, ethered, and it took three nurses to hold me down. Besides, I had been preparing for the event for weeks. And now, here I was having a tooth wrenched out with not so much as a by-your-leave. *Crunch!* The tooth made a dramatic bid for freedom, and there I was, sitting in the chair, with the kindly receptionist stroking my brow. The whole operation, from start to finish, took one minute flat.

"Bite on the cotton wool, now darlin', and if it bleed during the day a lickle, bite on a tea bag. Forty dollar, if you please, miss."

"But won't my face puff out like it did last time I had a tooth out?"

"Nah."

I felt around with my tongue.

"Isn't it supposed to hurt?"

"Sometime it don't, sometime it do."

"B-b-but, won't it *start* hurting in a minute?"

"Naw, sweetheart, you can live a normal life for the rest of the day."

I stared in stupefied dismay, unable to reply.

The dentist turned out to be right. For the rest of the day I felt not even the merest twinge of pain. The episode, however, put me off going to the doctor's in Jamaica. Boko remarked that if I were to go with a bad arm, the doctor would sit me down, then I'd see him opening a drawer out of the corner of my eye, and out of the drawer he would produce a saw, which he would proceed to sharpen.

"Just hold your arm out, so, miss. It won't hurt a bit."

The people I have told that episode to, are convinced the dentist had used "obeah" to quell the pain.

Obeah in Jamaica, and indeed throughout the West Indies, is held in the greatest of terror. Every evil that befalls, be it failing an important exam, or being struck down by disease, is blamed on obeah, an African oriented form of sorcery.

"Linette was in hospital for months after her new baby, because someone obeahed her." "Uncle Lindsey's plants never grew in his garden because of obeah," were the kind of phrases I heard often throughout my visit. No one ever seemed to know who put the obeah on, but obeah it surely was. Some people told me they had paid a small fortune to good Obeah Mothers to have the evil spells removed. Obeah is not a superstition, it is a fact. Few Jamaicans admitted that they didn't believe in obeah, and the ones who did were lying.

Obeah is the bane of Jamaican life. It creates a suspicious world where your neighbour is blamed for the smallest accident. Strangely enough, the only obeah people I met were good Obeah Fathers and Mothers. They were small, hunched people with piercing eyes and intense mannerisms. Soon I came to the conclusion that hardly anyone actually put the obeah on, but many made and spent money taking it off.

"But dey *do* put it on all de time!" insisted Middle Mannie. "I see frogs with padlocks on their mouths around de Court House. When Hobeah Mudda put lock around de mouth of frog, it mean dat de witnesses will get confused and start prattling nonsense. It happen hall de time. Me know a lady dat halmos' die in childbirt' but luckily 'er sister got de spell tekken hoff by going to a good Hobeah Mudda, an' got a lot of 'erb an' spice dat she bwile up into a soup. When de lady heat uff it, she cure."

"She heated it?"

"Nooor. Me seh she heat hit."

"Oh, *eat* it."

The thought struck me that Jamaicans are the only people in the world to *'eat* their food before they *heat* it.

"An' check now for instance. One time me loss me job, an' my gyalfrien' hin de same week! Days don't sweet widdout me job, an' nights don't sweet widdout me loving 'oman. Me believe still me inna jam bad, bad. So what me a do? Me gwova to Hobeah Mudda, an' she tell me hov hall de jealousy an' evil t'ought dat some ginnal 'ave for me. So she mek me tek off me cloth dem, an' get in a bath, an' she wash me down wid hall kind medicine an' 'erb. Tree day later, me fine a job, an' me sweet gyal come a knocking at me door, seen?"

"But how do you know you wouldn't have got your job and your sweetheart back anyway?"

Middle Mannie shrugged and bit his bottom lip. We had discovered a cat's head in the garden that morning, and he had been telling me it was the work of obeah, and I was staunchly pretending I wasn't in the least bit scared. Some woman was jealous, Middle Mannie insisted, and was trying to spring mischief upon me. The people of the house were only vaguely concerned. It was believed that a foreigner was immune to obeah, especially a foreigner with as much white blood as myself.

Sometimes in the warm, sticky evenings, Middle Mannie would point out which bats were the reincarnation of certain relatives.

"Nuff respect me 'ave for de ratbat dere. Me huncle dat, y'know."

The children became very excited by the idea of Duppies and Rolling Calves. To see a phantom calf, its legs bound in chains and breathing fire, means a pitiable spate of bad luck. A Duppy is a ghost that in Jamaican folklore rides with its head on back to front upon a mule, holding onto the tail.

"But dat just stupidness. Duppy can look just like you an' me. You leave your window hopen hall night, den Duppy'll rise from 'im grave, an' come t'rough ya window. True a true y'know! Four days before you come, me see Duppy standing hover me bed, jus' watching me with eyes too terrible to look into."

Boko would roll her eyes in boredom whenever Middle Mannie started on about Duppies, bats or Rolling Calves, but such conversations kept me awake with feverish fright for nights on end. I would insist a child sleep in with me – a big mistake. The child would spend one half of the night making howling ghost noises and cackling monster sounds, and the other half saying, "Ahh! Haunty Zenga! Me never see a talipot so big! Watch 'im craaawl 'pon your back!"

Most of the folklore of Jamaica, be it obeah, omens, proverbs or sayings, comes from Ghana and can be traced back to the Ashanti-Fanti peoples. Yoruba and Ibo customs of Nigeria are visible in Jamaica, but not as dominant as the Ghanaian influences. Many words in patois can be traced back to the peoples of Ghana, who were brought to the island as slaves. The word "quashie" was originally a Yoruba term of ridicule for the Ashanti. The Ashanti name for the Yorubas is "Nago". It looks as if there must have been a great deal of quarrelling between the Ashanti and the Yorubas during slavery days because even now, in certain parts of Jamaica, I heard people use the word "Nago" referring to people who cannot be trusted.

Many customs I saw in Jamaica, such as throwing water or spirits on the ground in honour of the ancestors, I remember my West African father doing whenever he spoke of relatives, now dead and gone.

The slaves who had been brought to Jamaica in the seventeenth and eighteenth centuries were treated by their English slave-masters with brutal contempt and scorn. The lack of concern for the life of a slave is proven by the fact that the fine paid by a master for wantonly murdering his slave was almost one third lighter than the fine paid for harbouring a runaway slave. The slaves were merely chattels used by sugar-planters for making as much money as possible. Because of the inhumane treatment they received, disease, and the appalling insanitary conditions in which they lived, the average life of a slave ran to a few meagre years. The planters did not care unduly: they found it cheaper and easier to import more slaves from the West African coast, than bother to keep their slaves alive.

Although the West African influence lies deep in Jamaican culture, it is also true to say that "slave culture" is very much a Jamaican fact of life.

My sister and I were treated as English duchesses everywhere we went, solely by dint of having "fair skins". "Fair-skinned" black people were guaranteed posh jobs and affected snobby mannerisms. Even the language, a legacy of slavery, denigrates "blackness".

"Don't be so dark!" I heard a mother say to her daughter, meaning, don't be so silly. "High"-coloured means light-skinned, "good" hair is straight hair, and to be told you've got a straight nose is to be paid none other than the highest of compliments.

Judging by the telly, and the advertisements on the posters, it was difficult to believe that I was in a black country. The models in the newspapers, hostesses and the beautiful girls displayed on the posters were all as light-skinned as you can get, without actually being white.

Janice, and Barclay's sister who lived in the house, used to roar with laughter when they caught Boko or me doing the washing or washing-up: then they would drag us away, telling us that we were ladies, so we mustn't get our hands dirty. I found being dragged away from the sink, and being called a "lady" highly irritating, but I soon found it was far more unnerving to stand washing dishes, while an audience of horrified gigglers looked on.

Our accents and skin colour were a passport to having first place in any queue, and a seat on the mini-bus. It felt most odd to be treated like English royalty in Jamaica, after a lifetime of not being considered English in England. After a while I began feeling permanently guilty. So often, at a long queue in the bank, a person would turn to me, and with a polite duck of the head that almost amounted to a bow would say:

"You go firs' ma'am."

"No, you got here before me."

"Me know that still, but you go firs'."

"No, you go first."

"No, you."

"No, you."

And so it would go on, with all the other queuers urging me forward, turning my face shiny with flustered embarrassment.

I tried everything in my power to stop people from treating me in this manner. I wore old dresses, and tied my hair up in unkempt plaits, but still it seemed as if the red carpet was rolled out whenever I or my sister made an appearance. Delson's philosophy was "accept and enjoy". Only one person I met in Jamaica, whom you will read about later on, hated and resented me for my skin colour and nationality.

How anyone in Jamaica could like England was a complete mystery to me. England had uprooted Africans to work for centuries as slaves, destroying the lives of countless millions of people, so Britain could grow fat and rich. The Jamaicans still toil under a shroud of misery and poverty. However, for some reason, Mother Nature has endowed Africans and West Indians with an extraordinary gift of forgiveness.

The grannies, who dominate Jamaican life, sat around telling their families that England was the mother country, Jamaica her daughter. Nearly everyone I met had a touching love of England. I began to hate England after a few days in Jamaica, but that's not to say I liked Jamaica. I could never come to terms with vacant faces mumbling "foreigner" at me everywhere I went.

Walking through villages, a child would come from her house and watch me, followed by another child, followed by a mother and baby, until, after a while, it would seem as if the whole village were sitting or leaning against walls, arms folded, saying "foreigner", in flat voices. Not that I ever feared for my physical well-being. You could not wish to meet a gentler person than the average Jamaican citizen.

One hot, unbearably sticky night, I had been reading to the children for hours on end, and they were safely tucked up in bed. All except Desmond, that is, who was lying by my feet, kicking his legs up into my face, telling me I looked as ugly as Aunt Evadne (whoever Aunt Evadne was).

Dinner was ready and a leaden feeling of gloom crept upon me, from the stomach outwards.

Every night, for the past ten days, the bill of fare had been curried goat, rice, yams, plantains, green bananas, and coleslaw. The food would always be half cold by the time it was served and, more often than not, piled so high upon the plate that, if a monkey were to sit on top, its tail wouldn't touch the ground (as my father used to say). It was rumoured that somewhere in town was a jerk pork stall, but I was never to see it. Jerk pork is a delicious barbecued pork dish, usually sold by the wayside, or at busy market-places.

That night, however, after ten days of staying in to wait for cousins, I desperately felt like a change. Glitz, glamour and high life were what I yearned for. My one party frock which I had brought had left the suitcase once, and that was only for Janice to admire.

"Let's all go out tonight!" I suddenly announced.

Barclay and his sister spluttered in their plates. Janice choked on a piece of coleslaw, and Desmond threw a mildewed mango upon my sunburnt shoulder.

Only Middle Mannie continued to nibble at a scrag-end of goat, in an offhand manner. I think the statement had been of such outrageous character as to have stunned him into a state of shock.

"Why?" asked Janice, a good ten minutes later.

"So I can get a taste of Jamaican night-life."

"Where?" gasped Barclay.

"Anywhere. C'mon, Barclay, it'll do you good."

"But there's nowhere to go!"

Delson, who had been lying down in the next room, announced that no one was going anywhere at all, because the town was too violent for people to go wandering the streets at night. We could only go out, he decreed, if we were driven there and back in Barclay's mini-bus, and we did not go within a twenty-mile radius of Kingston.

With a great deal of shaking of heads, and anxious glances in my direction, it was agreed that *Big* Mannie ought to be fetched by Barclay, so he could escort us to a swish night-club, somewhere within the vicinity. Big Mannie was described as a Bungo-man or wild man, and one who "knew the scene". Janice's and my eyes locked. She had already told me in hair-raising detail of Big Mannie's exploits. A distant cousin of Barclay's, he appeared to have done his bit to bolster up the baby boom in the area.

With a flash of gold teeth, and gold medallions winking out from an open shirt, Big Mannie swaggered into the room. The place to be on Friday nights was, he declared, Pins and Needles, the Ultimate Disco Experience. Boko groaned, and said she could feel a headache coming on. Barclay and sister *had* to babysit, and Middle Mannie had to stay in to wait for his girlfriend, whom no one had ever seen.

"So it look like it jus' gon' be me an' you, sweet daughter," and slapping my thigh, Big Mannie pulled me out of my seat.

"Delson!" I cried in alarm, "you'll come, won't you?"

"No, not if it looks like Boko's going to have a headache."

"Janice?"

The reply was a glare thrown at Big Mannie, and a grumpy shake of the head.

"As me seh, jus' you an' me." A metallic molar glinted wickedly.

"And Boko, and Delson!"

"And me!" Desmond was emerging from his bedroom, dressed in a pair of gold lamé slacks, with gaping holes at the knees.

"Move an' go-weh!" screamed Barclay, removing a belt; and lashing wildly at a screeching Desmond, chased him back into the bedroom.

Grabbing the whip from Barclay's hands, I felt like giving up the whole excursion as a lost cause.

But Big Mannie was adamant. After recovering from the initial shock that the beautiful Boko was married to a man twice his size (Big Mannie was very short) he consoled himself in the knowledge that I wasn't, and although a somewhat sorry substitute, I at least had "fair skin".

"Come now sister, mek we gwarn!"

"Well, let's wait for Boko and Delson."

"I'm not going and that's that!"

"Boko," I said quietly, looking deep into her eyes, "who told the dinner-lady at school that you had donated your dinner money to the church fund, when really you had spent it on five Choc Top Woppas, all for yourself?"

Boko's liquid brown eyes misted over. Her mouth opened and closed in a strangled attempt at speech, but of course no words were audible. She resembled a drowning duck, on a dark and lonely lake.

"One – one moment, I-I'll be with you in just a sec."

The "dinner-lady" speech has never been known to fail yet.

Pins and Needles, the Ultimate Disco Experience, was a small, poky club with peeling wallpaper and dangerously rickety furniture. Two old men sat by the bar, drinking white rum, staring at us unceasingly. The music was a blend of syrupy ballads, and country-and-western. Reggae is not played as often as one might think in Jamaica. It is looked down upon by "respectable folk" as the music of the quashie dem.

So, with two old men, Jim Reeves at low volume, and a bar that could only boast of rum and Coca-Cola, the evening got off to a somewhat dismal start. The place was plunged in almost total darkness, thus saving me the trouble of not having to look at Big Mannie's gold medallions.

To spare my dear old mother's blushes when she reads this book, I will not relate the flow of earthy farmyard aphorisms, that were being whispered in my ears. Big Mannie was not a man to pick his words with subtlety. He was what is commonly termed as "wicked an' wil', like a crocodile".

Just as I was about to remember a pressing engagement, a tall, fine-boned man walked into the club, and looked around him in disgust. For a split second our eyes met, then he turned his glance westward and peered into the vacant corner of the club.

"Lickle Mannie, dat," growled Big Mannie.

"Who is he?"

"Neighbour, of course."

"Ah, of course."

Little Mannie mooched broodily over to our table and began to gabble an incomprehensible patois.

"So whappen sis'?" he finally enquired, shooting me a glowing-eyed gaze.

"Nothing much. Good club this, eh?"

"A wha'?"

"The club, it's good."

I was desperate for him to stay, and sensing how eager he was to leave, felt I had to make the conversation extra witty to hold his attention, and so that he would rescue me from the jaws of Big Mannie.

"A wha' she seh?"

"She seh club nice."

"Cl-cl-club n-n-n-?" and a great peal of laughter shattered the dreamlike atmosphere that Jim Reeves had so painstakingly created. Boko began to giggle, and Delson guffawed like a barnyard door slamming. Only Big Mannie, his jaw jutting, and chest thrust forward, remained coldly impervious to the sudden bout of jocularity.

"Me like, like, like de high gold sister you tek hout wid you tonight, Big Mannie. She well funny. It a good sign to see Henglish woman with Jamaican humour."

"High gold?"

"You! High gold, dat what dey seh, y'know."

"Ah."

"Soon's me see you with Big Mannie, me see you must 'ave good sense of humour, but when me 'ear the joke you a tell, aooah!"

Big Mannie, who had asked me to marry him several times so he could be guaranteed British citizenship, patted my shoulder, and with a breezy "Me soon forward," was gone. He was not missed. Little Mannie and I chattered on about every subject under the sun. Neither of us could understand the other, but it didn't seem to matter.

He turned out to be unemployed, and was looking for someone to pay his way to England. Everyone in Jamaica between the ages of sixteen and sixty, was looking for a way to leave Jamaica and procure their stay in either England or America. Jamaica was merely a transit land, where people stayed only until a relative or friend could send for them, and pay for their passage out. Little Mannie was no exception. He was visiting the neighbourhood, staying with relatives, but lived in the Blue Mountains, in a log cabin with his crippled mother. The nearest neighbour was a cousin of his, who apparently lived in a small hut in the mountains, about a mile away from Little Mannie's cabin.

So we sat in the dinginess of the Ultimate Disco Experience. Little Mannie and I chatted about his ambition to become a "Hot Shot" in London, and I related my ambition to see Montego Bay, and the other hot spots of Jamaica.

During the long walk home Little Mannie and I lagged behind Boko and Delson, telling stories to one another, and giggling. I found him fascinating. He was the only Jamaican male under the age of seventy-nine who had not asked me to marry him and set him up in a posh apartment in London. What he was looking for was a "Bups" or "Bupsy", in other words a Sugar Mummy, and anyone who lived in the villainous area of Brixton (a place he had heard all about from Jamaican television), was certainly too short of the readies to be able to set him up in the style to which he hoped to become accustomed.

"What more, my gyalfrien' wan' fe come to Hengland too."

"Girlfriend?"

"Eh heh."

"Oh, I-I see."

Life can be like that sometimes.

By the time we reached our bungalow the night was pitch black. Little Mannie promised that he would take me to Montego Bay the next day.

I could hardly sleep that night, so excited was I. Even a nasty-looking talipot only produced a medium-sized scream, not the usual kind that would wake the whole household and cause the fat old woman from next door to hammer on the wall.

Next morning, I wolfed down the macaroni, salt fish and hard dough bread. When he saw Little Mannie walk down the pathway dressed in cut-off shorts and a Lawrence-of-Arabia style towel around his head, Desmond began a manic belly dance.

"Why you no go school, yout' man?"

"I *do* go school."

"Ah, that all right then. Because if you *do* go school, it mus' mean that you're at school now."

"That's right, I *am* at school now, mister."

"I'm glad fe hear 'bout that. For one frightening moment me thought you were playing truant. But there's ongle one ting you're missing, lickle bwoy."

"What that?"

"A *schoolmaster*!" and with that, Little Mannie picked up the stick that Delson had previously been using for torturing lizards, and chased a giggling Desmond around the yard.

Little Mannie was instilled with that essential quality that every Jamaican needs in order to survive – a sense of humour. He laughed when we missed the Montego Bay train that day, and his sides buckled when we found that it had been derailed the next.

"So Montego Bay is off yet again," I lamented, fingering an unworn bikini. To console me, Little Mannie said that he would take me out for a meal that evening. After a monotonous diet of curried goat for two weeks, I was glad of the change.

I was surprised to see Little Mannie wading through a mountainous pile of rice and curried goat when I called for him at his house that evening. When I reminded him we were going out for a meal, he brusquely replied that he'd come out to eat after he'd finished his dinner. I angrily refused his offer to join him, and at last we set off into the warm night to the Talk of the Town.

The exterior of the Talk of the Town was a flashing display of pink and purple lights. The inside, however, was small and poky with a disco bar, and a squalid dining-room (empty of customers) at the back. We sat on lop-sided chairs and studied the four-page menu. The Talk of the Town apparently sold everything from fish and chips to obscure Malaysian pâtés. The Chinese speciality was "suey mein".

By and by an inordinately grumpy waitress plodded towards us and stood scowling into space. I ordered "suey mein" and the waitress began to gabble a stream of Jamaicanese at us, looked at me and giggled, then stomped off.

"What did she say?"

Little Mannie was playfully tearing bits off the menu. "She say they nah have no food."

"None?"

"None."

We sat for a good five minutes in morose silence before we burst into fits of laughter.

On our next try for Montego Bay we took a taxi to the railway station. Unfortunately, the taxi driver filled the car with six other passengers who insisted on being deposited first at far-off destinations. By the time we reached the station the inevitable had happened once again.

"Don't waste yeyewater dawta," ["Don't waste your tears, girl"] soothed Little Mannie, on seeing my dismay. "We a-go zoo hinstead. Mek we get a bus a Kingston." I agreed.

In the packed mini-bus, on the way to Kingston, we laughed over people's heads about what could go wrong at the zoo. With my limited English sense of disaster, I suggested it would be closed. Little Mannie, however, with his native Jamaican intuition, said that the animals would not be in cages but running wild. While the bus swung this way and that along staggeringly beautiful country roads at ninety miles an hour, Little Mannie and I kept the passengers amused with our tales of the horrors-to-be at the zoo.

To get to the zoo you walk through the wonderful Hope Gardens. Hope Gardens is an enormous tropical park in uptown Kingston. Never have I seen the like: lush palms, lily-ponds in brilliant bloom and exquisite flowers. All these wonders lie beneath the misted Blue Mountains. Surprisingly enough, we were the only people there.

After a delightful stroll we found ourselves at the zoo and paid one dollar (about fifteen pence) to get in. Little Mannie and I looked at one another, our faces registering disappointment. Nothing had gone wrong. The zoo looked beautifully laid out, although devoid of people. It was not only open, but had cages by the score.

The first cage we looked at had a large sign reading "Indian Coney". We peered in, but found no sign of the coney.

"What is an Indian coney?"

"Me nah know – it not there."

"Well, is it a snake, elephant, guinea-pig, fish, or what?"

"C'mon, Mr Coney, beg you reveal y'self to me an' the lady!"

But the Indian coney appeared to be suffering from an advanced state of stage fright. The next cage had no sign – and no animals. The rest of the cages followed suit.

"Is why we nah guess *then* what seem so hobvious *now*? De zoo have no hanimals!"

To tell the truth, I don't think I've ever enjoyed a trip to the zoo so much. Looking at all those empty cages and laughing with Little Mannie made my holiday. Somehow or other a tiger had found its way into a cage, and so had an enormous python, but apart from that, our pleasure at staring into empty cages remained unmarred.

After the thrill of our day at the zoo, I gave Montego Bay up as a lost cause. No bus, train or cousin would take us, so I felt it best to admit defeat. I would buy a guide book about this elusive stretch of beach, describe what I had read to my friends in England, and pretend I'd been. No self-respecting tourist can admit to not having seen Montego Bay.

But Little Mannie overcame all obstacles, and soon we were savouring some of the magical delights that Jamaica had on offer. Dunns River Falls, a dramatically beautiful waterfall, and Ocho Rios, a lovely spa in the north of the island. But getting around was difficult.

If you are without a car in Jamaica, getting from A to Montego B. is rather like phoning the Social Security about a delayed giro: a hazardous task, but worth it in the end. The Jamaican scenery is the most lovely sight in the world. Lush palms and banana trees surrounded by exotic flowers, all in vivid colours. You only have to go one minute out of town to see fabulous mountains, rivers, lakes and gorges. Owing to the lack of transport Little Mannie, who became my interpreter/ handsome escort, either took me around on foot, walking for miles at a time, or on the mini-buses. The competition between the mini-bus drivers is so great that the drivers grab you, shouting: "Kingston! Manderville! Spanish Town!" The strongest of the lot will seize you and frogmarch you towards a tiny mini-bus, packed solid with people. "B-but I don't want to go to Kingston!" you protest as you are wedged between a tight-lipped old lady and a basket of green bananas. "Is where you a go?" "May Pen!" But it's too late. The bus hurtles down the road at breakneck speed. Evel Knievel is the idol of the Jamaican driver. The bus finally deposits you at a remote town, leaving you almost too dazed to inquire how to get to where you actually wanted to go.

"I always imagined that Jamaica was chock-a-block full of Rastas and reggae, but in actual fact, I've only seen about two Rastas, and have hardly heard any reggae."

"If you mean de man we saw jus' now, he's not a Rasta, himma mad man who don' comb him hair, and reggae – well it jus' de ragamuffin dem who listen to de stuff."

"Also, there's no teenagers here."

"'Course there is!"

"No, what I mean is that everyone under the age of eighteen is a child, and anyone over is an adult. You don't get yobs roaming the streets at night, or hanging round street corners shouting abuse at passers-by, like you do in England. In fact I've never come across a more decent bunch of teenagers in my life. Standing up for you on buses and calling you 'Miss' the whole time. It's wonderful! You can even shout at them in the streets without them answering you back."

"What's a yob?"

"A young person who goes about in a gang making trouble."

"Like a gunman?"

"No, more like a – well, when your bups takes you to England, you'll see them hanging around shopping precincts."

"What's a shopping precinct?"

Everything about England fascinated and thrilled Little Mannie, and everything Jamaican repelled him. Jamaica is a very unloved country. Very few people make a go of the good life there. Instead of building up a better Jamaica, Jamaicans save up every penny they can earn, and shoot off to England or the States, leaving bitter wives or husbands behind. Little Mannie, however, was keen to take his girlfriend with him. I had never met the woman, but I didn't like the sound of her. Every now and then he would disappear for a few days, and return to say that he had *had* to see her otherwise she would have felt neglected.

The days he was not around, I would do nothing, save play endless games with the children and run down men with Janice. Janice's philosophy was that men are like dogs: they must be kept well under control.

"You show a dog who's master from very hearly stage, then the dog will respect and obey you at all times. Give a dog too much kindness, and dog'll bite you. Same with a man. Treat them mean to keep them keen!"

Maybe Janice's philosophy was the one we all ought to follow, because Janice's husband never left for work before he had washed the clothes, prepared the evening meal, and given his four children a bath in the wooden shower house in the garden. I would watch him through lazy eyelids. Janice never expected me to do anything save give her any clothes of mine that she took a fancy to.

Kidnapped in the Blue Mountains
JAMAICA

*W*aiting for Little Mannie one day, I received an unpleasant shock. A tall gangly young man mooched down the pathway leading into the scrubby garden, stopped, and stood scowling at me, blinking in the sunlight. I was sitting on the wall, with four children on my lap, and Petty sitting between my legs.

"Who are you, and what do you want?" called Desmond, in a cheeky little voice.

The stranger glanced scathingly at the child, muttering some vile Jamaican oath under his breath. A tiny black pig began to root around his feet, grunting, and covering his already blackened shoes with slimy filth.

"Where Zvomba? Me-a tol' to see some gyal name Zvomba."

Petty instantly became wary, and clung round my legs, whimpering like a young whelp. Like me, Petty very obviously did not like the look of this young man, who continued to stand in the middle of the garden, a Rasta cap stretched over his picky hair; his features puckered into a permanent scowl.

"If you mean Zenga," I said, placing Kuba and the youngest child on the ground, "then I am she."

"You!" he asked incredulously, as though he couldn't believe that someone could have played so cruel a joke on him as to have sent him to see so nauseating a person as myself. "You Zvomba?"

"ZENGA, yes."

He gave me one long lingering look of distaste, as though deciding in his mind whether to turn tail now or carry out his mission.

"Well you see it like this, still. Likkle Mannie 'im seh 'im cyan come today, on account of 'im gyal frien' get cross 'cause she no see 'im no more since you come 'pon de scene, check? So 'im sen' me fe tek you hout today. Him seh him sorry (an' so am I)."

That last "an' so am I" bit was rather unnecessary, I thought, but of course I didn't say so.

"So you're taking me out?"

"Likkle Mannie say me got to."

"Where are you going to take me."

"A-wha'? Me cyan hunderstand your H-e-n-glish haccent." "Henglish" was drawn out very slowly, so I could fully appreciate the contempt in which he held the word and all it stood for.

"I said, 'Where are you going to take me?'"

"Ah, Likkle Mannie 'im seh to tek you to Negril. 'im give me likkle bit-a money too. 'Im want me fe drive you in me cyar."

"I see."

"Don't go, Aunty, me wan' you to tek us racing again!" said dear little Petty.

"Go, go! And take me with you!" cried Desmond.

The young man and I eyed one another with mutual distrust. On the one hand I did not like the look of him, and knew that a day spent with so malevolent a creature would be sheer purgatory, but, on the other (and equally important) hand, Little Mannie had given the man his hard-won dollars to take me out: dollars which would never find their way back into Little Mannie's pocket if I were to send the young man away with a flea in his ear.

"Ya naw 'ave fe come if you naw wan' to."

"Who are you? A relative of Little Mannie?"

"Eh heh, cousin. Ya come hor not. As me seh, you naw 'ave fe if you naw wan' to."

That was it. Just to spite him, I'd go.

"Sorry, kids, I'm off."

Desmond began to throw tiny stones at me, and Petty refused to untwine from around my legs.

I went into the house to say my goodbyes to one and all. Janice insisted on coming out into the yard to "check up" on the young man, just to make sure he wasn't a member of the quashie dem, a rough neck, or a Rude Boy.

When we came back into the garden, we were surprised to see that the man had vanished without a trace.

"Him got back in de cyar," said Desmond, pointing to a battered old car parked a little way off.

Janice walked towards the car, and peered rudely through the windows. The young man glared back through a pair of mirrored shades that he had seen fit to put on in our absence.

"The man is a ginnal," came Janice's verdict, as she pulled her head back through the car window. The man, who had obviously heard, accepted Janice's snap analysis of his character with a blank stare.

"Me know 'im, y'know. 'im nem's Lilbert."

"Is he really Little Mannie's cousin?"

"Eh heh, but me naw like 'im, y'know. De man dibi-dibi, y'know, lazy, an' well spiteful. No one like 'im. Not heven Likkle Mannie. See the face 'im got now? Long and mean? Well that's the way him stay, y'know. Watch him. See? Check the nasty look 'im throw 'pon you."

Lilbert did not appear to be enjoying the turn the conversation was taking.

"Get in the cyar now, man, or I jus' drive off."

"You won't have a good time with a man like that. Careful of your gold jewellery, an' keep a close eye on your handbag."

"You coming hor not!"

"Alright. Goodbye, Janice, thanks for the advice."

"No problem," she said, as I climbed in the car, which had begun to rumble down the road. "And remember! Any trouble jus' jook 'im in the eyes!" she screamed out over the screeching engine. I turned to catch one last glimpse of Janice making stabbing motions with her two fingers. I winced. Lilbert hunched his shoulders and we clattered down the dusty road.

"So – er – how far is Negril?" I asked after we had driven for over half an hour in silence. The countryside looked beautiful, mountains and lakes on either side of the dusty road.

"So 'ow you know about Negril?"

"Didn't you say we were going to Negril?"

"Yeah, that's what me seh, seen, but first me got fe go check me cousin dem."

"What cousins?"

"Is why you hask?"

"If I'm going to see them with you, I want to know who they are."

"Why you wanna know? You no know dem."

"How far do they live?"

"Kelletts."

"Where's Kelletts?"

"Look! Why you keep hasking hall dese damn troublesome questions! Me seh me goin' to see me cousin dem, an' if you naw wanna go, den get hout now! If you do wan' go, den jus' sit in de cyar an' be 'umble."

There then proceeded a long and painful silence.

"So 'ow come you got such a posh H-e-n-glish voice. You tink you is a real fine H-e-n-glish lady?"

"Oh yes, just like Lady Diana."

"So you'd like to tink."

"I don't really think, I was just teasing you."

"So what you tink you are? You talk like dat to make your-self look big?"

"No, I talk like this, because that's the way everyone who was born in the South of England talks."

Lilbert mumbled something which sounded suspiciously like, "Shut ya bloodclot," but I didn't press the point.

"Actually, Lilbert, I've suddenly developed a bit of a headache. Could you possibly drive me back to Clarendon, I don't think I really feel up to seeing your cousins, my head is splitting."

"Hall white people tek on these headaches an' ting an' ting an' ting. Dat jus' part of de penalty you 'ave to pay for being white."

"But Lilbert, you know I'm not white, stop being stupid. Listen, I'll pay you to drive me back, and I'll tell Little Mannie that you took me to Negril, if you like."

But the spirit of spite overrode Lilbert's spirit of avarice. He stubbornly pretended not to understand what I was saying, and continued to drive with the speed of a meteor, almost crashing into countless trees and shrubs.

I began to get that tingling feeling of terror, the sort of feeling you get when you're driving with a maniac in the middle of Jamaica. However, I didn't panic, but merely sat and was 'umble.

Soon we found ourselves in the very poor, rickety town of Kelletts.

A large, grubby market-place sprawled in the town centre, the market women with a few shrivelled vegetables lying miserably on pieces of rag.

"Er – em – Lilbert?"

"WHAT!"

"Sorry – nothing."

"If you naw 'ave nothing fe say, den why open your mout?"

"Well, actually, I *was* going to say something. Am I allowed to talk?"

"Don't joke about with me, man. You got somptin fe seh, jus' go ahead an' say it. What's the matter? You 'fraid of black men?"

"Not 'specially. Why, are you?"

The car slammed to a halt.

"Right! Dat's it! Me naw love hall-a dem joke you-a play 'pon me. Tek your bag, a' gwaan hout de cyar. Ya hear me nah!"

"I hear you, but I don't believe you. I'm not leaving this car. Anyway," I continued, with justified indignation, "what have I done to deserve this burst of grumpiness? All I've done is to ask you if you're scared of black men, which is exactly what you asked me, and why that should annoy you, the devil alone knows."

"You jus' don't hask a Black Man a ting like dat."

"I don't see a black *man*."

Lilbert's lips tensed dangerously over his long teeth.

"You naw see a what?"

"A fat man."

"A-wha' you say 'bout fat man?"

"Oh, nothing special. Only that I don't see one."

Lilbert blinked in confusion. "You naw see naw fat man?"

"No, why? Do you?"

"Do what?"

"See a fat man."

"What fat man?"

"Any fat man."

Lilbert pondered for a moment, then started up the car. It was obvious to both of us that the conversation had reached saturation point.

The cousins' house was on the outskirts of Kelletts, a small cottage with a corrugated iron roof and a cosy interior, aglow with red and pink lacy doilies and a picture of the Last Supper, so large it all but covered a whole wall.

The door was opened by a very pleasant looking middle-aged lady, wearing an attractive curly wig. She grinned a glinting gold-toothed smile at us, and led us into a tiny concrete porch at the back of the house. Two pretty young girls, who I presumed were her daughters, sat on the stone wall and immediately jumped up to clear a space for me.

"Hello, hello, hello," fussed the older woman. "Come in, sit down. Lilbert! Why you so late? You s'posed to carry Nanny to doctor's today by nine-thirty. It way gone midday now. She miss her appointment hall 'cause of you. Bwaay, you is bad, y'know! Sorry to quarrel like this in front of you, miss." She turned to flash me a brilliant smile. "What you like to drink? A cold beer? Sorrel?"

"Sorrel would be lovely, thank you."

"Eee! EH! Listen to the nice, nice Queen Henglish!"

"You from Henglan'?" asked one of the young girls, in awed tones.

"Cyan you tell by her fenky, fenky ways?" muttered Lilbert, sourly.

"Don' speak like dat in front of the lady!"

I couldn't resist raising a smug eyebrow in Lilbert's direction.

"Go get her a sorrel."

"What sorrel?" asked Lilbert, removing the mirrored glasses and narrowing his eyes at me.

"The sorrel! Go get it!" Scowling and muttering, Lilbert slunk off into the kitchen.

"So, darlin'. Is how you get to know Lilbert? I wouldn't have thought a lady like you know someone as rough as that. Me know he's me nephew an' all, but him been a rough boy from mornin'."

"I can be quite rough myself when the mood takes me!"

"You!" A dainty chorus of laughter ensued.

"You ever see the Queen?" asked the elder of the two girls, then blushed quickly, and averted her eyes.

"A-wha' you seh 'bout de H-e-n-glish Queen?" Lilbert was once again in our midst.

"No, I haven't seen the Queen."

"'Ow would she see the Queen? Queen naw associate with people like dat!"

"Tattup, Digga! What wrong with you! An' why haven't you fetched the lady a sorrel?"

"Me nah see no sorrel."

"Winsome, you get it den."

"Yes, Mama."

"Hall de Queen is, is a parasite an' a vampire. A blood sucker. No respect at all me 'ave for Henglan' nor the Henglish Queen."

The woman almost crossed herself at being in the midst of what amounted to blasphemy.

"The Queen is the mother of us all!"

"Wha' Henglan' hever done for us, sept make we slaves an' keep us in poverty? What white Henglish people dem done for we," he continued, shooting me a deathray look, "sept keep us poor an' miserable, an' come to our country as nasty white touris' dem. Me naw love dem, y'know, Haunty May, me naw love dem at all."

Aunty May looked at me in shocked bewilderment, expecting me to speak up for England, thus leading Lilbert through to the paths of righteousness, where he rightfully belonged.

"I'm sorry to say this, Aunty May, if it's going to upset you, but I agree with Lilbert. What *has* England ever done for Jamaica?"

"But how can *you* say that, sweetheart? You're Henglish your-self!"

"True a-true, y'know. She *well* H-e-n-glish."

"I don't know about *well* English, but –"

"Here, let me show you the photos I've got that me nephew's sent me of the changing of the guards. An' there's a nice one of the Tower of London. Jus' wait one sec." And she bustled off into the house.

Lilbert sat with a face like thunder, lighting cigarette after cigarette.

"Me nem Wendy," said the girl, as she entered with a posh jug of red sorrel, and some glasses on a tray, "an' that me sister, 'er nem Sarah."

"De Henglish woman dere, nem Zvimba," spat Lilbert.

"Zenga."

"Zenga! African nem dat?"

"Yes."

Lilbert sucked his teeth loudly. African names, the Queen, and English people were apparently not his cup of tea.

Wendy moved timidly towards me, and asked in a high-pitched voice, "Will you send for me?"

"What, to come to England?"

"Eh heh."

While I was desperately thinking of a way to get out of having to refuse, Aunty May swept in like a breath of fresh air, and began fussing about with dog-eared postcards of London sights. At this point, Lilbert got up, and mooched sullenly towards his car.

"Ooo! That's lovely, Aunty May. Yes, I *have* been there – er – one second – Lilbert! Oh Lilbert!"

Lilbert ignored me, carried on sloping through the house, and continued in a carward direction.

"Lilbert! I thought you said you were taking me to Negril."

"Where?"

"Negril."

"Who?"

"NEG-RIL."

"Ah naw, me naw wan' go there."

"But –"

"Me – a go home now. You stay here if you like. Seem like you really hen-jaay talking 'bout Henglan', an' you see Haunty May, she too really hen-jaay talkin' 'bout Henglan'."

"But you've got to drive me back!"

"Why?"

"Because I've got no other way of getting back."

A triumphant snarl lit up his face for the moment, then melted into the normal sour Lilbertian expression.

"Den if you're coming, come."

If only I knew the man just a little bit better, I muttered to myself, I could kick him on the shin as hard as possible, but at the moment he's too much of a stranger, and besides, how do I know he wouldn't kick me back?

"Well, just let me say goodbye to Aunty May."

Lilbert's reply was to climb inside his car and rev up the engine.

Saying goodbye to Aunty May took a lot longer than I thought. I gave her and her daughters my address, and continued to chat about England, the Queen and Prince Charles, for a good ten minutes. When I finally got back to the car – it had gone. And so had Lilbert.

"Lilbert!" I called rather hopelessly, knowing that, with the speed he drives, he would be at least a mile away by now. There was nothing to do but drag my dejected body through into the back porch, and continue drinking sorrel, until the day turned to dusk and the crickets began to chirrup.

"Never min', darlin'. You can halways rest the night here. We have a nice bed for you. You won't mind giving up your bed for the lady, will you, Wendy."

"No," said Wendy eagerly. By now, I had long since given up the struggle, and had promised to see what I could do as regards sending for Wendy, Sarah, and Aunty May. I had also given Wendy my straw hat, which she wore with coquettish charm. Any minute now, I kept thinking, the talipots will be out, and then what will I do? How can

I scream in comfort, with these people who think I'm so respectable? Whatever will they think of me? And what about everyone at home worrying about me?

At eight o'clock we all trooped into the living room to watch telly, and who should be sitting, staring at the switched-off TV set, but Lilbert.

"C'mon. Me gon' drive you home now."

"Digga, you all right?" said Aunty May, casually.

"Cool," came the reply.

Someone switched on the telly, and to my delight they were showing one of my favourite Ealing comedies.

"H-e-n-glish flim – rasclot," said Lilbert, and walked quickly out of the room. I wasn't going to let him get away so nimbly this time, so I followed him with alacrity, bidding hasty farewells to one and all.

"What made you decide to return?" I asked, when I was safely in the car.

"Listen now, right. Me naw like the way you keep screaming an' fussing about the way me drive, check? If you keep on making demma noises, me gon' put you out the cyar, and let you walk, seen?"

"Digga," I said, trying to sound as matter of fact as possible.

"Naw call me dat, so. Honly me *friend* demma call me Digga."

"And relations, and I'm practically a relation, aren't I?"

Lilbert didn't reply. Instead he began to hum, and my sixth sense told me there was something sinister in that hum. It was not the pleasant, happy-go-lucky hum of the man who lives in peace with his car; no, it was the deep, volcanic hum of a man thinking, 'I have a woman in my car who I really dislike, but never mind, I have something really horrible in store for her.'

I thought it wise to keep my mouth shut.

We drove and drove for three hours in the pitch blackness. Surely this was not the way home?

"Lilbert?"

We had not passed a town or village for so long, I was beginning to get extremely edgy.

"Lilbert? How long will it take for me to get home?"

"Who's goin' 'ome?"

"Well, I was hoping it was going to be me. You see we're not on the phone, and everyone will be getting worried about me, and besides," I added, using my trump card, "everyone knows I went out with you, so they may get worried about you too, and *call the police* or something, when they realise that we've both disappeared."

"Naw dey won't," he replied, and then grinned, "'cos Likkle Mannie tol' me to book you into a hotel in Negril for de night."

I deflated visibly. Lilbert's trump was certainly a lot higher than mine.

"But Little Mannie is going to get very annoyed when he realises that you didn't take me to Negril."

"But you're gon' seh dat we-a *went* to Negril."

"No, I'm not."

The car screeched to a halt in the looming darkness. Lilbert's eyes pierced through the penetrating night.

"Yes, you are."

"Oh yes, so I am. Sorry about that, slip of the tongue and all that."

Lilbert hummed a satisfied strain, and started up the old bone-shaker once again.

"So er – sorry to trouble you again, Lilbert, sir, but where are we going now?"

"To your destination."

"Ah – I see."

"But one ting me wan' tell you before we do. Me naw like your ways, y'know. Naw like dem at all."

"Oh. That's a shame, why not?"

"You tar Henglish."

"Well, of course I talk English, I don't really know any other languages, except a little bit of Russian. If I speak a few smatterings of Russian for you, from now on, will you drive me home?"

"Don' try fe be funny, man. Me nah seh ya *talk* Henglish, me seh ya *tar* Henglish. Too Henglish."

"Well there's nothing I can do about that, I'm afraid. Just out of interest, by the way, do you make a practice of kidnapping all the people you meet who strike you as being too English?"

"Me naw kidnap you, gyal, me-a gon tek you to a place, den me-a go tomp you, an' dap you until you whistle like a peanut stand."

"Peanut stand?"

"Peanut stand."

"I didn't know peanut stands whistled."

"Well soon you-a gon' find out jus' *how* dey go whistle."

I can't say it was something I was looking forward to with much spark of anticipation. The man was clearly completely potty, and I've been told often enough, that, when it comes to handling completely potty people, courage and calmness are the key words. What I've got to try and do is get out of his car and make a run for it. If only the

Jamaican countryside had more traffic lights dotted about here and there, how easy it would be to skip out when the lights turned red.

"Your Aunty May seemed a nice lady."

"Haunty May is too hard aise."

"Yeah, she struck me as being that as well."

Humour him, I thought.

Soon we came to where I recognised as being the outskirts of Kingston. A few people tried to flag down our car for lifts. I made frantic 'help! Get me out of here!'-type faces at them, but one and all shook their heads sorrowfully, muttering "Foreigner lady demma halways inna dem waters." "Inna ya waters" is another way of saying "drunk".

One thought that comforted me was, 'He can't actually kill me, or do anything too awful to me, because he'll have his whole family to answer for, plus Delson's family.' Long ago, I remember being soothed by thoughts such as these whilst waiting behind the door which led to my headmaster's study. He can't actually kill me, I used to think: cripple me for life, possibly, but I know I'm going to get out of that study alive.

Looking at Lilbert's face unnerved me somewhat. His eyes had taken on a puffy, red quality, as he began to light up a stick of the bad stuff.

"Oh, by the way, Lilbert, if you're driving through Kingston, could you please stop off at a place where I could get something to eat, I'm starving. Then you can take me to this destination-place you were talking about after I've had a good –"

"Kibber ya mout'. The place where me now gon' tek you has got no food, no drink, an' no sweet ting to please ya eye. Besides, when me-a t'rough with you, the las', las' ting you go tink 'bout will be putting food in ya belly."

I wiped a few droplets of sweat from a furrowed brow, and gulped a few times. Not that I quite believed him, of course. I was sure that whatever he did to me, a nice piece of jerk chicken couldn't possibly go amiss. I gulped a few more times, then gazed out of the window through glazed, unseeing eyes.

After what seemed an eternity, we pulled up outside a looming, black mountain.

"Dak ya ras, man! We here."

"Where?"

"At the place where we stop."

Lilbert swung out of the car, opened my door, and took a tight grip of my left arm, pulling me roughly outside into the muggy darkness.

"Move up de 'ill, gyal."

"But I can't see where I'm going!"

"Me seh move!"

"Yes, Mister Lilbert, sir."

We struggled awkwardly up the mountain, dense undergrowth on either side of our trail. Lilbert took a tight grip on my arm all the while, pulling me forever upwards. Our faces and clothes felt as if they were being lacerated by numerous branches and creepers. I could not see anything at all, save the tiny golden glow of the ganja spliff that Lilbert held clenched in his teeth. I was dying to ask Lilbert where we were going, but somehow it didn't seem the time nor the place to break into a babble of desultory chitchat.

"Get in now, 'oman."

"In?"

"Get in the house, nah, man. Move!"

As I peered into the blackness, I managed to make out an old, broken-down wooden shack. Lilbert pulled me into it and instantly lit a kerosene lamp, which he placed on a table. The room was small and pitiful, smelling of damp wood, the only furniture being a mattress on the floor, a heavy oak table and two wicker chairs with no seats.

"Now me garn fin' somptin nasty, nasty fe your retribution. You stay right 'ere in the room, and don' try any of your crispy, crispy Henglish stupidness while me garn."

"Do I have to be retributed?"

"As me seh, don' try fe hescape, 'cause you won't have no luck at all. The bush thick it thick, y'know, an' dere's a whole heap o' poisonous snake, an' poisonous lizard, so don't tink you can get away easy. Halso, bush too thick to move."

"So the outline is, you get retribution instruments, while I keep the home fires burning, or words to that effect."

"Don' joke wid me nah, man, unless you wan' dead."

Dead is the one thing that I particularly didn't want at the moment, so I pressed my lips together and sat rather painfully on one of the seatless wicker chairs. I tried not to look at the damage that had been done to my lovely turquoise dress.

Lilbert brushed himself down, and walked out of the door, in search of nameless tools of torture. I sat by the table, watching the lamp flicker, and wondered not only what I was going to do, but why I had got into his car in the first place. The night insects were making a terrible din. Clack-clacks were clack-clacking, and crickets, frogs and snakes were chirruping, croaking, and hissing respectively. I looked through the doorway. I could no longer see any sign of Lilbert, but only a blackness alive with tropical night noises.

What, I asked myself, was worse? To be retributed by Lilbert, or to be bitten by poisonous snakes, not to mention poisonous lizards, although I must say poisonous lizards sounded a bit doubtful to me. Anyway, whether they existed or not, I wasn't prepared to risk it.

Suddenly I saw something that made my heart's blood turn to cold. A talipot, of Hammer House of Horror dimensions, sat crouching by the kerosene lamp.

"Aaagh!" I grabbed my handbag and ran into the thick density of undergrowth, my feet occasionally squelching into muddy pools of inky water. I ran and ran, blinded by fear and darkness. Then through the trees I saw a light. Was it near, or very far away?

"Help! HELP!" The light glinted as I ran towards it. I had an awful feeling I had gone full circle, and by a hideous twist of fate was now back at Lilbert's pad, and would soon be finding myself being retributed until I whistled *à la* peanut stand. Before I knew it, I was by the log cabin. A man stood in the doorway, holding a glowing oil lamp.

"Help me! I've been kidnapped by a –"

"So whappen dawta? You naw go Negril today?" said a very familiar voice.

Maybe I *was* back at Lilbert's.

"Negril? But how did you know –"

"'ow me know, Zenga? It was me who send Digga fe carry you hover Negril. Still, don't waste yeyewater now. If you change ya mind, you change your mind, innit."

I stood in the darkness, stunned. Where had I heard that voice before?

"Come in de house, now, man. Don't jus' stand there so, lookin' like loss duppy!"

"Little Mannie!"

I flung myself into his arms, overturning the oil lamp, and making him lose his balance in my excitement.

"Cool out, sis'! What all the commotion about? Get in the 'ouse, now, man, an' mek me mek you a nice cuppa tea-bag Henglish tea jus' 'ow you like it, grey an' tasteless."

"But Little Mannie! My dear one, my Grecian knight. My Nordic god in the mist! How come you're here?"

"Is what you mean how come. Where else could I be?"

"But I've just made a narrow escape from your cousin Lilbert, who was just about to retribute me."

"Lilbert? Who Lilbert? Oh, you mean Digga!"

"He lives just up there!"

"Well, of course he does. An' dis where me Mudda live, y'know. Shame you didn't tell me you were going to drop by, or I would 'ave made sure she'd be awake so I could introduce you to her. You an' 'er would get on sor well. So why you decide to drop in so late?"

We went into the little cabin, and sat in the living room, a small room with a cosy sofa and a wooden what-not in the corner. Little Mannie re-lit the lamp, and sat next to me, putting a brotherly arm around my shoulder.

"Cooday, cooday! Jesum piece! Araty roots, man!"

He stared at my face in stark horror.

"What's the matter?"

"Is what gone wrong to your face, lady? You look like someone done mash you up widda machait!"

On hearing these kind words of sympathy, I burst into an unchecked flood of tears. Little Mannie brought me an overflowing glass of white rum, and re-placed the brotherly arm.

"Digga done dat?"

"No, it happened when I was being pulled up the hill."

"Oh! he try fe beat you! Now me see! Funny, that."

"Well, I'm afraid I don't see the joke."

"Nah, what me mean still, is, it funny that I'd forgotten how much 'im 'ate Henglish foreigner dem. Hever since 'im get deported, himma de-spise foreign Henglish person."

"Deported?"

"Ah yes. 'Imma come fe Henglan', an' marry a white woman for convenience. 'Imma pay de lady two t'ousan' dollar, an' the lady boyfriend, 'im tell police, an' police dem call himmigration, an' himmigration they go sen' 'im back. Since den, the man hate-hate foreign Henglish people. Sorry me forget."

"That's all right. Don't mention it."

"You wan' fe go back?"

"I want to go back."

"Well you can't, 'cause me no 'ave no way fe drive you back, but tomorrow mornin' hearly, me an' you will get a bus back to Clarendon, seen?"

I nodded.

"Now then. Lie back 'pon de couch while me-a check de room for talipot dem, an' see if you can get some rest."

Soon a coat was thrown over me. A cup of tepid tea was placed at my elbow, and a soothing song was being sung by Little Mannie:

> Raise your hands if you wanna be sanctified,
> Raise your hands if you wanna be sanctified.

It was a song I recognised as being in the Jamaican hit parade, and I found that when sung in Little Mannie's gravelly tones, it provided just the source of comfort I required.

"Heh! Little Mannie?"

"A-wha'?"

"You don't think Lilbert's going to come back with the retribution kit."

"Dead imma dead if him does."

"Thanks, goodnight. Oh, by the way, I hope I'm not doing you out of a bed."

"Me-a go sleep wid me Mudda. By the way, if you see me girl-friend, beg you not to tell 'er dat you spent de night here. She well vex 'bout you. In fact it all 'cause of you me force to tek 'er out today y'know."

"Oh, you poor thing! Where did she force you to take her?"

"To see some of 'er relations in country. Bored me-a bored y'know. Her cousin an' her Auntie dem, chat, chat, gossip, gossip, her sisters pickney demma runnin' all around the floor, making too much nise; one of dem 'ave a toy drum an' de other 'ave a toy gun, an' between dem both they wake Count Drac 'imself. Hall de while, me-a runnin' up an' down, from kitchen to front room wid plate hafter plate of food dat her granny was pilin' on. Den de granny she run hout of food, so she send me to market to buy about fifteen pound of goat, an' twenty pound of rice. When me come back wid it hall, the gravalicious ol' lady hask ME to cook it up for her! So me spen' the nex' two hours cooking up food for dem all, an' when me finish, all-a dem blasted fambly seh, 'Naw! We naw wan' no more food. Belly full already.' Den 'er granny start up shouting at me saying I should never press food 'pon people, saying, 'Bwoy! Kill you wan kill dem?' Rhaaatid! Gyal me tell you, me well vex. Anyway, don' keep me up hall night. Me feel fe sleep now. Good night, sleep tight, an' wake up sober."

"Goodnight, Little Mannie."

The night noises, that before had sounded like the demonic laughter of imps from hell, now lulled me into a blissful sleep.

A brilliant ray of sunshine had been shining on my face all morning, but because I had been asleep, I had worked it into a dream. Nazi Gestapo were shining lights into my eyes, shouting in guttural tones, "Peanut shtanden peanut shtanden peanut shtanden!"

I opened my eyes to see an old lady wearing a floral cotton dress busily sweeping the floor with a brushwood besom.

"Mornin', darlin'? It so nice of you to drop by and see your old haunty."

Where was I? Oh yes, Little Mannie's mother's house, which means I must be in the Blue Mountains, and the lady must be Little Mannie's mother.

"Good morning, Ma'am, thank you very much for letting me stay in your nice house."

Little Mannie's mother continued to clean the floor with an energy that belied her frail old body. There was no food in the house, she told me, only an egg which the hen had laid that morning. Her grey green eyes surveyed me sharply.

"Are you African?"

"Yes," I replied, "my father was from West Africa."

"Me know dat, lady. He dead now, though."

"How did you know?"

"Lot o' ting me know, and dese . . ." pointing to her eyes, ". . . see. Wash in the river. Haaron will show you where to go."

I walked outside into a beauteous paradise. Behind the log cabin was a wooden shack, from which soft voices filtered through. Little Mannie and a twelve-year-old boy were squatting by a stone oven, boiling an egg in an aluminium pot.

"Sis' Zeng! How's it hanging? Meet me nephew, Haaron. Haaron, show sis' Zenga where to go for beard."

"Beard?"

"Eh heh."

"What do I need a beard for?"

"You naw have beard in the morning time?"

"I don't have beards at any time."

"You *never* have beards?"

"Not that I've been aware of."

"Henglish people dem don' have beards?"

"Not the women."

"But the men do?"

"Some do, but most of them don't . . ."

I won't go into this conversation any deeper, because it lasted for a very long time. The gist of it was, beard meant bath, and I am afraid to say that I left at least two of the Jamaican population with the impression that the English are "the great unwashed".

The river I bathed in was a rocky blue torrent, aswarm with red and silver fish. Aaron walked down the hill with me, followed by a speckly pig whom he called "Bacon Bill". A tall slim Rastafarian cowherd, swishing a whippy stick, led a herd of cattle to pasture.

"See me huncle dere. Imma live not far from 'ere," squeaked Aaron.

When we got back to the cabin, I insisted Little Mannie's mother eat the egg. Her house was so sparsely furnished, and she was so pathetically thin.

"Please marry me son, ma'am. Tek 'im to Hengland, an' mek 'im rich."

"I'll see what I can do."

"Send for him – and Aaron."

"I'll think it over."

Little Mannie began to sing the wedding march, then laughed loudly with embarrassment. I began to laugh as well, in equally mirthless tones.

"See how she bend double an' cackle like laying hen. What she don' know is dat to laugh in the face of oppression –" and little white sparks seemed to fly from her eyes, "means *death*!"

"Cool, Mummy, we naw laugh at you, we laughing at weself."

His mother began to rock back and forth, squatting on the ground, rhythmically picking dust off the floor. Aaron fetched a damp rag from a pail and mopped the old lady's forehead with it.

"Come, sis'. Mek we go weh."

Little Mannie led me from the cabin, and we took a long pensive walk through the Blue Mountains. Neither of us spoke, but everything had changed. No longer could we laugh and joke together, and from that moment on, we were never so free in each other's company.

"Mek we getta train to Montego Bay," he suddenly announced.

I agreed, although my heart was not really in the adventure. We took a mini-bus to May Pen, and from there caught a train to Montego Bay. It was one of those enchanted days when everything seemed to go right.

The train was cool and pleasant, with hawkers walking up and down selling everything from cool drinks to fried fish and bammy, a local fried bread. As we approached Montego Bay, I saw a sight which startled and amazed me. Another train, seemingly designed for tourists, pulled up alongside ours, and in the carriages were white tourists being serenaded by Jamaicans wearing Morecambe and Wise style Latin American costumes, shaking maracas and singing "Island in de Sun". Girls walked up and down the train selling very expensive batik materials to the tourists, who crooned and clucked over the "genuineness" of it all. Rastas in their hundreds milled up and down selling wooden carvings, jewellery and shoddy looking ornaments, all at inflated prices.

Little Mannie and I gazed at each other in utter surprise. So *here* were the tourists, and this is what they apparently do. They don't go to the churches, the markets or wander around the towns. They go on guided tours everywhere, being entertained by bogus "Jamaican culture".

"See the Rastaman dere. What we call 'professional Rasta'. Jus' hang round the tourist dem, trying to be as Jam-eeya-can as dey can be."

"So they're not real Rastas?"

"Kiss me neck, what's a real Rasta? How me see it, still, a real Rasta is a man who smoke up all the sensi 'im can lay 'im 'and on, den follow tourist dem around giving demma taste of what dey all like to tink of as local colour. Halso dey honly go wid white girl, dem."

"Does that annoy you?"

"Not so long as dey keep clear me path."

"But what sort of a Jamaica are the tourists seeing?"

"A fantasy one."

Our train had stopped beside the tourist train, and a few hopeful women, wearing long, flowered skirts and brightly coloured bandanas, filtered over towards our carriage, holding up various bits and pieces for the passengers' inspection. No one in our train was interested, the travellers being mainly sleepy old ladies.

Then, from out of the blue, a muscular Rasta swaggered towards Little Mannie and me, and ordered us to buy a hideous carving of a demented goat.

"Me nah want de goat, man, it got Denga fever, an' I'll get sick if me so much as touch the diseased ting, so gwarn," said Little Mannie righteously.

"Buy de goat, now man, selling cheap."

"Beg a favour, man, bury de ting, but make sure it a Christian burial or its duppy'll haunt you forever."

"A wha' you seh, man! Me made de goat wid me hown 'ands. Me nah like the way you say, y'know, you talk like a white man."

"Eh eh, brer Dreddy, dat jus' where you wrong. If I was a white man, I would 'ave bought de ting, den dey'd have to fly me in ambulance plane back to Miami to be treated for the hillness that that goat would surely hinfect me wid."

The Rasta gave up, and touted the goat elsewhere. If you ever hear of a case of a person with Denga fever caught off a wooden goat, you'll know the Rasta finally had some luck. The train chugged back into action, and, after a five-hour journey, we were in Montego Bay.

I climbed from the train to view the scene – and gulped. An unpleasant little town tainted with the worst traits of tourism. People clustered around us, trying to sell us rubbish at exorbitant prices.

We had to pay to go on the beach, and pay through the nose to use the beach niceties, such as showers and deckchairs. The beach was surrounded by grey, ugly hotels. Tourists lay about like beached whales, whining in loud American accents that they couldn't leave the beach because it was too violent in the town. "Those people y'know . . ." and they gave Little Mannie a meaningful look. Little Mannie (looking resplendent in his floral beachwear) sucked his teeth.

"Kiss me neck. Y'see why me naw like tourist dem."

I could see, but pointed out that I too was a tourist.

"Nah, you's foreigner."

Can't say fairer than that.

So after an hour lying in the scorching heat, bloated tourists on one side, menacing skyscrapers on the other, we bought expensive ice-creams, and jumped into a taxi. The driver began to shout at us when he realised that Little Mannie was Jamaican and so wouldn't fall for his tale that the Jamaican tourist board had set a rate of fifty dollars a mile. Fifty dollars seemed a cheap way out of Montego Bay, so we hopped into the taxi, caught the train, and sailed back to Clarendon.

The next day Little Mannie took me to the Craft Market in Kingston, where I bought a ridiculously large number of souvenirs, mainly water pots and carved heads.

"The only person who would want anything so ugly in dere house, is me Mudda, an' dat only 'cause she mad . . ."

"Well, then your mother can have them."

"A-true?"

"A-true."

"Zenga."

"What."

"You is a real lady."

"I know."

"But if you tink you can try fe bribe me Mudda outa forcing you to marry me, you may as well save your money."

But he took them, and caught a mini-bus to his mother's house in the Blue Mountains, and I never saw him again. Nor did I ever hear from him because Little Mannie, one of the brightest men I have ever met, was illiterate.

On our last day in Jamaica, there was a huge kerfuffle. Barclay was driving passengers around in his mini-bus, leaving only Big Mannie to drive us to the airport. Big Mannie said that he would not drive us for less than five hundred dollars. Because none of us had anything even approaching so enormous a sum, it began to appear that we would have to stay in Jamaica for ever.

Just as we were preparing to unpack, and learn patois, Lady Luck knocked on the door in the portly form of an old lady who announced herself as Aunt Evadne. After cursing Big Mannie's name, and the name of his children, she produced a roll of notes, and peeled off five hundred-dollar bills, which she duly handed over to a wide-eyed Big Mannie.

"Here, tek the money, bwoy, an' may you never 'ave a day's luck wid it."

"Tank you, Haunt Evadne, miss," he mumbled, visibly deflating.

Barclay, Janice, Middle Mannie and naughty little Desmond all stood on the porch to wave goodbye to us.

"Me put a goodbye Aunty present inna you cigarette pack," said Desmond, dolefully. "But you not to hopen it till you on de plane."

Desmond seemed so unbearably subdued. Only a vague glimmer of cheekiness stirred somewhere behind the eyes, reassuring me pleasantly that underneath it all, the old fighting spirit lived on.

Oh, how I'll miss you all, I thought, but how glad I am to be leaving you. Oh, Jamaica, land of religious, careworn people. As I sped through Kingston's ruinous streets for the last time, I had a strong conviction that something must be done fast, but what? Somebody has to do something to make Jamaicans love Jamaica, island of the world's most exquisite scenery.

Boko fell asleep on the way to the airport, and Big Mannie asked me again if I would marry him.

I lit a cigarette out of nerves, and what should fall out of the packet, but an enormous dead talipot.

"Desmond!" I shrieked. "I'll kill the blighter!"

Failed Poets and Too Much Tacos
THE DOMINICAN REPUBLIC

*T*he morning I was to fly off to the West Indies, Marcia woke me up with the breakfast, a cup of tea and an aspirin. A rumble of thunder rolled quietly in the distance. A bad omen.

There are always things you think you've forgotten to pack. These are usually lying at the bottom of the suitcase after you've turned the whole house upside down looking for them, then there are the things you actually *have* forgotten to pack, and those are laid neatly by the suitcase in readiness. There they lie until you return. My white suit which I had bought especially for the trip was lying in a plastic bag by the bed. It never saw the Caribbean.

Marcia became very excited after she had drunk her morning coffee.

She fluttered about arranging my hair in neat plaits, and even gave me her pretty green comb to put at the side of my head. I took it out again. Green is an unlucky colour.

"Let's hope you'll come back to England with all the superstitions knocked out of you," she muttered, placing the comb in her own hair.

Rap! The mini-cab had arrived.

"Oh well, Zenga, this is it."

"Marcia, how am I going to cope without you? Can I phone you all the time?"

"No."

"Thanks. I'll call you as soon as I get to Santo Domingo."

A brroom of thunder shook the block.

"No, it's not a bad omen."

"Oh, Marcia —"

"Look, get out! You'll be late."

I took up my small suitcase and handbag, and walked out of the flat, looking appealingly at Marcia, hoping she'd persuade me not to go after all. She merely scowled, so I followed the grumpy Nigerian mini-cab driver down the stairs to the lift.

"Hey!" Marcia flung the door open. "Your airline tickets!" She threw me a bundle of tickets kept together with an elastic band.

"Oh my goodness, thanks, Marcia. Goodbye!"

"Bye."

"Bye, Marcia!"

"Bye."

"Bye!"

"Get out of the house now before you miss your plane."

I stepped into the lift.

"Bye, Marcia!" I yelled. The door closed. A faint "bye" caught my ears as the lift clanked downwards. My journey had begun.

The mini-cab had first to pick up my mother who lives near Ladbroke Grove.

The sky was still dark, and now the rain was pouring down in great globules. I knew exactly what my mother would say when she saw me. She would say, "Ach! What a mess you look. Straighten yourself up, my girl!"

My mother, born in Paris of East European parents, is known as the "Tigress of Kensal Green". The love I bear for her is not unmixed with awe and trepidation.

Her house looked so dinky and chintzy from the outside. Glowing lights behind lace curtains, peeling stucco over the door. Even though the windows of the cab were firmly wound down, the noise of my brother's screaming came through loud and clear. I glanced at the driver, hoping he hadn't heard, or if he had, he wouldn't connect the shrill sounds with me. But the cabbie's face was immobile and shuttered. Maybe he had a brother who screamed as well. He beeped his horn and waited, drumming his fingers on the steering wheel in time to the high-life music that was playing in his cassette. A man with a squeaky voice was singing,

> "When woman get a shake up on a Saturday night,
> Man wigga wigga, and everything all right."

Normally I get pleasure out of telling mini-cab drivers where they come from, and laughing at their look of surprise when they say, "How did you know I was Ibo?" (or whatever) but that day I felt too tense. What if my brother continued screaming for another hour? How would I ever catch the plane?

"Aaagghh!"

The door of the house flew open, and four dogs ran out into the road, followed by my mother, my three-year-old nephew, and my brother Lancelot, who let out a shrill scream. My mother grabbed the stodgiest dog, a King Charles Spaniel, and I leapt out of the car and called my two Bichons Frisés. They bounded towards me, yapping, licking my face, and covering my blue dress with muddy paw marks.

"I knew this would happen! I knew it! It's all your fault, Mamushka. I told you not to open the door so quickly before I'd had time to tie those bedevilled curs to the banisters! It's an accursed day, I can tell. Nothing's going to go right." Lancelot stood by the door, cursing aloud to an unfeeling world, his face a hollow mask of despair.

"Oh shut up, my son, and catch Genghis," said my mother calmly.

"Blood oath! What villainous treachery is this? If a mongrel dog runs wild and free in a thunder storm, then black deeds of trickery are afoot. Oh hell! Oh heavens! Aaagghh!"

"Oh for goodness sake, you're as bad as Zenga – oh hello, Zenga, ach! What a mess you look. Abbas will feel ashamed of you when he sees you. Never mind, at least my boy will be getting away from all this rain."

"But, Mamushka, this is thunder! What sort of an omen is that?"

"An accursed omen! I know I'll never see Zenga again." And Lancelot stood with his head on the door frame, and wept silent tears. My mother, nephew and I ignored him, and shooed the last of the dogs into the house. Finally we succeeded in shooing Lancelot and nephew in as well, slammed the door, and made our way to the car.

"Zenga!" Lancelot stood with the door a fraction ajar. "Have you got the horseshoe?"

"Yes."

"The crucifix?"

"Yes."

"The star of David?"

"Yes."

"Keep them with you at all times for blood's sake!"

"I will. Goodbye, Lancelot."

"Oh, Zenga – look at me just one more time so at least I'll be able to remember what you looked like when that fateful telegram arrives."

We stared at each other, then I climbed into the car. The driver's face was as expressionless as ever. As we moved forward I turned to wave at Lancelot, who waved back, and shoom! What seemed like seventy dogs pelted into the street barking and howling, followed by Lancelot, followed by my nephew.

"Please don't scream, Lancelot, everything will be all right, I'll look after you," I heard my nephew squeak as we turned a corner and splashed down the road.

The posh side of Notting Hill Gate was our next stop, to pick up my middle brother, Abbas Yusef. He was to accompany me to the first three countries of the trip, leaving for England after we had spent a few days in Dominica.

When we arrived at his luxurious bachelor flat, Abbas was of course not nearly ready for us.

The driver agreed to wait for an indefinite amount of time whilst I and my mother mounted the wet steps leading to the flat. The door swung gracefully open, and there stood Abbas, wearing a green silk dressing gown, tied at the waist with enormous tassels. He arched an eyebrow at us as though we were the last people he expected to see.

"Mmmmm?"

"Abbas, my boy! You look sick! How are you? Have you been eating properly?"

"How sweet of you to offer words of such comfort. Do come in, Mamushka."

Abbas went behind a peacock-blue Chinese screen, and emerged after a long time clad in a baggy cream suit and a white Panama hat. I felt too nervous to laugh at him. Fragments of my dream kept coming back to me. It had something to do with an aeroplane. My mother, however, laughed heartily, first at Abbas, then at the mini-cab driver who had been waiting for half an hour.

Abbas also had only one small suitcase which he tossed into the boot, and away we sped, past Marble Arch and Victoria. London had begun to bustle, black with shiny umbrellas and dark-suited men. How I love you, London! At eight-thirty we were at Gatwick Airport.

Why is it that as soon as you step into an airport a nameless dread grips your heart with vice-like talons? You could have been looking forward to your holiday for weeks, and yet as soon as you hear that echoing female voice blaring over the intercom about Gate Sixes and Terminal Sevens, you feel like turning tail and beetling back to Brixton, or wherever it is you've come from. If just one airport official knew anything at all, it wouldn't be so bad, but all of them giving you a cynical curl of the upper lip when you ask with tear-filled eyes the way to the check-in, is heart-rending.

We sat in Gatwick Village eating a very expensive breakfast, with my mother fussing over Abbas in the most ludicrous manner.

"Poor Abbas! Are you sure you're eating enough food? You look so thin."

"Of course I am eating food, Mamushka, why, I eat nothing else."

"Have you got your malaria tablets?"

"Any mosquito who ventures near me will need the medication, not I."

"Here, have my egg. Eat, my son, eat!"

Seeing the way she treats my brothers makes me feel very glad I was not born a boy. Abbas and I sat silent, whilst my mother chattered on nineteen to the dozen, telling me how lucky I was that Abbas was accompanying me, and how I *must* look after him and make sure his clothes are washed, he eats enough, and he doesn't get led astray by scheming temptresses. Abbas sat playing with a cold fried egg, a wry smile playing about his lips. The thought of scheming temptresses had obviously struck a chord somewhere.

And then a light began to flash and it was our time to board. My stomach began to churn, and I was seized with a terrible fear that I was never coming back again. Somehow, somewhere, I was going to die. I clasped my mother tightly.

"Mama-léb, Zenga, pshol von! Look after Abbas – Abbas, are you all right?"

"Not if I know Zenga's going to behave like this all through the trip."

"Goodbye, Abbas, take care of yourself, and be careful what you eat. Steer clear of fish, milk and, of course, sausages. Make sure you phone me once a week. Oy yoy oy yoy oy yoy. Don't run about like a kakkelak, already. Goodbye, goodbye! Enjoy. Oh, bye then, Zengchutska, ech, shmendrik!"

Abbas, impatient to leave, waved a dismissive hand and disappeared through the bleeper thing that makes a funny noise if you're carrying guns or wearing expensive jewellery.

"Oh well, Mamushka, this is it! Look after my dogs, and write lots of letters telling me everything in detail. I'll miss you."

"Yes, yes, make sure Abbas gets enough sleep. My boychik never gets enough rest. Ah haida! Maybe I should never have allowed my son to go away with a clay goilem like you. Ach vay!"

And that was the last thing my mother said to me. Maybe I'd never see her again. Why couldn't I be normal, and look forward to this trip?

Abbas and I didn't talk very much to one another as we boarded the plane. All I could think of to say was how much I was dreading the trip, and so I thought it wise to keep my mouth shut.

Now I don't know if I've told you this before, and if I haven't, maybe you've already guessed, but I'm terrified of flying. I never know which is worse, taking off, landing, or being up there. I'm convinced the plane only goes up by fluke. A tube train doesn't suddenly start going up in the air, so why should an aeroplane? The whole thing's too absurd to be true.

I felt pathetically grateful to Abbas. What on earth would I do without him. Seat-belts clasped, Abbas flipped through airport magazines, and watched through lazy eyelids air-hostesses donning life-jackets. The plane whirred a bit, went slowly round a few corners, then whirred again. Then it made a gallant attempt to move and stopped. Suddenly it lunged forward, jerked, and finally let out a slow, dismal death rattle. We were all told to get out. I had an awful feeling someone was going to ask us to push, but luckily we just had to wait for seven hours in the airport lounge until most of the passengers got fed up and went home.

Of course, from then on, everything went wrong.

We flew to New York and waited for six hours at Kennedy Airport, then on to Miami where we finally arrived at six o'clock English time. Passengers were shouting at Cuban airport officials about their luggage. Where did the myth spring up that Latins are fiery, and the English self-contained? Big, boozy Englishmen yelled loudly at petite Cuban women, who replied in cool, polite voices. Maybe the English have changed, but I suspect they've always been stormy and have kept it a secret.

Only Abbas, fast asleep, sitting bolt upright, resembled Tutankhamun in a moment of soporific serenity. How could he sleep? Life's too tense.

During the plane ride over to the Dominican Republic next day, Abbas looked up from his book of Dryden's plays, and said, "There's something rather fishy about the Dominican Republic."

"Why?" I asked, startled that Abbas could come out with such a statement.

"Because no one's ever heard of it. People assume it's either in Spain, Central America, Africa or Asia, but other than that, they neither know nor care about its whereabouts."

"What's its claim to fame?"

"It had an evil dictator called Trujillo who came to power in 1930, and after a reign of terror, he was assassinated in the early sixties. He hated black people and slaughtered thousands of Haitians."

"That doesn't sound very promising."

"But according to Amnesty International, it now has a better record for lack of political violence than anywhere else in the world."

A very attractive Dominican lady seated in front of us, told us in near perfect English how well she remembered Trujillo's oppressive regime. He did everything in his power to make the Dominican Republic look better off than neighbouring Haiti. Roads leading from Haiti were perfect, but only for a mile or two, so that the visitor could gape at the difference between the two countries. Santo Domingo, the capital, was dressed up to look splendid during his dictatorship, she said, so that tourists could favourably compare it with Haiti's capital, Port-au-Prince.

"Dressed up?"

"You know, hideous buildings put up everywhere."

She told me that I would never get by in Santo Domingo unless I could speak Spanish, and offered to teach me my first two words of the language. Unfortunately I had forgotten them by the time I reached Santo Domingo.

The immigration officials were friendly and chatty, not that I could understand what was being friendlily chatted because their English was only slightly better than my Spanish. Unlike me, they had not forgotten their first two words.

British passports baffled them somewhat. A short, stout man copied down my London address on a form, but for nationality he wrote "American" in big red letters.

"No, *señor*, British."

"*Si, si*," he said, flipping me a lecherous wink, "*Americana*."

Abbas, who had also gone down for posterity as an American citizen, merely laughed, and we stepped out of the airport into a gaggle of young men. They pulled us and twisted our clothes out of shape, begging us to hire one of their cars. So thrilled was I at being called "*señorita*" that I was sorely tempted to hire a car from one of them.

"When I've gone back to England," thundered Abbas, dragging me towards the taxi rank, "then you can hire cars off handsome young men even though you can't drive. You can even hire aeroplanes from them. But when I'm around, I must insist that your behaviour takes on a semblance of sanity."

I only half heard him. I was too busy looking out of the window at the rain-soaked streets.

From the airport we drove through miles of wide palm-fringed streets, seeing very few people, and then, in another instant, we were in the heart of Santo Domingo. Everything looked so peculiar and old-fashioned, like a weird Spanish town of the sixteenth century. Winding little streets and alleyways meandered through quaintly lop-sided flat-roofed houses. The buildings were enhanced by a crumbling effect, painted in gay pinks and greens. Picturesque narrow streets were thronged with people selling fruits, cooked meats and trinkets, on makeshift stalls. Mothers with raggedy, barefoot children sheltered in the doorways of the dilapidated old shops, the rain falling upon their faces, turning their hair to snake-like tendrils. A group of little shoe-shine boys scurried underneath an orange stall, their bare feet black with watery sludge. Huddled together, they laughed loudly at the ingenuity of their hiding-place. Everyone looked so warm and so cheerful, with brown complexions which the lady on the plane had described as "*mestizo*" or mixed blood, very similar to my own skin colour, only enriched by the sun.

"It looks so poor!" said Abbas.

"It looks so Spanish!" came my reply, as indeed it did. The ladies wore their hair scraped back in true Carmen style, some with a hibiscus pinned up at the side.

"*Scusi Señor* – is our hotel very far from town?" The driver shrugged and switched on loud Latin American music. He was a stolid man, with a complexion of such brilliance, he made Abbas look a little grey and lifeless.

The taxi swerved round a bend, and we found ourselves on the sea-front, chugging slowly behind a stream of long American jalopies which billowed out great clouds of black smoke.

My mother had said that the pure, Caribbean air would do Abbas good. I would have done anything to see her here now, witnessing Abbas winding up the windows and coughing hoarsely. I smirked, and lit another cigarette.

The sea-front was one mass of ugly modern buildings, hidden behind tall coconut palms. On the other side, a dark, ominous ocean lashed and foamed. Just my luck if it were to rain the whole time.

Our hotel, a tall concrete building, was about a mile away from the town centre. Staggeringly beautiful girls stood at the reception, tall and brown, with long black hair and flashing eyes. The prettiest of the lot peeled back her lurid red lips into a smile, and fluttered false eyelashes at Abbas. Abbas tipped back his hat with a thin gold pen, leant upon the desk, and began to chat with her, tut-tutting softly every time she mispronounced a word. Standing rather foolishly in the middle of the room with my cases, I began to wonder whether I was going to like Santo Domingo after all. Abbas was right. There must be some reason why no one's ever heard of it, and I was determined to find out what it was.

The hotel's decor struck me as being surprisingly heavy and old-fashioned for so modern a building. A few opulent Dominicans sat crossed legged on the leather divans, smoking and drinking brandy, murmuring in soft Spanish. There only appeared to be one other foreigner, a very dark man, with a shaved head, and gold nose studs. Maybe he was American.

Eventually Abbas tore himself away from the dark-eyed señorita, and we made our way to our room, a musty affair with thick, carved furniture. Abbas popped into the shower, and I lay on one of the beds, and switched on the telly. A black Benny Hill, wearing a beret, was making crude jokes in saucy Spanish to loud canned laughter. Seeing him roll his eyes, and leer into the camera, made me lament that I had never learnt Spanish. Then a beautiful woman appeared on the screen, and began to sing Salsa music in a shrill voice. She sounded a bit like Lancelot had done that morning – or was it yesterday morning? Time had suddenly jumbled itself up in my mind.

Abbas emerged from the bathroom in an African shirt, and cool blue trousers.

"When did we leave England? Yesterday, the day before, or this morning?"

"Don't worry about that now," he said, clapping his hat upon his head, "let's go."

I took up my Spanish phrase-book, and we went out to explore. The rain had cleared somewhat, and the seaside looked quite pleasant. How glorious it was not to have to wear a coat. A little buggy sporting a red fringed canopy, pulled by a mule, clip-clopped alongside us. Seeing me stare in entranced rapture, the two old men sitting in front pulled up alongside us and began to persuade us to get in, in streams of Spanish. I pulled out the phrase-book and frantically fumbled with the pages, trying to find out how to ask how much they charged, but, for the life of me, I couldn't find the right phrase. "Where is the station?", "Where is the American Embassy?", even, "Will you kiss me, please?", but "How much do you charge?" could not be found for love nor money.

"Forty pesos," one of the old men said in a sudden burst of English. Forty pesos is about five pounds, so I jumped in, dragging a reluctant Abbas in beside me.

We drove to an exquisitely beautiful old fort, where Christopher Columbus's son had once lived. All the architecture around the area was centuries old, with cobbled streets, and beautifully maintained buildings. The beauty was so pure and breathtaking, it transported the visitor back in time to an age of luxury and gracious living.

The mule-buggy men waited outside the historic fort, while a guide who spoke unintelligible English showed us around, up and down the winding old stairs.

Opposite the fort was a museum, built in the sixteenth century, guarded by savage-looking soldiers.

When we had looked around for about half an hour, we walked back to the buggy.

"Eh! Wite! Wite! Eees eye-tee pesos," shouted our guide.

"Eighty pesos?"

"*Si*, eye-ty pesos."

Abbas told me not to pay him so much, but I did without a word.

The mule-buggy men then charged us two hundred pesos because they had waited outside for us.

Before Abbas and I came to the conclusion that Santo Domingo was a dud, and that most people were crooks, we decided to walk about a bit, and give the place the benefit of the doubt. The night was warm and starry as we strolled past ancient buildings alive with olde worlde charm. It seems as if the Santo Domingan army is so large that there's nothing for the beefy young soldiers to do save stand outside all public buildings looking menacing, large guns slung over their hips.

The soldier standing outside the cathedral looked exceptionally pompous and informed us in haughty Spanish that we weren't allowed in. Undeterred, we sneaked round the back, and came across a group of nuns dressed in white, holding candles as they walked slowly into the cathedral, singing in celestial tones. We watched them, awestruck, as they glided through the huge oak doors of the house of God, until the last fluttering white veil disappeared inside.

It was a more sombre, spiritual Abbas and Zenga who then made their descent into the heart of Santo Domingo. The town is built on a slope which meanders down towards the sea and, from almost every road it is possible to see the sparkling ocean.

The town centre simply seethed with wild activity. Tiny little shoe-shine boys ran around ringing bells, grabbing passers-by by the sleeve, touting for custom. Malnourished children, knock-kneed and bare-footed, sold every knick-knack imaginable, from shoe heels to yo-yoes, which they demonstrated with gusto. The street life was quite astounding in its electrifying gaiety. Courting couples sauntered arm-in-arm, weaving in and out of the shops, which were still open at eight in the evening.

Latin American music blared from nearly every building, the ancient stones crumbling slightly every time an especially loud "Arriba!" blared out. Open-air cafés, bars and restaurants were crowded with flashily dressed young people. The gaudily coloured, flat-roofed houses, replete with shutters and pretty little courtyards, kept their doors and windows open, making life very sweet for a Nosy Parker such as myself. I spent a highly pleasant evening peering at the old men and women who sat in the antiquated cheeriness of their living rooms, surrounded by religious artefacts and colourful decorations.

Abbas seemed to be in a state of shock the whole evening through. When I finally asked him why he was looking more and more like a stunned cod, he heaved a sigh, and turned a glassy-eyed glance in my direction.

"Every one of them is a walking dream."

"Every one of whom?"

"The women. Never have I seen such a vast accumulation of beautiful women."

"Oh them, they're all right, I s'pose."

"Carmens one and all. Swaying and wiggling along the cobbled streets, rich brown skins, superlative figures, faces of unmatched loveliness –"

"All right, all right, I get the message."

I couldn't disagree with Abbas, the women were certainly one of the most striking sights that Santo Domingo had to offer. The men, in comparison, were short, squat and a trifle too bandy-legged.

For once in my life I found myself in a world where all the inhabitants were the same colour as myself and, apart from looking a lot uglier, I looked no different from anyone else. I can't say I was overliking this state of affairs.

The rigid colour hierarchy of Jamaica did not appear to exist here. Pale tans to mahogany browns mixed with total ease.

How safe it all seemed, and how buoyant and beautiful, with exotic plants lining the streets, and cluttered little craft shops. Orange juice was freshly squeezed before your eyes, and real leather was sold in place of plastic. Being so old-fashioned meant a total absence of all that is hideous and mass-produced.

Everything, from handmade leather bags to cups of coffee, was ridiculously cheap. Maybe I'm in a time warp, and soon all this will disappear, I kept thinking. The historic architecture, ladies with flowers in their hair, horses and traps – can they all be real? A paradise land which time forgot.

A tacos bar beckoned, and soon we were seated at a small table outside in the street, sipping tequila cocktails. Abbas lounged back, arranged his shirt so the folds flowed over his chest, and settled back to watch the señoritas as they swanned past us, leaving a trail of drowsy perfume in their wake.

"Careful, Abbas, remember what Mamushka told you about scheming temptresses, and besides, it's a penny to a quid that they've all got hot-blooded male relatives with stilettoes between their teeth."

"Don't worry about me, I can shift for myself. So, there's six million people in this country, what's it like being the ugliest of the lot?"

Before I had time to reply to this profound question, a wild-eyed young man joined us, and seated himself between me and Abbas. Thinking he was a beggar, I immediately began to fish for my purse. He uttered an outpouring of heartfelt Spanish, then gazed at us with brightly intense eyes.

"*Non comprehendo, Señor.*"

"*Americano?*"

"*Británico.*"

"Ah! I did not see you were foreigners, please excuse."

"Don't mench."

"All I see is that you both have deeply spiritual faces, and I was wondering if you would like to hear some of my poetry?"

Abbas and I had not enjoyed the tacos, nor the two pizzas that the waiter had eagerly pressed upon us. Although it made me feel slightly better to know that the beautiful women couldn't cook, we were in need of a diversion, and so sat back to listen to the poetry.

"First, before I begin, I must ask where you are from."

"England."

"I do not know England, but I know of Russia."

"My grandfather was Russian, more or less."

"Ah! Now I understand: the face! The Russian face, pure in its surrender, but marked by cruelty!"

Abbas and I perked up a bit. It's not often you hear a poet being as poetical as that.

"I write all my poems in English, but I like to write about Russia – and about Africa."

"Our father is from West Africa!"

"Yes! Yes! Now I see. Now everything hides in its own little place, then rises and falls! The cruelty of the Russian, combined with the nobility of the African, and there they sit, barbaric in their splendour."

He tossed back a lock of dark brown hair and surveyed us through heavily hooded eyes. His skin was sallow, jaded by sleepless nights.

"Never yet have I had my poems published, but maybe you," and here he looked directly into my eyes, "can copy them down, and take them back to your country and publish them for me."

I whipped out a pen and paper and sat in readiness.

"I'm going."

"Abbas! You can't go! There's a failed poet here, ready to pour out his very soul, and you just walk away! Where is the African nobility that the poet here hath spoke of?"

"African nobility, my foot. I'll meet you back at the hotel."

I agreed nervously. I had a strong suspicion I wouldn't be able to find my way back to the hotel, and only hoped that the failed poet would be worth it.

"Please, get my poems into print in your country. I do not require money, only fame and recognition. My name is José Lopez."

I wrote down the name, and the poetry began:

> "Sound for stuff the white wings flowing
>   Flowing all through time and stress
>   Our freedom, liberty is going,
>   There's nothing here but our repress.

"On platforms rickety he stood upon
Looking pompous, big and thick,
But when his bottom jaw fell open,
These are the words that came from his lip."

"Yes, it's really good! Anyway, I've got to go now, my brother's –"

"'Russian peasants of the world unite!'
For Liberty and such.
For freedom, tovaritch, we must fight
A little, but not much."

"Mmmm, yes. Anyway, I must be g –"

"Great cheers swoll from the swelling band,
The serfs went wild with –"

"Swoll?"
"Yes, it means swoll."
"But there's no such word as swoll."
"But of course there is such a word as swoll. It is in the English language. Anyway:

Great cheers swoll from the swelling band,
The serfs went wild with joy.
Until the master, whip in hand
Beat the nerve out *of* the boy."

"Well, I must say, that was really very good. Must dash, thanks very much, I really enjoyed your poetry."
"Waiter! *Dos cafés por favor.* Now, I want you to hear the poem of Africa."
"But I can't! I promised to meet my brother!"
"This is also in English; all my poems are in English."
"Well, I'm awfully sorry, but I don't understand English."
"You must listen carefully to this poem, because it has layer upon layer of untapped truth."
"But I'm –"

"The Lion sprang, the zebras ran
Over the plains of Africa.

> The leopards spring
> Along the thing
> Walking outside the moors,
> Does the moon?"

"Ah, that's lovely. It brought tears to my eyes. See you lat –"

> "But why? I see the lion ill,
>   Walking, motionless and still
>   Leaping, waiting, watching, but –
>   When do the water-tigers strut?
>   Crocodiles of Eastern plains –"

"Thank you, Señor Lopez, but I really must be –"

> "Does the moon?
>
> The bears gallomph in proud array,
> The sun shines on the African day.
> Pigeons fly, I know not where.
> Do you see the grizzly bear?
> Does the moon?
>
> But open hearts of languid pain,
> Awake, for heaven and hell again.
> Listen and look,
> The beautiful brook
> Flowing, tinkling passed the moors.
> I can see a man, but –"

"Let me guess, 'does the moon?'"

"'Does the moon?' Well, do you think my poems stand a good chance of getting published in a country such as yours? A country where maybe they have a fuller understanding of art?"

"I promise I will do all I can, Señor Lopez, but now, I am afraid I really must be off."

"But do you not want to hear my poem about the Cossacks in the mist?"

I leapt up in alarm, and started at a brisk trot down the street.

"I'd love to but I'm in a tearing hurry. Goodbye!"

His eyes turned red with despair.

"But, madame! Have you copied them all down?"

"Yes," I called from the other end of the street, "word for word!"

He beamed a satisfied smile. "Thank you, thank you, and you will see that they are published?"

"I promise I will do my best," and with that I scuttled away, past the prostitutes who minced up and down, flicking their hands behind them in highly suggestive ways.

I have often heard of failed poets, but never before have I heard of a poet being as failed as that.

A cluster of glamorous women stood before a tall man who appeared to be holding court, booming in a loud voice about the slump in the agricultural economy of the Dominican Republic.

"Abbas! There you are! I'm so glad you're not too far away."

"What are you doing here spoiling all my fun!"

The girls giggled at the sight of me, and quickly dispersed.

"They couldn't understand a word you were saying. Even *I* couldn't! Anyway, how come you know so much about the economics of the Dominican Republic?"

"Common knowledge. Surely you know all about the agricultural exports of the Dominican Republic."

"Well, yes, that is to say, yes and no."

Abbas passed a hand over his brow, and we continued on our way.

By the time we reached the sea-front it was almost midnight, and the surge of activity showed no signs of dying down. In many of the bars, male singers dressed in gleaming white sang Latin strains with gusto. They all seemed to look like Big Mannie, which, as you can imagine, put me off going into any of the bars. The steamy gusts of air blowing in my face brought memories of Jamaica back to me in waves. It seemed strange to think that Jamaica was so near by. Which two countries could be more different? Jamaicans, with their heavy African influence, reflected the continent of their forefathers in their art, religion, and lifestyle. Here, in the Dominican Republic, where was the legacy of the African peoples who were brought to this island? Why had the Spanish culture smothered the African until it had died a death?

Before Abbas and I returned to our hotel, an unfortunate thing happened. Abbas tripped on an unstable curb stone, and crashed to the ground, rolling in agony, holding his ankle, and squirming with pain.

"Abbas! What on earth has happened?"

He tried to reply but could only groan, his face contorted with pain.

"Abbas!" I reached out a hand and tried to help him up, but he merely rolled over and clenched his teeth, beads of sweat appearing on his forehead. I stood impotently, staring, baffled and not knowing what to do.

Couples swished past us without giving Abbas a second glance.

"I'm going to call an ambulance," I said, but knew I couldn't actually do so when I could neither speak nor read Spanish.

"No, no, I'm all right," he said in strangulated tones. Abbas has been the same since boyhood. When he once caught pneumonia, he refused to believe there was anything wrong with him until he collapsed with exhaustion.

It was heart-rending to watch the normally suave Abbas rolling and writhing like a footballer, and why were those hateful Santo Domingans just mincing past without a second glance?

Trying to flag down a car, I found that the drivers all drove on without a word, after throwing Abbas a cursory glance. What to do? At last a car drew up, and a squat, balding man stepped out, and gently helped Abbas into his car. Abbas hopped painfully in, and sat in awkward discomfort on the back seat. We drew up outside our hotel which was a mere two-minute walk away from where the accident occurred.

'Oh, what a kind man,' I thought, as he masterfully guided Abbas out of the car, and to the door of the hotel.

"Eh! *Cinco pesos!*" he hissed, just as I was uttering my fourth "*Muchas gracias.*"

As I paid him I smiled a cynical smile. The only person to help had been someone who wanted money.

No one helped Abbas up to our room, and the pretty receptionist whom Abbas had been flirting with earlier on, even giggled, manicured nails fluttering over rouged lips.

"Sorry to do this to you, Abbas, but could you check the room for talipots before I go in?"

Every inch the perfect gentleman, he hopped in, groaning with every step, and searched under the bed, on the walls, and most importantly, in the bathroom.

"No, aaghh, there's – ouch – no – ooph – tali – oo – pots anywhere."

"Thanks," and I entered the room and prepared a cold flannel to place on his ankle, and gave him a cushion to prop his leg up with.

He fell asleep very soon, and I stood by the window, watching the black sea sparkling with stars. What if Abbas were seriously hurt? Suddenly I was gripped with a severe panic.

Santo Domingo, so charming, but so deep, with so much of interest going on under the surface that I could never hope to understand. I felt shut out, almost as if I were watching everything through a glass screen. How could I ever glimpse the true soul of a country where I couldn't speak the language, where the slightest chance remark was meaningless to me? Everything seemed overwhelmingly mysterious.

And what lay ahead?

"Oh, stop thinking so loud, you're keeping me awake."

I started. Abbas's face looked pitifully sunken. I gave him an aspirin and two malaria tablets and went to bed, after an abortive attempt at reading aloud to Abbas, who kept snapping, "Oh, shut up and let me sleep," after every sentence.

Sleep came slowly, but it is, as everyone knows, the mother of wisdom.

The next day, Abbas's ankle was no better, and now sported a lump the size of a half-submerged tennis ball. It took all my sisterly powers of persuasion to force him to hop into a taxi and go to the nearest hospital.

When we reached the hospital, a sprawling grey building, Abbas was led to a bed by a middle-aged nurse with dyed blond hair. There was a musty, incensey smell in the casualty ward, which was dark, dirty, but cosy, with pictures of the Virgin Mary and Jesus hanging crookedly on the dingy walls.

A nurse came to wheel Abbas into the X-ray room, and the sight that met my eyes almost prompted me to wheel him straight out again. A woman stood in the guillotine, her arms outstretched and her head poking through the jaws of the monstrous contraption. For one terrible minute I thought I was back in the Central Middlesex Hospital, until I remembered that the Central Mid. nurses didn't wear so much lipstick. The guillotine, as Abbas found out to his cost, turned out to be the X-ray machine. However, the atmosphere was so easy-going and relaxed that it was impossible to feel frightened for long.

After a considerable wait we were told by a serious, careworn doctor that the ankle was merely suffering from "*inflamación*". He prescribed some tablets and told us to pay at the reception.

Our taxi drove us to a chemist, and I checked the back of the prescription scrupulously to see if there was anything to tick saying I was covered by Social Security, but no luck. Already I was beginning to feel like an Arab in London in the 1970s, when street vendors in Knightsbridge charged £25 for a pound of apples.

The young woman at the chemist looked exactly like me, only ten times more beautiful. As she raised her liquid black eyes to mine, she simpered, as though to say, 'Oh look! I look exactly like you, only I'm ten times more beautiful!' No, I thought, I don't like Santo Domingo.

That night, Abbas's ankle was no better. He lay in bed, with a swollen foot held high above his head, whilst a very pretty waitress poured him tea, and taught him Spanish. So keen was he to rid himself of my company that I crept out of the hotel and walked up and down the sea-front, until I found myself in a night club. Flashing lights lit up the bright-eyed faces of the women, and the men swivelled frantic pelvises to the frenetic Latin dance rhythms. The club played strictly Salsa music, which I very much enjoy. Although I sat in the farthest corner of the club, deep in the shadows so no one could see my face, I still received much outraged attention when it was discovered that I had come alone. After sitting for a few minutes, sweating in the heat, and wilting beneath horrified stares, I left the club, and cantered back to the hotel. There are countries where a woman can go to a club on her own, and rollick till dawn, but, as I found to my cost, there are countries where she can't.

With Abbas permanently abed, I felt very much alone, and still felt I could not enter into the spirit of the country. I had not made any friends, save the failed poet, partially because very few people spoke any English. The only people I really got on well with were the shoe-shine boys. Never having had a shoe-shine before, I found that I enjoyed the experience so greatly, that before long my shoes were receiving a shine three or four times a day. I dazzled like glass from ankle to heel.

Eager little boys, aged from six to twelve, chattered on in bell-like voices about current affairs, their families, and anything else that popped into their heads. For some reason I could understand them, and they could understand me. Maybe this is because children tend to be so much more expressive than us jaded old grown-ups. They were all extremely honest, charging only about 5p and when once I offered one of them the equivalent of 50p the child waved his little arms in alarm, shouting, "*No! No!*"

Only one little boy, an eight-year-old urchin, wearing a pair of raggedy shorts, tried his luck at swindling me. I was sitting in an outside café, in a lovely sixteenth-century square. A short mustachioed waiter was busying himself around my table, plying me with extra sugar lumps and saucers and hanging around for an extra tip. All of a sudden, two little boys appeared, an eight-year-old with a wooden shoe-shine kit, and his little brother, a striking child with enormous eyes and a tangle of curls.

The waiter began to shout at them to leave his customers alone, but I held out a gleaming foot, and the child got to work. I threw a coin at the little brother, and the effect it produced was quite amazing. He grabbed the coin, kissed it, held it up to heaven, then crossed himself with it. So tickled was I by this little show, that I threw him every local coin in my purse. The small boy repeated the action with enormous verve, then stood to attention, waiting breathlessly for the next coin.

The shoe-shine boy meanwhile, was upping his price with every toss of a coin. The waiter's eyes bulged with envy. He, who had served me so impeccably, only got a few pesos, and here were these two upstart ruffians receiving extortionate sums from this senseless tourist just for playing the clown! He stood and watched the proceedings with a great deal of injured pride.

"Your shoe-shine is *mucho caro*," I said to the boy, who bulged out his eyes and twisted his face into ludicrously grotesque contortions.

"*No, no!*" he squeaked in a nasal voice, "*Barato! Barato! Barato!*"

"I am just going to give you *dos pesos*," I joked. This remark caused him to throw himself over his shoe-shine kit, and burst into loud, mock wails.

"Oh, all right, then, twenty pesos." The boy's back shook with loud false crying.

"Oh, very well, *cinco pesos*." He leapt into the air and began to dance. His little brother, who had not received any money for the last few seconds, continued to stand as stiff as a soldier, gazing at me with round eyes. All my local coins had gone, so I gave him an English penny. The waiter, who had been loitering around, his eyes green with jealousy, suddenly grabbed the child and wrenched the penny from his hand. Far from throwing himself on the ground and sobbing in feigned exaggeration, as his elder brother would have done, the tiny boy merely threw the waiter a pleading look of resignation.

"Give him back his penny, bully!" I said, but the evil waiter smirked, and sauntered off with swaggering gait.

"Here, have a two-bob bit instead, it's worth a lot more," and I handed the boy 10p.

"*Gracias, gracias!*" and he went through the same kissing and crossing routine, then stood to attention once more.

Meanwhile, the shoe-shine boy had shined up my shoes so brightly that I put on a pair of sunglasses to look at them. Then I pretended

I'd gone blind, and began to stagger around the café, spurred on by the laughter of the two children, and all the other children who had gathered round to laugh at the grown-up who was making a fool of herself.

Only the waiter remained untouched by the comedy of the situation.

A few days later I walked to a travel agent to book a plane to Haiti. Although it is part of the same island, it is impossible to get there by boat or bus. On the way up the hill I passed a shanty town alive with throbbing cheerfulness. Women washed clothes in great buckets, shouting and laughing. Children ran in and out of their cardboard and corrugated-iron houses, and vendors, shouting for custom, sold sugar-cane, fritters, old and new clothes.

Salsa music boomed from practically everywhere. It was quite possible to look inside the homes at the makeshift beds, and the tatty books that lay here and there on the floor. The smell was quite fearful. Maybe eighteenth-century London smelt similar, except for the cars, which caused an unbearable fume. Most of the cars appeared to run by pure magic, belching out great clouds of black smoke. The vegetation had a rather dusty, dirty look about it. Tropical vegetation still frightened me, it all seemed so massive and alive.

Before I got to the travel agent, I had to buy something important from the chemist's.

The chemist's was the most overstaffed shop I have ever come across. A group of girls clustered around me, and asked me what I wanted. I was almost too embarrassed to ask, knowing they wouldn't understand my English, and my Spanish would be so bad they wouldn't understand that either. In the end, after a long practice with the guide book, I muttered, "*Paños higiénicos,*" and the entire shop fell apart with fits of laughter. Two girls, choking with mirth, clung to one another in helpless hilarity, almost collapsing to the ground. 'How I hate you,' I thought as I watched them through narrowed eyes. After a five-minute spell of screeching laughter, one of the girls handed me a package, and continued to giggle as I paid, then carried on guffawing as I scuttled out.

"What ees all de laughing about?" asked a young man, as I stepped outside. "Were you telleeng da funny yokes?"

"Sort of," I replied, and hurried on towards the travel agent.

The travel agent could not believe that a sane woman such as myself could willingly wish to travel to Haiti.

"But why?" he kept saying, rubbing his red eyes with amazement.

The assistants in the agency shuddered at the very mention of the word Haiti.

I had noticed that all the English-speaking people I had mentioned Haiti to, had shaken their heads, and told me that no person in their right mind would venture into a country like that. Even the manager of the hotel had shaken convulsively on hearing Haiti's name, and had said, "You and your brother must be the only two people in the world who would want to go to such a place."

Not that anyone was willing to say why it was such a horrific country, but the very mention of Haiti never failed to cause a tremor.

There must be a certain animosity between the two countries, because for the Dominicans a visa was required, but for the British, it was simply a case of booking a flight.

I tried not to think about Haiti too much, for when I did, a deep, sickening fear would run up my spine, and render me almost paralysed.

Abbas would never be well enough to come with me; I was going it alone.

The day before I left Santo Domingo, I took a taxi to the zoo. A tiny train took me around the tropical park, affording me a splendid view of a few fine, noble animals, ambling around in spacious cages. A far cry from Kingston, only this time I was alone, with no Little Mannie for company.

Behind the zoo was a scraggy hill, with an enormous shanty town crawling up the side in a jumble of cardboard and sticks. If it rained, I thought, then whoooosh! Everything would surely be swept downwards into a sodden heap. Kids played cricket with sticks and rolled up newspaper, and tumbled down the hill. How odd it seemed, that the people who swung their way up the winding steps to their makeshift homes actually lived there. They looked so smart and well done out, the men in sleek pressed pants, the women dressed as glamorously as ever; it was difficult to believe that their houses were piles of cardboard and not much else. Maybe it's nicer living there than in a Brixton tower block. At least it's sunny, and there's never that dreadful sense of being shut in on a freezing cold day.

The sun went down in a glow of purple and red, and a star began to shine through.

Abbas was fast asleep when I reached the hotel and I felt unbearably homesick. I had not got the hang of the Dominican Republic at all. Maybe I'd never get the hang of any of the islands. I tried to sleep, but a menacing voice seemed to growl, 'Haiti, Haiti, Haiti' over and over again. I switched on the light. It was four in the morning.

"Abbas. Abbas. Abbas!"

"Uh, who, where, what?"

"Sorry to wake you up."

"What's happened?"

"I'm not going to Haiti tomorrow. I'm too scared."

"We'll see."

"Well, I'll go, but I'm warning you, if it's too frightening I'm not leaving my hotel room."

"All right, goodnight."

"In fact, if it's too frightening, I'm coming straight back again."

Abbas opened a bloodshot eye.

"What are you so afraid of?"

I thought for a while.

"Unbridled brutality."

"Oh, I see, well turn out the light and go to sleep. G'night."

Drums in the
Caribbean Night

HAITI

A swirling mist totally enveloped me, and I realised I was lost in the forest. I trod very slowly, my feet sinking into the swampy undergrowth. Where had Abbas gone? Suddenly a bright red demon shot out at me from behind a tree, spiked a claw-like hand on my shoulder and said, "Welcome to Haiti!"

"Wake up, Zenga," said Abbas, shaking my shoulder, "time to go, Haiti awaits."

"But I just can't, especially after reading Graham Greene's book about Haiti."

"Well, if you took any notice of Graham Greene, you'd be too frightened to go to Brighton."

I took his point.

Once in the bathroom, I stood in front of the mirror for several minutes, practising my "voodoo dead-head" look. I had decided a long time before that if anyone tried to voodoo me, I would voodoo them back with equal vigour, and with the voodoo dead-head look that I could switch on at a moment's notice, the Haitians could not fail to hold me in the utmost fear and trembling. A voodoo dead-head look is easily acquired, but takes a lot of practice. The chin is brought down almost to the neck, the right eye is bulged whilst the left eye is narrowed, and the lips are twisted wickedly. On London tube trains, where I have frequently tried out the look, it has gone down a storm. A city businessman has even been known to vacate his seat, so powerful is the effect of the look.

Why was I so afraid of Haiti?

The reason was simple. Everything I had ever heard about the country was horrifying.

Think of Haiti, and what comes to mind? Voodoo, the Tontons Macoutes, mad dictators, and zombies. Besides, before I left, I was told by well-wishing friends that the Haitians would make very short work of me because I am a "mulatto", and the black population has strong animosity towards their lighter-skinned country people.

"The blacks will hate you, and the whites will *despise* you," I was told by a bright-eyed friend of mine, who always looks on the sunny side of life.

Before I left, Lancelot, my elder brother, who has read up on Haiti, told me that one night I would have to go to bed after having developed an inexplicably bad headache. When I woke up the next morning, I would be a zombie.

This seemed perfectly plausible, because it has been proven that zombies really do exist.

The houngan, or voodoo priest, gives a drug to the victim, which, in true Shakespearian style, produces all the symptoms of death. The heart slows down so drastically that no pulse can be found, and the breathing becomes so shallow as to be undetectable.

The unfortunate person is buried and mourned as if dead, but a few days later the houngan digs up the "corpse" and administers another drug, which revives the person to life. The living corpse, or zombie, is now totally devoid of will-power, and lives for ever after as a slave of the houngan.

Fear of friends or relatives being turned into zombies causes many Haitians to stab and break the legs of any person who dies suddenly under mysterious circumstances.

Yes, out of all the Caribbean Islands, Haiti certainly has the worst reputation.

Just before I left the hotel, Abbas gave me a present. A present, he said, that he had been planning to use himself, but because he was staying behind in safe Santo Domingo, he would bequeath to me. It was a cigarette lighter in the shape of a gun.

"Point it at the Tontons Macoutes when they get on your nerves. Keep it with you at all times, but don't start getting superstitious thinking your luck will run out if you lose it."

At once I knew my luck would run out if I lost it.

I would be lying if I said that my heart was not in my mouth. Before I left England, the telly was awash with gory pictures of the carnage that had taken place during the elections. A new president was to take office a few days after I had arrived. I hoped the mood of the country wouldn't be too hysterical.

"Oh, well, Abbas, this is it."

Abbas was sitting up in bed chatting to a voluptuous chamber maid, daintily eating a breakfast of mashed plantain.

"Very well, off you trot. Give my regards to Papa Doc."

"Papa Doc's been dead a long time."

"Oh, well, never mind, I'm sure you'll meet people just as bad."

With these comforting words ringing in my ears, I caught a taxi, and was soon sitting in the airport in Santo Domingo. The only drink available was a tepid 7-Up. Braving Haiti without the backing of a nice cup of tea was quite unbearable. Tea is the cradle of hope. The other passengers were en route to Miami: chuckling Dominicans, leading a hearty, chubby life.

As the plane took off, it occurred to me that for the first time in my life I was more frightened of arriving than I was of the flight. Two smartly dressed Haitians sat in front of me, looking like posh Nigerian law students. I was dying to catch their eyes and talk to them, but they let off such an aura of austerity, that I just didn't dare. Everything made me edgy. Air-hostesses asking about the seat-belts almost made me jump out of my skin, as did a lady opposite whispering politely that I was in the non-smokers, so could I please extinguish my cigarette. I hadn't seen any talipots yet, but I was sure they all congregated in Haiti, just as they did in Jamaica.

I began a letter to my mother.

'I'm warning you,' I wrote, 'I'm flying back at the first frightening thing that happens. You'll be glad to know that Doot-Doot (our pet name for Abbas) is not coming with me.'

My poor mother had been so afraid of letting her "boychik" go to Haiti with only me for protection.

As the plane swooshed down I felt more and more green around the gills. I was actually here, in Haiti.

Stepping off the plane, the glorious sunshine comforted and smiled upon me. For some reason I had always imagined Haiti to be cold and dark.

The first thing the immigration officials did was to confiscate my lighter, telling me briskly that on no account could I bring so dangerous a weapon into their country.

"Well, madame, is this the first time you have returned to the land of your ancestors?"

"My ancestors were not from here, they were from Nigeria."

"So were mine. So if you are not from here, why did you choose Haiti? Especially now – at such a time as this?"

"Em –"

"And alone? I shall pray that you will be safe."

"Safe? Why shouldn't I be safe?"

The official smirked, and began doing clever things with forms.

I walked out of the airport with my suitcase, not quite sure what to do next. How was I to find a hotel?

As I stepped into the sunny street, the first thing to catch my eye was a parade of brilliantly painted buses. The pictures painted on them are very similar to the paintings in fair grounds, and canal art, only more beautiful. The buses had wooden frames, ornately carved, entwined with fringes, fairy lights, and silver bells. They drove up and down the street in a blaze of colour.

"Oh, how lovely!" I gasped.

"You are liking our buses, *mademoiselle*? They are called tap-taps."

"Tap-taps?"

"Oui, *mademoiselle*. You are surprised I speak to you in English? How did I know, you were thinking? Well, *laissez-moi* explain. You dropped your passport on your way out, and here! I pick it up for you, and here! I hand it to you."

"Blimey! Thanks!"

"There is an expression that you have in England, is there not? I think it goes, 'the pleesha, is all mine.'"

"That's right. Thank you once again."

"Will you permit me the knowledge of your name?"

I told him.

"And I, *mademoiselle*, am Jean-Claude de la Vallière."

"*Enchanté, Monsieur.*"

"Please, *madame*, you speak very bad French which is most displeasing to the ear. Allow yourself to speak English."

"Oh, all right then."

"I expect you are waiting for the car."

"No."

"*Le taxi?*"

"No."

"Then what are you doing standing here in the middle of the road? I am thinking it must be because you are waiting to meet your death by the hands of a tap-tap driver!" He burst into a sudden fit of the giggles and I turned, surprised to see that I had encountered my first taste of Haitian humour.

Jean-Claude was a tall, skinny, very light-skinned man wearing a suit which could have come straight out of Savile Row. Form-fitting grey silk, with ruffles at the collar and cuffs.

"You have anyone to meet?"

"No."

"You have no one to meet, and nowhere to go? Are all English women creatures of such strange habit?"

"I am looking for a hotel to stay in."

"If you are looking for a hotel, you won't find one here."

He burst into another fit of laughter and I joined in, always prepared to do as the Romans do.

"Please, *madame*, please allow me to drive you in my car to find a hotel. I live in Pétionville and I am sure I can find you somewhere nice to stay."

That sounded like a good idea, so we set off in his long silver car, and slithered down the road, behind streams of tap-taps.

"I am thinking it would be best for you, *madame*, if you were to close your eyes on the way over."

"Why?"

"Because the sights you will see are not very pleasant."

A cold shudder shook my spine. Maybe I shouldn't have come after all.

Tin shacks stood amidst piles of refuse and slime. Large imposing men and women sold old tyres, rags, and what looked like lumps of burnt plastic. Women, miserably dressed in tatters, with enormous straw hats, worked with a furious energy, not a cheerful, bustling energy, but an urgent, almost hysterical energy. Tiny kids, half-naked and filthy, carried large tin cans on their heads and weaved their way along the muddy pathways, scattering pygmy goats as they stumbled in the piles of dirt.

Haiti is not much larger than Wales and is connected to the Dominican Republic, together forming the second largest island in the Caribbean. Could two countries so close to one another really be so different? Where were the smiles, the jokes, and the children playing imaginative games that abounded so freely in Santo Domingo?

The shanty towns of Haiti are bleak and hopeless, with an overwhelmingly desperate squalor.

"Stop the car," I said suddenly, "I want to get out."

Jean-Claude, who had been driving in silence, stared incredulously at me.

"Get out? You mean out of the car? But we are in a very bad area. You do not know what these people are like. They are not nice educated people like you and me."

"Please, *monsieur*, please stop the car, that I may see for myself."

Jean-Claude pulled up at the side of the road, where a man, covered in open sores, lay with his head upon a pile of burnt sticks.

"They'll pull you to pieces if you go among them!"

But I was slamming the door, and stepping over a nursing nanny goat, who lay half-asleep on the dusty kerb while a kid sucked furiously at a shrivelled udder.

"Retain the handbag in the car, at least. You will never see it again if you do not!" shouted Jean-Claude from the car window, his bright silk shirt gleaming in the sunlight.

I walked on oblivious. I knew no harm could befall me. There is nowhere in the world where the population beats up tourists for nothing, and besides, I was wearing the Star of David.

At first, a few children stared in dumbstruck amazement at me, then all at once they ran towards me, shouting, "Ssss! Dollar! Dollar!" I backed away, slid into a rusty bicycle wheel and fell into the arms of an old lady, who helped me up, then composed her features into a pleading expression and said, "Sssss. Dollar." Three men, attracted by the noise, ran towards me, and instantly joined the "Ssss! Dollar!" parade. Soon it seemed as if the whole world were surrounding me, screaming for dollars.

People ran from their homes to see this crazy Mother Christmas character who was apparently scattering dollars like confetti.

A small child took a dollar from me, and ran screaming with delight to his mother, only to be grabbed by a man claiming to be his "tonton", and the precious dollar was forcibly removed from the grubby little fingers. As the old saying goes:

> The rain it falleth on the just and also on the unjust fella,
> But mostly on the just because
> The unjust's nicked the just's umbrella.

The sad fact was, it was always the biggest and beefiest who would push in front and beg the most fiercely, leaving the ones in most need cowering in the background. So it always seemed that I gave the notes to the most strapping people who looked scowlingly at the money, then at me as if to say, 'You have everything, I have nothing. Is this paltry amount all you can cough up?' The gourde is the official Haitian note, but US dollars are what the nation craves.

It was impossible to walk around and nose about, because I was being besieged on all sides. After a few minutes of being shouted at and begged, I pushed my way towards the car.

"You must be the disciple of the King."

I turned to see an old lady with stick-like arms, leaning against her shack.

"I know of no king," I replied.

"You have not come this way to see the King?"

"What king?"

"Why, the King of Haiti, of course."

"Haiti has no king."

A young man began to laugh mockingly.

"Of course Haiti has no king," he sneered. "The man she speak of is craize. She see you, and she think you must be his friend. Give me a dollar."

By now I only had traveller's cheques, so I pulled open the car door and climbed in. About a dozen hands thrust themselves through the window, covering Jean-Claude's pearl-coloured seats with mud and grime.

"Wind up ze window!" he shouted in panic, and we zoomed forward. Children chased our car, yelling for dollars until they disappeared into clouds of dust.

"What did I tell you, *madame*. These people are ignorant and miserable. All they will want is your money, but they will hate you for it. Give them money, and where do you stop? It is not wise for you to go to such places too often."

"But, Jean-Claude, I have seen something that has impressed me beyond all measure!"

"What did you see? A dead body?"

I ignored the remark.

"The *art*. Even the most decrepit hovel had some form of art work in it, even if it was just a newspaper table-cloth cut up into patterns, or chalk designs on the floor. I've never seen anything so beautiful."

"Oh, I see. So you like naïve art."

"I hate the phrase 'naïve art', even if it is the official term for it."

"How sensitive you are, *madame*. These people have not the same culture as you and I. You are European, and I am a member of what is known as the Haitian élite. We share the culture of the European, but the people here have centuries to go before they catch up with us."

"I seem to recall," I murmured, "a South African Boer saying exactly the same thing to me in a bar in Piccadilly. Now listen here, Jean-Claude. If you want me to let you drive me around, and find hotels for me, then less of this 'I'm so superior' nonsense. It grates on the nerves."

"But there is such a thing as the concept of superior and inferior races. Have you never read Darwin?"

"Darwin can go to the bald devil."

"But Darwin said that –"

"Darwin said that inbreeding of races produced half-witted mutants. That's Darwin for you. In any case I don't believe that the race of a person can in any way determine intelligence or any other qualities. All it determines is colour and certain physical characteristics."

"What are you? Christian, socialist, or what?"

"Why do you ask?"

"Because you have the most strange ideas. What you don't understand is that someone has to keep the people in their place. There are over five million people here in Haiti, that's five hundred and twenty people to the square mile, and the population is increasing rapidly. Seventy-five per cent cannot read and write, and the country is supposed to be the poorest in the Western hemisphere. Mulattoes only make up a tenth of the population. The new president, Madigat, is a very good man. He is friendly with the Americans and understands that only military force is needed to control the people."

"Did you like Papa Doc?"

"Ah yes, he was a good man *aussi*. He came in with the idea that he was '*noirist*' er, excuse, do you know what I mean by '*noirist*'?"

"Yes, 'for the black people'."

"Quite. My family panicked when he first came to power, but then he married a mulatto woman, and when his son, Baby Doc, came to power, he also married a mulatto woman, until the whole government was entirely on the side of the mulatto élite. We did very well when that family was in power."

"So as long as you're doing very well, you think dictatorship is a good thing?"

"Please, *mademoiselle*, please do not be so hard to me. What can be done with these people? Did you not know that eighty-five per cent of the population belongs to the voodoo cult?"

"So?"

Jean-Claude looked at me out of the corners of his eyes. "You must be a socialist," he said.

I stared out of the car window musing on what Jean-Claude had said, and also upon the woman's statement about the King of Haiti.

Pétionville, home of the Haitian élite, is a suburb of Port-au-Prince, set atop a rugged hill. Our car crawled up behind a tap-tap which belched out great clouds of sooty smoke. The Pétionville houses beggar description. Mansions in absurdly contrasting styles stand behind iron bars, with savage dogs slavering in the courtyards. Arabesque palaces, giant gingerbread houses and marble Taj Mahals flashed past us as we bounced down the dusty streets.

The élite were not to be seen. Only men and women balancing incredibly large baskets on their heads, stepping gracefully along the stony streets.

Down below, the view was a breathtaking haven of palms and flowers, although lacking the dramatic splendour of Jamaica.

"Here is quite a nice hotel. You can stay here if you please. I would invite you to stay in my house, but I am fearing you will cause a fuss when you see the servants, and will start giving them money, causing much confusion."

"How astute you are, *monsieur*."

"I suppose, next you are going to say that you hate all white people because of how they have treated the blacks."

"I could never hate any person because of what they look like or where they were born."

I can be unbearably noble at times.

The hotel was a pretty white building in the colonial style, surrounded by pink flowers and palms.

"Thank you very much for the lift."

"My pleesha, *madame*. I would be happy if you would come to dinner with me this night. Then we could go on to the casino."

He handed me a card which I pocketed, and I clambered out of the car. A few men tried to carry my luggage, but I easily fought them off. Because I only had one small bag, they soon became discouraged. A tall, solemn man greeted me, announcing himself as the manager, Monsieur Le Roi.

"Do you have a room for a couple of nights?"

"I have seven rooms for the rest of your natural life."

"One room for a couple of nights will do me fine."

Monsieur Le Roi showed me to my room, and then made me a cup of tea in the lounge. As I sipped the delicious brew, it suddenly struck me how much I craved a Chinese meal.

"Haiti is very unhappy at the moment," the manager remarked glumly. "The opposition has called for a strike because of the new president. Nobody voted him in. It is not that he is a bad person. He is very intelligent. He has been to university and is highly educated, and is far too clever to go in for politics. A smart man like that should have become a doctor or a lawyer."

On the walls hung eighteenth-century pictures of Haitian women dressed in Georgian attire.

"Who are those ladies?"

"Ancestors," he replied, and continued to talk of Haiti's perpetual suffering.

The reason Haiti has retained so strong an African influence, he informed me, is because when Toussaint L'Ouverture started the revolution in 1798, the life expectancy of an African slave was three years. This meant that when the French were booted out of Haiti, most of the inhabitants had only been on the island for a very short time. Because so few of the people had time to take on any of the European customs, Haiti has retained a purer African culture than any of the other Caribbean Islands.

Even so, it must be said that there is something about Haiti which strikes one as being slightly English, far more so than in Santo Domingo, although why there should be an Englishness about Haiti, which has never had anything to do with England, is difficult to say. Many people seemed to speak English, and a lot of the signs and posters were in English. Monsieur Le Roi appeared to be very knowledgeable about England, and even asked with concern about the riots in Brixton. To the Santo Domingans, on the other hand, England was so obscure that they probably all thought, 'What's wrong with this England place? How come no one's ever heard of it?'

"So what is the first sight you would like to see in Haiti? You must excuse my curiosity, but you are the first guest I have had in a long time. No one wants to come any more because of the election violence and because of AIDs, which the Americans believe, or say they believe, started in Haiti. I know of no one who suffers from AIDs, but the whites love to blame any ill that occurs on black people."

We sat silent for a time.

"Well? Where would you like to go?"

"The Iron Market."

"You are a fool to go there, *madame*. You will not like it."

"Why not?"

"When you are more used to Haiti, then I would advise, but now, no."

But I knew that getting used to Haiti would prove as difficult as getting used to a wild-eyed schizophrenic. I had only been here for a few hours, and already the scenery, the people and the atmosphere had been changing with mind-boggling rapidity. After the horrors of the shanty town that morning, how could a mere market surprise me? Especially the Iron Market, which was advertised in the guide books as being an exotic wrought-iron indoor market, originally crafted for a Bombay bazaar.

So, while Monsieur Le Roi shook his head, I waltzed off, and waited for a tap-tap in an elegant square.

"Will you pay for me?" asked a pretty miss, who stood beside me.

"What for?"

"Le tap-tap. I have no money."

"Of course I'll pay."

"*Merci, madame.*"

We stood for a while in companionable silence, watching an old woman balancing a can of oil on her head.

"*Madame*," the girl flashed me a bright smile. "I have no money at all. I am very poor. Can I be your maid? I will wash your clothes, clean your house, and look after your babies."

"I'm sorry, I do not need a maid, I'll just have to pay for the tap-tap."

A jangle of bells, and a tap-tap appeared, called *Le Réaliste*. All the tap-taps had religious or moral messages emblazoned upon the sides.

I squashed up in the back, and stared out of the window. The other passengers all seemed preoccupied with their own sombre thoughts. Only the man in front of me turned to smile. I smiled eagerly back. His handsome, broad features reminded me warmly of a roguish blues singer I had once fallen in love with in New Orleans.

"From where are you?" he asked, crinkly eyes all a-twinkle.

"London."

"Ah! And to where you go?"

"The Iron Market."

"Ah, oh!" he expostulated, sounding very Nigerian. "I too? I go to the Iron Market! We shall go together."

"Oh yes! How wonderful! How kind of you!"

"Anything, anything I will do to help a sister from overseas; you do not mind me calling you sister?"

"I should say not, brother."

"Black people must help one another, not so?"

"Absolutely."

"Your parents are Haitian?"

"No."

"But you look Haitian, sister. See how you come in important times. A new president is about to take office, and all the shops are closed because of the strike."

All the shops seemed to be open, but I thought it best not to mention the fact, and risk offending a brother and a friend. What a nice place Haiti is, I thought, how cruel the world has been to lie about it.

All of a sudden – bang! Our tap-tap rattled into the midst of a seething throng. I alighted gingerly and almost collapsed. The stench was so strong it could be cut with a machete. Bad vegetables and excrement along with general decay all helped to produce a smell which could knock Gabriel out of heaven. Huge, fat women wearing gigantic straw hats sat in the street, packed like sardines, selling maize, manioc, rice and tobacco out of giant sacks. Men pushed and shoved one another in their eagerness to sell everything under the sun, from old clothes to tiny pink pigs. Children scampered around hawking for trade, holding bits of junk, their desperate eyes darting like minnows. The atmosphere was so intense, it was all I could do to stop myself fainting. Tap-taps edged haltingly down the main street emitting mighty billows of pitch smoke, which hung in the air creating a permanent grey smog.

"See there," said a voice behind me, "a vegetable." I wheeled round to see my friend from the tap-tap. I had completely forgotten him standing beside me.

"And this," he said, picking up a padlock which a child held up for inspection, "is a padlock."

I pushed my way forward, picking my feet awkwardly over streams of sewage which ran in the gulleys. Looking above me, I saw a wrought-iron building, a terrifyingly imposing sight, looming like a mighty spectre. Moving was very difficult, not only because of the wedge of vendors who squatted in the street, but also because the beggars could seemingly sniff me out like dogs, and were climbing over the human barricade to get at me, thrusting shrivelled hands before my face.

Just let me get to the indoor market, I thought, treading on the tail of a scabby dog, and everything will be all right. At least the sun won't be draining the very marrow from my bones.

"That is a lady selling things," I heard the tap-tap brother mutter, as I all but fell into the indoor market.

"Pregnant, pregnant!" an old man shouted in the doorway, waving a spavined turtle at me, "you will soon be pregnant!"

I resisted the urge to slap his face and staggered into the Iron Market, more dead than alive. Looking around in horror, I saw that it was far worse inside than out! The proverb, "out of the frying pan into the fire" took on a new and hideous meaning. A darkened dampness filled the air, and even more people were huddled into the space, shouting, pushing and jabbing me in the ribs. Without warning, about five beefy young men each grabbed a limb of mine (if that's possible), and began to pull me in different directions.

"Help!" I gurgled, in strangulated tones.

"I have art for sale! Come and look."

"No no, *madame*. My art is much nicer, look, look!"

"Not until you have seen *my* pictures!"

"*His* pictures! He has rubbish pictures, *my* art is what your good heart can love!"

"Help! Help!"

"That is a lady selling things," muttered Mr Tap-Tap.

"Help me! Someone!" My left leg was being pulled out of shape, and I could feel a shoulder being slowly wrenched from its socket. And to think I once went to the London Dungeon to laugh at the dummies being stretched on the rack.

Just when I thought the fates were about to take the final snip, a rich female voice rose over the din.

"Leave her alone! What sort of men are you that you can molest a poor woman for the sake of a few gourdes!"

It worked like magic. Instantly two arms and two legs were dropped as if red hot, and I found I was being led gently by the hand of a strong, motherly woman. The men gaped in outraged amazement, as we disappeared into a tiny cubicle.

"You see, *madame*, you are a woman, I am a woman. We understand one another. Here are my paintings. Please buy as many as you like."

"B-b-b-buy your p-p-p-p –"

"Yes, this is art."

I looked at the paintings which hung on the dank walls. Exquisite oils in such colours my heart stood still. It was like being in an ancient Egyptian sanctuary, where weary Pharaohs rested after a long day's plague of frogs. A lovely blend of pinks and purples, depicting village life, fabulous animals and religious ceremonies.

The lady sat on a wooden stool, watching me with hawk-like eyes, rivulets of sweat running down her face.

"Which ones do you like?"

"Well, *madame*, because you saved my life, I will take the one of the leopard, and this one, with the woman working in the paddy-fields."

"Fifteen dollars each – heh! Get out! Get out! *Allez-vous-en!*" and she leapt out of her seat and made for the door, brandishing a broomstick. To my shock I saw the doorway was alive with faces, staring at me with dollar signs lighting up their eyes. On seeing the woman they scattered like canaries in a cat show, and I bought my paintings.

The woman, who had previously been treating "her art" with the tenderness of a new-born babe, now took up the paintings, wrapped them up in dirty old newspaper, and flung them carelessly towards me. The soothing charm was turned off like a tap.

'I'm in for it now,' I thought, as I walked out from behind the partition and into the crowds, feeling more and more like Little Red Riding Hood by the minute.

"*Madame! Madame! Madame!*" This time the crowds were so dense, and so seething, I found my long nails came in very handy as I clawed my way through the throng, the acrid stench all but knocking me unconscious.

All I could think was, 'I've got to get out of here, one more second and I'm dead.'

"There is a man," a familiar voice sounded behind me, "buying rice." Mr Tap-Tap was right next to me, throwing a dazzling smile in my direction.

"Tap-tap!" I yelled, staggered out of the market, and jumped into the first tap-tap I saw.

"Heh! Wait! I have been your guide. You owe me twenty-five dollars."

"What?" The tap-tap stood still, unable to force its way through the crowds.

"I have guided you. You owe me money."

"Guided me?"

"Yes, I have been expertly explaining to you what everything is. Please give me money."

The young "art" men who had followed me into the street began to laugh loudly at us, enjoying the joke of the naïve tourist who was about to be swindled. Luckily the tap-tap lurched forward, and we joggled down the road, clouds of blackness enveloping Mr Tap-Tap and the art dealers. I neither knew nor cared where the tap-tap was heading.

"Where is it you are going, young miss?"

The man asking the question sat opposite me, holding a baby in his arms which could not have been more than three days old. How unhealthy for the poor little mite, I mused, to lie in a tap-tap which pours toxic fumes into the air.

"You are going to see the King, yes?"

"Who is the King?"

"You do not know the King?"

"I don't."

"Excuse." And that was all I could get out of him. Even after a good few minutes of ardent questioning, he would not reveal any information about this King.

The tap-tap lumbered down a long street of decaying buildings, filled with people sitting behind glowing coal fires selling roast peanuts and strips of fried pork.

I got out when we reached the harbour, and instantly struck up a friendship with four very naughty boys, one of whom stripped off all his clothes and dived into the dirty water. A large ship chugged dolefully away, looking as splendid as a seventeenth-century galleon.

"I am the father of these boys," explained a toothless old man. "If you have any money to give them, please give it all to me. Where are you from?"

"England."

"England. How many children has Prince Charles got now?"

"Two." There you are, I said to myself, see the affinity the Haitians have with England! Even the little boys were given English names, George, Albert, Clive and Benjamin.

I sat for a long time by the harbour staring out into the sea. As the darkness began to descend, I made my way back to where I hoped a tap-tap could be caught, along a wide street with a few art dealers selling some amazingly beautiful paintings. They hounded and begged me so much I began to wonder why they didn't just grab my handbag and make off with it. It would have been so simple. There were no policemen anywhere in sight, and I was so obviously all alone and defenceless. If they believed I had an infinite amount of money in my bag, then why not just take it? But the minds of the people didn't work along those lines. Robbing and stealing were totally alien to their natures. Only a mind as tainted as my own could have conceived such an idea.

It was only when it became completely dark that I realised that I had forgotten the address of my hotel. Not only that, I had forgotten the name of the place where it was. I had a vague idea it began with a "V" but apart from that, my mind remained a total blank. I hunted for the card that Jean-Claude had given me, then it dawned that I had left it in my jacket pocket, and my jacket was, of course, in the hotel.

Port-au-Prince suddenly began to look very sinister. There were very few people around and very little street lighting.

After a while, all that was visible was the glimmer of an occasional charcoal fire, glowing at the side of the street. I walked up and down greeting everyone I met. "*Bonjour,*" they replied politely back. What I really wanted to say to them was that I was lost, and could they help me find an hotel whose name I had forgotten, but that seemed a bit much to ask *anyone*, let alone people whose English was slightly hesitant. 'The best thing to do,' I told myself, 'is to make my way back to the harbour and sleep on the grass patch by the sea, and by the morning my mind will be clearer, and I will know what to do.' Nothing, I knew, was ever so bad in the morning.

So with my old newspaper wrappings under my arms, I wended my weary way back to the stretch of ocean, which now glinted wickedly in the moonlight. Tonight the moon was huge and yellow. No one was around when I reached the grass patch, which disappointed me sorely. Company was the one thing for which I yearned.

I laid my head down upon my handbag, and settled down to a night's kip, curled up on the damp grass.

How glorious 'tis to lie 'neath the stars on warm, fragrant nights! One becomes but a babe of the rich earth, tucked in Mother Nature's cradle.

Just as I was reaching the climax of poetical reverie, an incomprehensible flow of Haitian Creole exploded from above.

"*Je suis très* sorry, but I'm afraid I don't understand."

"*Español?*"

"English."

"You are English?"

"*Oui.*"

"Then why is it you are speaking French?"

I squinted up in the darkness, dimly making out the silhouette of an old man dressed in red leggings and padded jacket. His hair shone silver in the moonlight.

"My English is not good. Why do you lie alone in the outside of the world? Is it that you have no lead in the head?"

"I am lost."

"You are not affeared to lie in one of most dangerous place of Port-au-Prince?"

"Well, now you come to mention it, aagh! I'm *terrified*!"

"What do you wish to do with your fear?"

The question stumped me.

I stood up beside him and looked at his face. His cheekbones pointed out at different angles, throwing grotesque shadows around his eyes.

"If you nowhere have to go, then come to me and my lady, we will let you sleep with us this night. It is a lot bad that you sleep with money below your head. Come and walk with me."

We began what turned out to be a long journey through Port-au-Prince, through narrow streets, and past the Iron Market. Three women, huddled together by charcoal embers, began to laugh when they saw me and the old man, and struck mocking poses as we trod past them.

"I know why the lady do that thing. She know you?"

"No, why?"

"Because she say she know you are friend of me."

I was too dazed to care what she said. Everything suddenly began to seem surreal and unreal. Women laughing at me for no reason seemed to fit in quite well with the natural order of things in Haiti.

"What you know of the King of Haiti?"

"The King? I keep hearing people talking about the King. What does it all mean? Who is the King of Haiti?"

"The King of Haiti is Toussaint L'Ouverture of course. How is it that you do not know of Toussaint L'Ouverture, the most blessed and perfect man of your peoples? It is *dégoûtant* you do not know!" The old man limped slightly as he walked, stopping to mumble curses as the few people we passed turned to jeer at us. "Sssss! Dollar!" could be heard softly from amongst the shadows.

"We defeat the French long time ago, 1801 was the first full year of rule. So great was military power that Toussaint L'Ouverture captured all Santo Domingo. The whole island was under black rule, and the white people afraid and respectful of us. We stronger than any of them.

"The French did not want Haiti to become powerful black nation. We recruit Dessalines. Dessalines fierce lieutenant, and he help to drive French away."

The more the old man talked, the quicker he limped, and soon I could hardly keep up with him. We hurried through run-down streets of old brick houses covered with peeling political posters. Squat grey houses stood in all the charmless squalor of Dickensian London. Something fanatical about the old man, something so uncanny, made me ask myself whether I was doing the right thing in following him. This was no ordinary history lesson he was giving me. But what was it? What was he trying to prove to me?

"Napoleon send Leclerc to Haiti to make pact with L'Ouverture. Leclerc married to Napoleon's sister Pauline. They live in Cap-Haïtien. Leclerc and Pauline very wicked people. They captured and bought to France."

"Captured who?"

We had reached a dingy house. The old man slowly creaked open a crumbling wooden door. He shouted something in Creole, and we walked in. My blood ran cold at what I saw. The room we found ourselves in was crammed from top to bottom with wood carvings, pictures and sculptures of Toussaint L'Ouverture. Imitation cannons and guns stood by the walls, sparkling with a newly polished finesse. Over grinning wax dummies were draped three-cornered hats and Georgian clothes. Something was odd about the mannequins. Obviously home-made, the expression in their faces was one of madness and evil.

It then became apparent that everything in the room looked odd and misshapen in some way. The pictures on the walls were strewn with unearthly figures, although looking perfectly normal at first glance.

I turned to look at the old man and for the first time noticed that he himself was dressed in eighteenth-century costume. Sweeping a hat from one of the dummies, he clapped it upon his silver head.

My legs almost gave way in confusion.

"They captured me! But I say no to white rule. Take me to France, but I get away, and come back to Haiti. Now my home is here, where I am King."

"Yes, your, er, majesty." I made a low bow, then looked intently at his face. The fanatical expression had mellowed into a soft, regal smile. I backed away very slowly to the door, but was cut short by a shrill woman's voice coming from the next room.

"My lady," said the King, striking a lordly pose.

A woman of extraordinary beauty sailed into the room, and surveyed me with brilliant opaque eyes. She was clothed in a shabby white dress with a white headshawl bound neatly over her hair. With one hand resting on a bronze cannon, she addressed me in a soft Creole, then continued to scan me with a mixture of fear and curiosity.

By now I felt completely drained.

"I'm sorry, *madame*, but I don't speak Creole or French."

"You are a foreigner?" Her English was almost accentless.

"Yes."

"Why do you come to my house? You are here for interest in my father?"

"No, I got lost so he said I could sleep here for the night."

"Are you here to laugh?"

"To laugh?" The idea of laughing seemed so alien to my nature after everything that had happened, that I almost laughed. "Of course I am not here to laugh. I couldn't find my hotel, and was about to sleep outside by the harbour. Your father came to help me, that is all."

She peered at me very deeply, then suddenly relaxed, and smiled a sad, sad smile.

"Please sit down, *madame*. *Papa*, sit down also."

We seated ourselves on the floor simultaneously.

"My father is not a well man. I hate the people to laugh at him. Always I am sad. Please do not stay the night. He is more unwell in the night."

In a way, I was quite glad she had said that, because the last place I would wish to sleep would be in a house so full of ghosts and strangeness.

"Sit with us a while, but leave before the owls."

"Yes, I will."

We sat on the floor not speaking, listening to the faint strains of the Haitian music which filtered in from next door.

"You speak excellent English, did you learn it at school?"

"You see we are not rich. I did not go to school. The English I learn is from the guests at the hotel where I work."

At the sound of the word "hotel", a warm glow shot through my body.

"But you cannot have many guests. At the hotel where I am staying, the manager says that I am the first guest he has had in a long while."

"My hotel also. Only one guest we have who come this morning. Monsieur Le Roi was very pleased."

"Monsieur Le Roi?"

"Yes, he is the manager of my hotel. I am a maid."

"Tell me where your hotel is, because it is the same hotel that I am staying in."

"Pétionville."

"Pétionville! Of course! How do you get to Pétionville?"

"Tap-tap. I will come with you, and we will find the tap-tap."

I almost felt drunk as the girl and I stepped into the street and down a long lane towards the Iron Market. Men and women stopped in their tracks to jeer and mock her, using powerfully expressive Creole. The woman marched past with queenly dignity ignoring the spiteful remarks so skilfully that I began to wonder if she had actually heard them.

Soon we were by the Iron Market once again, and in a few minutes, a tap-tap rolled along. The woman asked the driver in Creole to put me off at the right stop, then made to leave. I pressed a handful of notes into her hand, which she looked at with quiet disdain.

"Thank you, *madame*, goodbye."

The tap-tap driver nudged his friend, and they began to sneer quite openly at the young girl, who swept along, head held high. How cruel people can be, I thought, as I watched the lonely white-clad figure move slowly away.

The men in the tap-tap began asking for money and leering with such ferocious intent that I decided that if ever there was a time to use the voodoo dead-head look, it was now. One eye narrowed, and one a-bug, I lowered my head and pierced them all with a terrifying gaze.

At first the men stared in rapt excitement, then as one man, they burst into peals of shattering laughter.

"She is trying to afraid us!" one man yelled, quivering with uncontrolled hilarity.

"To afraid us? Is that what she's trying to do? Ha ha ha!"

I shrugged, scratched the back of my head, and lit a cigarette. At least I had given it a try, and it had worked in so much as they were laughing at me so hard, they had forgotten to ask for money. Poorest country in the Western hemisphere Haiti may be, but there is nowhere else in the world where the people enjoy such good laughs.

When I finally reached the hotel, it was locked.

I banged on the door so hard that in the end the long-suffering Monsieur Le Roi opened up, wearing a long nightshirt, with a Wee Willie Winkie style nightcap on his head.

"Oh, it's you," he said with unnerving calm. "I thought you must be killed."

"No, no, alive and kicking. Sorry to wake you so late. Goodnight."

There was a power cut in the city that night, so I spent the rest of the night trying to avoid looking at the metal figure of a devil giving birth to a mother and child on the wall, which flickered in the mysterious candlelight. The horns of the devil seemed to change shape all the time, and the light played such funny tricks on his legs, that at one point I could have sworn he was moving towards me.

"You're a funny old place, aren't you Haiti," I said, before falling into a dreamless sleep.

The Devil Woman
and the Zombie
HAITI

*I*t didn't take me long to get used to Port-au-Prince. I grew to almost like the roguish style of the Haitians, and after a while I was falling in love with every child I met. And there was art simply everywhere, which was quite astounding. Even in the humblest of cafés, chairs and tables were carved, ceilings decorated, and every inch of the walls was painted and sculptured in the most exquisite patterns.

All day I lay in wait for the King of Haiti's daughter, but I never saw her or her father again. It was time for me to move on and explore the island, but I had no idea how to go about it. No tourist office appeared to exist, so in the end I decided the best thing to do would be to pack my little bag, head for the road, and hitch a lift. Destination: Cap-Haïtien, in the north of the island.

Monsieur Le Roi was shattered to see me leave, and begged me to stay, even to the extent of offering me free cups of tea, but I explained to him that I had a sick brother in Santo Domingo who needed me, so could not be away for too long.

"Santo Domingo, hah," and Monsieur Le Roi all but spat in disgust.

Hitch-hiking is usually a very humiliating business. Cars pull up beside you, take one look at you, then drive off again scornfully. You begin to feel like the wildest kind of maniac, whom only a fool would have in their car. In Haiti, however, the opposite is true. The very first car I flagged down drew up beside me and the door was flung open. A middle-aged man with all his teeth missing, climbed out of the car, threw my luggage in the boot and delicately helped me into his battered little car. Very few cars were around, the most popular form of transportation being the ever trusty tap-taps, so I thanked my stars that the driver of the first car to pass took pity on me.

The day was hot and dry, and I had felt I could not walk another step.

"Do you speak English?" I asked the driver, whom I had already thanked for minutes on end in English.

"*Non, non*." The driver shook his head, and began to chuckle softly to himself.

"I am going to Cap-Haïtien, are you allonsing anywhere near there?"

"Cap-Haïtien," he repeated, in exactly the same accent as me, then shook his head again and tittered.

"You do not know Cap-Haïtien?"

"You do not know Cap-Haïtien? Ha ha ha!"

Oh, well, never mind, eh, I told myself, at least I'm seeing the country. And seeing it I was. The scenery, first desert, changed quickly to lush greenery, then to barren mountains, and before we knew it, we were back in scrubby land, where only cacti grew. The sea on the coast was too turquoise to be true, shimmering like a sheet of crystal.

The villages we passed were pure African in appearance. Compound huts with thatched roofs, and delightful little chicken coops in the yard. Apart from the odd pigmy goat and fowl, animal life was not very plentiful in Haiti (unlike in Jamaica). A few bossy little egrets chased the cattle and goats who lazily swished them off with irritated tails.

Most of the houses in the countryside were painted in pretty colours;

some even sported little gables over the doors, lending them a Russian cottagey feel.

It was obvious who was doing all the hard work in Haiti. While the men stood about in huge gangs watching cockfights, or messed around trying to "guide" tourists, the women walked for miles on end with produce on their heads to sell at the markets. All those working in the paddy-fields were women, bent double, with their ragged dresses hitched to the thighs. Slavery has not been fully abolished in the West Indies, it is only that today the slaves have no masters. But why is it the women who work the land? It was certainly not because the men were lazy: never have I seen so much energy as in Haiti, no, it must be a sense of uselessness that the men feel, as they do in Jamaica. Besides, it was probably the men who were painting the tap-taps, and creating all the beautiful art work that was so apparent in this strange, enchanting land.

I noticed that many of the women went topless, which surprised me somewhat. I kept having to tell myself that I was in the West Indies, and not in Africa. Even the scenery looked African.

"Je suis très thirsty, Monsieur."

"Très thirsty, Monsieur."

I mimed a drink, then clasped my throat, the man looked at me and laughed, as though to say, 'yes, very funny, what other amusing things can you do to entertain me while I drive?'

I gave up. The heat was dry and intense, and I was sure my tongue was swelling, as tongues always seem to do in books about the Sahara desert. What if we never stopped and I began to dehydrate and died of thirst? I could imagine the man laughing as I collapsed on the floor of the car, probably mimicking me into the bargain. Why was it that the guides and beggars could always speak perfect English, when it would have been far better for me if they couldn't, but the ones who were driving me for miles to unknown destinations were unable to do aught but snigger. Life is a cruel, bitter, barren sea.

The man suddenly began to ask me something in an animated Creole, which, to the uninitiated ear, sounds very much like a West African language. I said *"oui"* in reply. I hoped he was not asking me anything to which *"non"* would have been more appropriate. After another half-hour's journey, past women washing clothes in the stream, the man began to ask more urgent questions. *"Oui, oui, monsieur."* Maybe he was asking me if I wanted to get out, and would just drop me off in the middle of the pitted, pot-holed street.

And then, like a beacon in a dark mist, I saw a splendid hotel. The man drew up beside it, jumped out of the car, and gallantly opened the door for me.

Soon we were sitting by the crystal sea, having just finished the nicest Creole lunch I have ever tasted. The man remained silent all the while, not bothering to make conversation, biting into the delicious fish with gusto.

About seventeen men dressed in waiters' uniforms sat at the other end of the room, smoking and gossiping. Myself and the kind man who was driving me were the sole diners. Seizing my chance to find out what was happening to me, I asked one of the waiters if he could find out from the man where we were going.

"I am broke, give me a dollar," came the waiter's reply. I gave him a dollar, and watched as he went into a long conversation with the toothless man. Every now and then, they would turn to stare at me, then continue to talk, heads pressed tightly together. After a while, the waiter looked up at me with soulful eyes.

"He says he will be your guide for as long as you need him. He says he is poor person who has no money at all. He wants you to give him a lot of money, then he will do much to help you. Give me another dollar."

"But tell him I do not have a lot of money to give."

"Hmmmmm." The waiter pocketed the dollar, and murmured with the man. They turned to me and shook their heads.

"He says you *are* rich. He says he can't describe the riches."

"Ah, I see. Well, ask him if he will take me to Cap-Haïtien."

"Where?"

"Cap-Haïtien."

"Oh! Hah, hah! Le Cap." He bent his head forward, and emerged a few minutes later to say, "Le Cap is where he is going anyway. He wants to know your name. His name is Ricard. Give me another dollar."

I duly handed over another dollar, tipped the rest of the waiters, and hurried away with Ricard. More waiters appeared from nowhere, clamouring towards me, hands outstretched.

When we reached Ricard's car, we saw that little boys had spread palm leaves over the windscreen to keep the sun from turning the car into a veritable oven. I felt no qualms about giving them a large tip.

On and on we drove, into the heart of Haiti. As dusk began to fall, the leaden sound of drums could be heard from the villages. Some of the houses had devils painted gaily on the sides; devils adorned in carnival attire with brightly coloured ribbons trailing from their heads.

Little children chased our car yelling the familiar "Pssst! Dollar!" Older children played long African-style flutes which emitted a hollow, haunting sound. Women, walking back from the fields, sang West-African-sounding chants, in perfect harmony, clapping their hands, enormous sacks balanced on their heads. Cockfighting was a most popular sport. Twice, Ricard leapt out of his car to join the group of men who crowded by the wayside, screaming with merriment at the sight of cocks pecking each other to pieces. Once he even grabbed me by the hand and tried to wrench me out of the car, so I too could witness this delightful spectacle, but I sat firm, feeling very sorry for the cocks and slightly sorry for myself, sitting alone in the dark.

Left to themselves, men become wild beasts, I thought, sourly. It is only when women are around to quell them that they turn vaguely human, and at these cockfights, there were no women in sight.

When the darkness fully descended, the drums could be heard loud and clear, boom-da-da-booming away from the interior of every village.

The cemeteries are monumental affairs, almost as large as the villages, with high tombstones, painted in vivid colours. I have heard that the heavy tombstones are specially designed to keep houngans from making zombies of the dead.

Baron Samedi, Lord of the Dead, is said to walk through the cemeteries at night, wearing a top-hat and long black coat. Looking at the weird shapes that the graves made in the moonlight, I could well believe it. Baron Samedi is very similar to the Christian idea of the devil, a humorous, wry character, full of sly tricks. No one dares walk in the cemeteries after dark, for fear not only of bumping into Samedi, but also of encountering the zombies as they are led back to their open graves by the sorcerer, after a night's slave work.

Haitian roads are very bad. Gaping holes appear where you least expect them. For much of the way, Ricard and I followed a tap-tap filled to bursting point with men and women, many standing for miles on end. Most of the tap-taps had a section in front for animals, as they travelled to and from the market. The tap-tap driver seemed to know all the pits in the street, so we skidded and slid around them all, following the tap-tap's every twist. After a while, I got so used to tap-tap fumes that fresh air began to make me feel dizzy.

Lights appeared dimly in the distance, then vanished, only to re-appear again a long time later, looking as far away as ever. We had been driving for twelve hours.

"Le Cap?"

There was no reply. Ricard was to drive me, I was to pay him money beyond the dreams of avarice. Talking did not come into the bargain.

Gradually the drumming stopped. We were in the suburbs of Le Cap. The houses began to look rather grand, looming in the blackness, as we sped past them. Ricard's little car did us proud. All of a sudden we came to two imposing gates, and with a jolt we were in Cap-Haïtien. Never have I seen such street life! Simply everyone was out in the roads, talking, jostling and selling things, standing by burning charcoal fires. Churches of every description lined the streets. Catholic, Evangelical, Pentecostal, and denominations unknown to me, such as the Church of the Celestial Fathers, and the Brotherhood of the Twelve Martyrs. Many of the names were written in French or Creole, so I had no knowledge of the religions of the masses who spilt out into the streets to worship. I wanted to stop and listen to the singing, but Ricard drove on.

"Heh!" A burly policeman stopped the car, and began to speak in Creole to Ricard. I sat trembling in my seat, hoping he would not notice me. Slowly, he peered into my window, and addressed me in Creole.

"*Non, Monsieur, je ne pas parle Français.*"

"*Non Français! Je parle* Créole," he snarled, and rode off on his motor bike.

I was pleased to see that the Haitians had a healthy dislike of the French who have so ill-treated them in the past.

On the green, wild activity was taking place. Drums boomed, flutes blared, and people sang in ghostly screams. In the darkness, I could see shapes dancing and leaping into the air. Could this be a voodoo ceremony?

Ricard drove very quickly from the scene, as if not wanting me to witness another second of the ceremony. Finally, after a short drive through the narrow streets, we stopped our car outside a grey Victorian building, set back in a garden of palms and long grass. A swinging sign over the gate advertised the house to be an hotel. Ricard grinned a gappy smile at me, and helped me out of the car, leading me gently through the overgrown garden, and into the hotel.

The bar was totally surrounded by African *objets d'art*. From floor to ceiling, wooden women in African costume were carved and painted, carrying pots on their heads, some looking very merry, and some crying.

Because there was another power cut, only white candles and oil lamps were used for illumination. A young lad with a bad squint slouched out of the kitchens and stood gazing dumbly at us, chewing on a stick.

Ricard spoke to him for a few minutes and the boy nodded.

"Ze man want for you spend night, you are to understand. Says you sit, eat and drink in ze 'otel, and he come for you in one hour, you are to know."

"Thank you very much. *Au revoir, Monsieur Ricard.*"

But Monsieur Ricard had silently stolen away.

The young boy stood by the kitchen doorway chewing, his eyes half-scornful, and half-laughing at me.

"*Bonsoir, bonsoir, madame.*" A short, bonny little man clattered into the bar, his arms full of dusty wine bottles and bottles of sack.

"Do you speak English?"

"I speak English better than anyone you are likely to meet in this sad country. You have been following the elections? See how the Americans have put another of their puppets at the head of our country. We do not like the man, and yet here he is, trying to ruin us all because of the USA. Does that not make you feel sad?"

"Very sad indeed. How much for a room?"

"You know, my child, I do not understand why you foreign women travel all alone, when you don't even learn the language. You are asking for trouble to fall on yourself. You must not be so trusting. Ten dollars."

I sat by the bar for a long time, chatting to the manager, and looking nervously at the black cobwebs in the corner. Little red beetles and cockroaches raced about, playing in the dust. Whenever I needed a light for my cigarette, the bovine young boy would fetch me a piece of glowing coal from the stoves, and charge me a dollar.

"So why is it the rest of the world hates Haiti?"

"Because they don't like the idea of a black Republic that is doing well, so they try to bring it down to its knees."

"But," asked the manager, seemingly unsatisfied with my reply, "why don't they like the idea of a black Republic? How can we ever grow into a strong nation if the rest of the world refuses to trade with us? If they shun us like pariah dogs?"

I told him that in England there is an old cliché that Africans cannot rule themselves, which became emphasised because of the atrocities of General Amin. The fact that several European rulers past and present have been guilty of equally terrible massacres seems to have escaped the notice of many self-righteous Europeans.

The manager nodded sagely and introduced me to his daughter, a teenage girl of surly aspect.

"She will cook for you. What would you like to eat?"

"Something with lots of meat and rice and things like that."

"But, *madame*! You know you are the only guest we have here. How do you think we have meat and rice for you to eat?"

The young boy sniggered, and choked slightly on his stick.

"Well, what do you have to eat?"

"Alicia could go down the road and give you peanuts, sugar cane or oranges. That is all I can do."

I declined the offer, preferring to sit by the bar drinking beer, and lighting cigarettes from charcoal embers, a dollar apiece. The use of charcoal for cooking and heating purposes has tragically been instrumental in the destruction of the Haitian forests. The peasants have reduced much of the land to barren waste.

Ricard was punctual to the second, bouncing into the bar, a gappy smile upon his jocular face.

"He says where would you like him to take you," said the manager, after a brief chat with my night's escort.

"Dancing," came the instantaneous reply.

I needed to let my hair down that night, and revel in the spirited atmosphere of abandoned joy, West Indian style. So, slipping into the "going out" dress that I had taken with me for evenings such as this, I tottered into the steamy night behind Ricard. Although it was now nearly midnight, the street life showed no signs of slowing down. I hurried to the green where the drumming and singing had been going on, but everything had disappeared without trace. The small park, with its bandstand barely visible in the dark, was empty of people and was now creepily quiet.

Round the back of town, past elegant houses, was a steep cliff overlooking the ocean. How lovely everything looked, washed colour-less by the moonlight. Tiny sailing boats bobbed up and down on the sparkling jet waves. Even Ricard appeared to be moved by the sight, and stood silently by my side gazing dreamily at the ebony waters.

The night-club we went to that night was a far cry from the frantic confusion of the Santo Domingo discotheque.

On an outdoor dance-floor, couples waltzed in slow motion to deep, sombre rhythms. Gentility was the order of the night. Ricard limply held my wrist, I placed a perfunctory arm about his shoulder, and we swayed sleepily beneath the stars.

When I became bored, after a few hours, I bade Ricard farewell, and told him, through the barman's translation, that I would see him the next day. Ricard offered to walk me to my hotel but I refused. I could remember where the hotel was and, besides, I always seemed to have more adventures when alone. Adventure! Little did I know what was in store for me that night.

A large stretch of tree-filled land beckoned and, thinking it was a common or garden park, I wandered in, a song in my heart and a swing in my gait.

How nice it is to walk about in a pretty park in the middle of the night, I thought. Why, in England, are they all locked up, denying people the pleasure of seeing a park at its best, in the fragrant night? Maybe this is where the royal palace is, or perhaps I was in the grounds of a cathedral. By now I was treading through thick undergrowth, picking my way through tangled trees and shrubs. Unexpectedly, I tripped over what seemed to be a pile of brambles.

A gargantuan man holding a menacing gun stepped out from the bushes and boomed, "*Où allez?*" in thunderous tones.

I stumbled backwards and stood rooted to the spot.

"*Où allez?*" he asked even louder, removing the rifle from his shoulder.

All I could do was blink stupidly at him.

"*Où allez?*" Click. He cocked the barrel of the gun, and pointed it towards my chest.

It has often been said that when you really think you are going to die, you cease to feel fear. A sense of calm, they say, pervades you, and you wave a breezy cheerio to life as it flashes before you like a slide show. Don't believe a word of it. Take it from one who knows, when you really think you are going to die, you're scared stiff.

This is it, I thought, as I heard the click. I always knew I would die some day, but who would have thought it would be in Haiti, killed by a mad gunman, and all because I can't speak the lingo! It was only when I felt the pressure of the gun butting me in the breast that I found my tongue.

"Tourist," I rasped. "I am a naïve tourist who's lost her way." My mouth felt uncomfortably dry, and I had an awful feeling I'd wet myself.

"*Je ne comprends pas. Parle Français!*"

'*Parle Français!*' What did that mean? Of course, it meant speak French – but I didn't know any French. By now I was trembling from head to foot. Suddenly, in a flash of inspiration, one of the phrases I learnt at school flew into my mind.

"Esk er vous avez day le petit animal?"

He had asked me to speak French and, unfortunately for both of us, this was all the French I knew.

"Le petit animal?"

"I'm sorry, but I'm afraid I don't speak any more French. Can I go now?"

The rifle jabbed me a sharp one in the ribs.

I stood my ground, nausea rising and falling in my throat.

"Erch! Allez-vous!" And with a final shove of the rifle, the man waved me irritatedly away. Very slowly, I trod from the gunman on numbed feet.

As soon as I reached the exit, I broke into a run, and shot through the streets until I arrived at the hotel. The young cud-chewing boy was in exactly the same place by the kitchen door.

"Give me a shot of water," I gasped, "and a glass of brandy to wash it down with!"

The boy poured out the necessaries with slow deliberation.

Who was that man, and why did he want to kill me?

I was determined to find out on the morrow. The main thing was that I was still alive and, better still, I had not wet myself.

Next day, when Ricard turned up, I insisted he take me back to the park where the gunman had so rudely butted me. On arriving, I found that the "park" was the grounds of a government building, with armed guards standing at every post. I was quite glad that the darkness had prevented me from seeing the guard's face the night before, for when I saw their faces that morning, they appeared startling in their cruelty.

Cap-Haïtien is a very poor town, with very little industry. A filthy market, almost rivalling the squalor of Port-au-Prince's Iron Market, stood in the town centre. Bright pink pigs, trussed up and bound, were being loaded roughly into the backs of vans and horse carts. The native black pigs of Haiti were all killed by the Americans, who believed the animals to have swine fever. A great shame, in my opinion, because the pigs the Americans now supply the Haitians with are not nearly so hardy, nor, according to a market woman, so tasty.

None of the houses were painted, but they stood in genteel dilapidation. I made a vow, there and then, that when I accumulate fabulous wealth, I shall return to Haiti and paint all the houses in soft white. Cap-Haïtien has the potential for being a remarkably beautiful town, with a Frenchified splendour reminiscent of New Orleans.

A woman, looking ninety-six if a day, bald-headed, her face a network of wrinkles, was sitting by a stall in the market-place. Her breast, the only youthful part of her body, was exposed, and sucking eagerly at it was a five-year-old child. The woman, who must really have been in her thirties, held out a pathetic hand to passers-by, occasionally whisking the flies away. Beside her was a woman with a tin pot into which I glanced casually. Ears and skin lay in bloody profusion, covered with black flies. I stared, hypnotised. The evil-smelling, rancid meat was the culmination of all my nightmares. The woman sat smiling.

"*Acheter? Oui, madame?*"

I stumbled into the car, a broken woman.

Once safely inside, I closed my eyes, breathed deeply, and heaved a sigh.

"*Madame! Madame!*"

My eyes snapped open. Great lumps of fetid meat were being pushed through the window. I screamed. Ricard started up the car, and away we clattered, past the shoe-shine boys, who frisked around with tinkling bells.

We were off to Palais Sans-Souci, the royal palace which King Henri-Christophe had commissioned, but was unfortunately destroyed by an earthquake in 1842. King Henri had hoped to imitate the style of the sumptuous European courts of the day, and both the name and the style of Sans-Souci were based upon Frederick the Great's palace at Potsdam. Although Haiti was virtually destitute at the time, no expense was spared in the building of the palace. Precious woods to wall the rooms, chandeliers made from cut crystal, marble floors and imported finery from Europe were all used to enhance the lavish effect. Now it stands, a hollow shell, stripped of all its finery.

Henri-Christophe was one of the most flamboyant characters in Haitian history. Born a slave in 1767 in St Kitts, then a British colony, he went on to work for many years as a waiter in Cap-Français. His bravery and military skill only came to light when the battle for independence began and, very quickly, he became a high-ranking general. He became president of the northern state of the island in 1806, and in 1811 appointed himself king. The nobility of the court were given colourful names, such as Duc de Marmelade and Comte de Limonade. All the nine palaces Henri built are now in ruins.

During the last years of his life, Henri's mind became seriously deranged. He fired cannons during tropical thunderstorms, demonstrating to his subjects his power over nature. Obsessed that Napoleon would seize his state, he built more and more forts and palaces to ward him off. Napoleon never invaded.

When we reached Milo, the small town lying below Sans-Souci, Ricard told me through the lips of a little girl, that he would meet me by the sugar-cane seller in an hour's time. An hour hardly seemed long enough to give me time to trek the journey to Sans-Souci, and the twelve miles to the Citadel. Try as I might, I could not persuade Ricard either to wait longer or to join me.

Walking up the hill to the splendid ruins of the palace, I felt a bit like the Pied Piper of Haiti. Raggedy children followed me for a very long way, holding up bright fragments of jewellery. Babies, that in England cannot walk or talk (because they're babies), in Haiti are not only walking and talking, but asking for money in a foreign tongue. It is most impressive.

"Voodoo dolls, voodoo dolls," intoned a number of women, holding up flimsy rag dolls. The women, dressed in flowing cotton skirts, wore hopeless expressions. I was the only tourist around, and apparently I did not look the voodoo doll type, for they did not pester me any further. The pestering was done, predictably, by the men, who swarmed around me like vultures over a dead cat.

"You have to have a guide, *madame*, it is the law."

"The law! Leave it out, mate."

"But I speak the truth! You must have a guide!"

I looked them all over and resignedly chose the handsomest one to be my guide. He was a tall, wiry thirty-year-old, with thin, calculating features.

"That is good that you have chosen me. I am the one who knows most about this place. I will show you around Sans-Souci, then we have to ride a horse up to the Citadel. When we reach the Citadel, I will guide you around, then we will ride the horse back down, and you will pay me ten dollars."

I nodded. Ten dollars – about five pounds. Not too bad. I was very eager to ride a horse, having been a keen horse-woman in my youth, astounding the villagers with my masterful prowess in the saddle.

The guide, Yacoub, and I wandered around the ruined palace, mostly in silence, but every now and again, he would tell me things about the building that I already knew. He pointed out the very spot where Henri-Christophe committed suicide with a silver bullet, then laughed loudly at the foolishness of such an action.

"His palace guard joined the rebels in 1820, and because the man was mad, he was thinking that the only thing to do was to die. I would have joined the rebels as well, then I would have proclaimed myself King of the rebel army."

"Good idea, so would I."

"Suicide is not honourable way to die." Yacoub looked long and slyly at me from the corner of his eye. I wasn't carrying much money on me, but I could sense that to Yacoub, my handbag represented the horn of plenty.

"You wait here, now, I will get the horses."

Half an hour later, two tired old nags lolloped toward us, led by six men.

"I hope you are a good rider, because we have a long way to go, but they are good horses. I know them. You will ride Boogie."

"Who are the men leading the horses?"

"They are guides as well. They will lead us up."

"Can't we go up by ourselves?"

"Of course not!"

"But how can they walk twelve miles up a mountain?"

"It is their job."

I look back on that ride up the mountain to the Citadel with a blend of horror and relief. Relief that I know I will never have to make that journey again.

Villagers who lived in the mountain ran from their huts to scream for money for the whole duration of the trip. Never have I felt a bigger fool than when I sat upon the old senile horse, with one man in front, holding the reins, one in the middle, holding the saddle, and one behind, lashing the poor horse cruelly with a leather thong. The horse almost slipped down the steep mountain several times under the pain of the lash, and the more I shouted at the heartless "guide" the more he laughed, beating the horse with gleeful energy.

"*Madame!* Psssst! Dollar!"

Women with faces twisted with misery and starvation scampered towards me, pleading, and selling useless pieces of junk. I knew it was pointless to stop to give any of them money, for then I would be totally mobbed, as I was at the Iron Market, and even if *I* could take the pressure, my horse certainly could not.

If it hadn't been for the view, I would have given the whole thing up as a bad job. The palms, hibiscus flowers and humming-birds, aglow with a shimmering light, almost made up for the horrors all around me. The day was swelteringly hot, with a radiant blue sky.

"I must stop to buy some coconut water," I called to Yacoub, who was far ahead of me. His eyes lit up.

"Yes, of course. Stop! Stop!"

The men settled beneath a palm tree, and immediately put in their orders. One wanted oranges, another sugar-cane, and the rest preferred jelly coconuts. I hoped I could afford all this, for I had purposefully brought with me only a small amount of money.

Children surrounded me, smiling and begging. One little girl caught my attention. A creature of great enchantment, with a round face and sparkling eyes, she began rubbing against me like a cat.

"Oh, aren't you a duckling!" I gushed, swinging her up in my arms, and tickling her. I judged her to be two and a half. Her mother, a heavily pregnant woman, beetled over.

"I am the mother. My name is Mildred. My daughter's name is Angela. Give us money. We are poor. Do not forget me."

Angela squirmed prettily in my arms, and grinned sweetly. I placed her on the ground and gave her a dollar. She continued to grin and duck her head, and then a strange thing happened. Her elder brother approached us and also started to grin, posturing and posing before me. Angela, the tiny toddler, pushed him away in a conspiratorial manner, whispered frantically in his ear, then gave him a final shove. So doing, she smiled innocently at me once again, and nuzzled up against my leg. I was shocked.

"Leave her alone!" she had obviously been saying to her brother. "I'm the one who she thinks is really cute. Let *me* handle her and we're quids in!"

That so small a child could have such built-in slyness shocked me to the core. Was she trained to look sweet to bleed tourists white, or was she naturally adept in the art of crafty wiles? When she did not think I was watching her, she would give me looks of such bright intelligence that I was almost unable to believe my eyes. Seeing I was looking at her, her keen-eyed expression would instantly change to one of soft, guileless charm.

Her mother, Mildred, clacked over to us, pushing her seven children forward. They stumbled towards me, smiling sweetly.

"Just afford me to buy a dress. You see this all I have, and now in my state, it is small."

Her dress gaped widely from the waist upwards, revealing a swollen stomach which made her wasted arms look all the more pitiful.

"If I had money, *madame*, you could have it all, but all I have is fifteen dollars, and that all has to be spent on the seven guides," I said, although I said it to myself.

Having paid for the guides and my refreshments, I sat back upon poor Boogie, the tired old mare, and up we went.

Mildred and Angela chased after us, telling me that we would meet up again on the way down and next time, maybe, I would be more generous.

"Don't forget me," cried Mildred.

As if I ever could!

After four hours in the saddle, a gothic monstrosity became visible through the trees, high up ahead. The mountain grew steeper and steeper, and soon poor Boogie was twisting her legs painfully on the rocks, receiving a savage lash for her pains.

The Citadel was truly an imposing sight. Napoleon knew what he was doing when he steered well clear of the place. 200,000 men are said to have worked on it, and at least 20,000 lost their lives in the process.

It is a massive fort, iron grey in colour, standing like a haunted medieval castle at the very top of the beautiful mountain. Two hundred and fifty years ago, King Henri, to show off the total obedience and discipline of his army to a British diplomat, ordered a troop of soldiers to march off the side of the Citadel. The men blindly obeyed, meeting a horrific death. One cannot look at the Citadel without shuddering. The place is haunted by malevolent spirits and, as soon as I arrived, tired and saddle sore, I deeply regretted having made the long, hazardous journey.

Yacoub sat comfortably on an ancient iron cannon, ordering Coca-Cola for himself and the men, shouting orders to a lone vendor and swearing heartily in Anglo-Saxon.

"Come, woman, pay for the drinks! You think my men want to work for nothing?"

Too weak to resist, I coughed up, trying not to think too hard about the money Yacoub's "men" would need once this hell ride had reached its completion.

"Are you married?"

"No, Yacoub, I'm not."

"I am married, and I have three children, but that doesn't stop me from having very many mistresses. I like you. You are a good people. As you are not married, maybe you could let me come to London."

"Aren't you going to guide me?"

"Don't talk such stupidness! I'm tired. I must drink and eat. I like your figure. You are built like the Citadel, strong and solid. I like that."

"Thank you. Do you guide many tourists up here?"

"No, you are the only one we have had for a long time. You're all alone up here, just you, me, and the men."

"Ah."

I studied my nails with feigned unconcern.

"So what date was the Citadel built?"

"Look, woman! I told you not to trouble me with all this nonsense. I can't sit around in the heat wearing out my tongue talking about dates and things. Let me eat!"

A man had appeared from nowhere holding a plate of rice and peas, garnished with a tender meat stew. Yacoub ate with relish, flicking stray morsels into his mouth with a pretty pink tongue. I rather liked him in spite of myself, and insisted I share his meal. In true African style, we ate from the same plate with our dusty fingers.

"Right, is that belly of yours feeling satisfied?"

"Yes."

"Then we shall go and look at this Citadel."

We walked further up the hill, past lines of rusty old cannons. As soon as we approached the building I felt sick to the pit of my stomach. Something ghostly and eerie about the place seemed to drive me back. I stood in the entrance, too afraid to enter the haunted ruin.

"Come in, woman, what's the matter with you?"

"I'm frightened."

"What? Come on, come in and I will show you the place where the men fell over the walls and died."

"You go in, I'll wait here."

"I've never heard such fool talk in all my living days."

But I knew that the spirits that haunted the Citadel meant nothing to me but the evilest intent, so I sat on a mossy stone wall and admired the view.

Yacoub, laughing and cursing at the same time, sauntered back to his cannon seat, and chatted with the men.

An elf-like little boy approached me, his huge eyes staring out from his piquant face, and handed me a tiny posy of wild flowers.

"*Merci*," I said, "but I am afraid I have no money to give you."

He spoke in a sing-song Creole, and told me that he did not want money, and he understood that I was poor. Due to his skilful miming, I could understand every word he said.

I did a double-take. A Haitian boy who does not want money, and who actually *understands* that I am poor? Where's the catch? But I had become too cynical, and with this little child, there was no catch. We chatted about his family and friends, and he told me that although he didn't go to school, he had been taught to read and write by an old man who lived in the forest. We sat for a long time looking at Haiti as it spread before us, green with palms, and brown with infertile waste. I felt so touched by the present of the flowers, I could feel the tears welling up in my eyes.

"Heh! Woman! If you don't even want to go into the Citadel because of superstitious cowardice, then come down again."

"I will when I have finished talking to this sweet child."

"Sweet child? What child? Is it that you are mad as well as coward?"

The child had vanished. I called him, looked between the cannons, and searched behind the wall for him, but he had disappeared into the thick air. Maybe he was a fairy, or a ghost of one of the murdered children of bygone years. The posy was as fresh and fragrant as ever, and remained so for a very long time afterwards.

Boogie kicked and reared wildly on the way down. At one point I lost my temper, and began to shriek at the guide to leave her alone.

"Why did you have to come anyway? We don't need you to stand behind the horse, ill-treating it like this."

"Yes, you do! It is the law in this country. When tourists are riding horses, you need one in the front, one at the back, and one behind. I swear, it is the truth I am telling you."

Boogie and I snorted.

"I like you, I like you, I like you." Yacoub had trotted up beside me, and was clutching at my saddle.

I did my best to ignore him. We were back in Mildred's village, and I felt I would die unless I had a drink. I ordered seven coconuts for the men, and the men ordered oranges, mangoes and water-melons for themselves. I opened my purse, and to my horror found that I had only two dollars left. Every woman who had sold us the fruits wanted at least a dollar each. I was well and truly stuck.

"I shall have to go into town, change traveller's cheques, and return with the money," I told them, guiltily.

The women didn't seem to mind at all. Haitian honesty is as strong as Jamaican honesty, so with smiles and waves, I was seen off on my horse, and away we lurched down the stony hill.

"Don't worry, woman. I know that you were wondering how you could come back on the horse to this village, but I see that you are a good people. I will come with you to town, while you change your money, then I will take the money up to the women. Do you like me?"

"You're all right, I suppose." He was very handsome, rather like a film-star villain.

"Why aren't you frightened of me?"

"I'm not really frightened of people. I'm more frightened by tiny animals."

"And ghosts?"

"Yes, and ghosts."

"But I could have done anything to you up there. I would like you to be my girlfriend, otherwise I might get bad to you."

I laughed loudly at him. I was absolutely defenceless towards him, having no power at all. I wondered what it must be like to be white and have built-in power. If I was white, he would think twice before threatening me in so blatant a manner. The Haitian government would not take kindly to a guide maltreating a white tourist, but being black, I felt all the more vulnerable. Never show fear is the golden rule, so I continued to laugh at Yacoub who, after a while, laughed back with sheepish guilt.

When we reached the bottom of the hill, all the men began to shout at once, saying they needed twenty dollars each, and were not leaving until they received it.

Yacoub busily explained to them that he was coming with me to the bank at Cap-Haïtien and would watch me while I changed my cheques, and would ensure that they were all paid. The men glared fiercely at me, muttering strange Haitian oaths.

"So this is how it is!" One of the men raised his hands up to heaven in despair. "Sometimes I get paid for doing work, and sometimes I don't. I see it now. I am going!"

And off he went.

If I had told him I had thought the whole escapade would cost ten dollars in all, he would not have believed me.

A lone figure stood by a dented blue car. It was Ricard. His crinkly face lit up on seeing me, and he swung open the door of his car.

"This is Yacoub. Yacoub, Ricard."

The two men bristled like stray cats at the sight of one another. Far from acknowledging one another, they pointedly stared out of their respective windows.

After we had driven about a mile, Yacoub ordered Ricard to stop the car to pick up his friend, an army officer. The officer sat in the back of the car looking neither right nor left, and away we sped.

Behind us, straddled upon a powerful motor bike was a sombrely clad man, wearing enormous dark glasses. He followed our every turn, and smiled in a sinister manner whenever I caught his black shielded eyes.

"If I didn't know better," I murmured to Yacoub, "I would think he was the Tontons Macoutes."

"Shhhh!"

"Why do you say shhh?" I asked obtusely.

Yacoub flicked his eyes towards the army officer, and pursed his lips.

I looked back at the motor cyclist. Surely he could not be a member of the dreaded Tontons Macoutes, they went out with Papa Doc – didn't they?

When we reached Cap-Haïtien, the army officer shifted himself from the car and started up the road, with the motor cyclist hot on his heels.

"So what was that all about?" I asked Yacoub, in the bank. "Was that really the Tontons Macoutes?"

"You laugh, but it really was! They are out for my friend."

"So what is your friend going to do?"

"Maybe he will die."

"Are you serious?"

"How could I not be serious about a thing like that?"

We strolled out of the bank together towards Ricard's car.

"Tontons Macoutes means the same as 'bogie man' in your language. When the children are naughty, we say to them, 'Be good or the Tonton will come and put you in his macoute!' Macoute is a sort of satchel bag that you wear on your shoulder and tonton means uncle. I don't like what they did to me and my family."

"What did they do?"

"Never ask questions. The foolish questions you asked in the car almost got us all killed. Now give me the money, and I will take it back to give to the people."

"Make sure you give a lot to Mildred and her family, and to the lady who sold the coconuts."

I then handed over to Yacoub a sum so vast it doesn't bear thinking about.

"Ah! You are very good people, very good. I will pray for you. I will pray for a very long time. Can I come back to your hotel with you, or will that no-toothed goat be there?"

Poor Ricard stood by an art stall, smiling blandly.

"Yacoub, get back to the guides before they call the police on us both."

"To the guides? You joke! First I must go to see my girlfriends who live here, one by one."

Yacoub threw back his head and laughed. The last I saw of him was his bony form swaggering away through a group of artists, shouting greetings, and swearing in ancient English. Rogue though he was, I hoped I had not seen the last of him. I found his cocksure villainy so intriguing, he made my blood flow in the opposite direction. That being said, I desperately hoped that the money went into the right hands.

After leaving Yacoub, Ricard and I decided to take a little stroll around the town. Through some of the windows of one of the more chi-chi houses could be seen elegant classrooms. Standing on tiptoe and peering in soon became tedious and uncomfortable, so, after a few minutes, Ricard and I knocked at the head mistress's study and asked permission to look around the classes of the elegant little school in the centre of town.

The children were such goody-goody little prigs, I wanted to spank them. Neat uniforms, impeccable English and a swarm of upraised hands whenever teacher asked them a question. These were the children of the élite, and, as befitting the *crème de la crème*, they were perfect in every detail.

Only French is taught in the Haitian schools, and not the predominant language, but it didn't seem to matter, because no Creole speakers attend the schools. The maths that the six-year-olds were learning was way above my head, a blinding array of square roots and fractions.

Every child I met addressed me in the politest of tones. Ricard was most chuffed at being asked, "How *do* you do?" in crisp English. It was assumed he was my husband from London, and he was none too eager to deny it. He walked pompously around the classrooms, hands behind his back, his lips pressed tightly together.

For supper that night, we dined with a friend of Ricard's who lived in the centre of town near the cathedral. Our hostess, a bowed young woman, served us rice and pigeon peas in glum silence. I tried to speak French to her, but after she had ignored my question over whether she was in possession of a little animal, I gave it up as a bad job. In the corner of her small dark room was an altar, encrusted with papier mâché designs, painted in gold. Statues of the Virgin Mary, and of many Catholic saints, stood amongst white candles. In the very centre of the shrine was a tiny skull. I tried not to look at it, but something compelled my eyes to rest upon it whenever I looked up from my food.

Catholicism and voodoo are so intertwined in Haiti as to be one and the same religion. Madame St Michelle would call herself a

Catholic. The voodoo elements in her religion were practised but unspoken.

That night I slept at the large brick boarding-house overlooking the Cathedral. A tired young man wearing nothing but a pair of old underpants and a frown opened the door to let me into the building. My room was bare save for a bed with no blankets or sheets. I lay on the stained mattress, pondering on the good things of life, such as what it must be like to have a pillow, and why a cockroach was doing a breakdance on the floor.

Haiti was a fascinating country, and I would have liked to have stayed there for a very long time, but you need to be very rich to holiday in that weird isle, and funds were fast disappearing. I would need to return to the Dominican Republic the next day, and, with a bit of luck and a lot of money, the trusty Ricard would drive me back.

From the balcony of my room the next morning, I saw Cap-Haïtien come alive. Uniformed children hurried to school, and women walked tall and proud, balancing all kinds of produce on their heads. A medicine-man, wearing a long coarse grey dress with bags of herbs tied round the waist, ambled slowly around the square. The atmosphere was one of purposeful drive.

I had arranged to meet Ricard for breakfast in the dining-room of the Hôtel Christophe, the house where Pauline Bonaparte had once lived, the house that the King of Haiti had mentioned all those days before. Even when the hotel was pointed out to me by good-natured market women, I still could not find it. Surely it couldn't be behind the dense wall, sprawling with unsightly political graffiti.

"*Oui, oui.*" And a powerful woman gripped me by the arm and pushed me through the gates. I blinked as I beheld a splendid mansion set in a haven of gentle palms and flowers. The rooms were so luxurious, it was easy to imagine the sumptuous style in which Pauline Bonaparte and her husband Leclerc once lived.

Ricard was nowhere around. I was the sole diner, a state of affairs I had long since become accustomed to in Haiti. A small, skinny waiter fussed around me, polishing the empty tables, and filling up my tea cup. How boring a waiter's job must become when there are no customers to serve!

After the final wipe of the napkin, I hurried outside to see if Ricard was anywhere around, but no. For two hours I waited for the elusive man, but to no avail. I walked up and down the street, calling his name loudly. Children and sugar-cane vendors appeared, to laugh at me, but no Ricard.

Never mind, never mind, never mind, I repeated inanely over and over again. A tap-tap would take me to Port-au-Prince and even if it didn't, I could always get another lift. I plodded out of the town, wondering how and why Ricard could have deserted me when he hadn't even been paid yet. A gripping mystery story is in the making here, I thought. Before long, I had reached the gates of town, and was walking past a group of men wearing large straw hats and playing the giant African flutes that I had heard children playing in the villages. And then another sound caught my attention.

"Zanar! Zanar!"

I looked this way and that, but could not see the caller.

"Zanar!" A long silver car crawled between rows of tap-taps, and out of the window poked the head of Jean-Claude.

"Zoh, there it is!" Jean-Claude looked fresh and beaming, with a smile to match the glisten of his car.

"Where are you going, walking around on foot like a poor lady?"

I was so glad to see him, it was all I could do to stop myself from hurling myself into his arms.

"Port-au-Prince."

"And is it that you intend to walk. Ha ha ha."

"No, I shall get a tap-tap."

"But why do you not want for me to drive you back? I am leaving for Port-au-Prince this immediate."

"Well," I drawled, not wanting to appear too forward, "if you're going back anyway, and you're sure you don't mind . . ."

"Mind! Why, my dear young lady!" and a door was held open for me, in the most gentlemanly of manners.

"I was here on business, and now all is well. If we drive quick we shall be in Port-au-Prince before the four hours."

As long as I caught my plane which went at three, I wasn't really bothered what time we arrived.

Nothing of any interest occurred in the first two hours of our journey. Jean-Claude was quiet and slightly morose, hinting vaguely that his business venture had not gone as well as he hoped. I felt it was best not to pry too deeply into his affairs, so kept up a silence, before the bumpy roads and the hot sun lulled me to sleep.

"Zanar! Zanar! Awake, quick. Look."

I opened my eyes and stared at Jean-Claude, who was pointing to a black figure ahead.

"What is it?"

"A woman dressed as the devil. I thought you would like to see her. Funny, yes?"

Funny, no!

Walking with slow majesty by the side of the road, was a figure dressed in long black, tattered robes. On the shoulders was an enormous mask. It was the mask which shocked me fully out of my peaceful sleep.

The mask was made of goat skin, with slit red eyes, huge teeth, and long curling horns which twirled grotesquely upwards. Never have I seen anything so evil. Everyone who passed the devil held out their hands to pat. The devil clasped the hands of the passers-by in a ritualistic fashion, then wended her way.

As soon as the devil woman saw our car, she made an uncanny sign at us with her hand.

I crossed myself, truly affected by her intense power.

"It is good that we drive back to get a better look."

"No, Jean-Claude. No!"

But it was too late. Jean-Claude had wheeled round, and we were speeding down the dirt track back towards the devil woman.

When we approached her, she made another sign at us, this time with a larger gesture. The people in the street stopped to watch our car speed past, flitting cautious glances at the devil woman.

I knew we would have to pass her again, for there was only one road. I was deeply afraid. Something in me said that this was no pretence, the evil that radiated from this woman was very real.

When we passed her for the third time, she threw her arms up in the air at the sight of us, with such force, she resembled an avenging angel of war. Her red teeth glowed in the sun. As she lifted up her arm, the frayed black sleeves fluttered like bat's wings. The people on the side of the road stopped dead in their tracks to gape at us and the woman.

"Drive faster," I whispered, "let's get out of here as soon as possible."

"I am going as fast as I can."

"But you're not! You're slowing down!"

"*Mais oui*, I do not understand it, maybe we are out of petrol!"

I began to shake, gently at first, then it seemed as if convulsions were overtaking my whole body. The car drew to a halt only a little way away from the devil woman, and the devil woman had stopped dead still, and was looking at us, her arms all the time upraised.

"Move," I rasped. "Jean-Claude, for the love of God, try to get this car to move."

In the rear-view mirror I could see the devil woman walking very slowly and stiffly towards us, her face so terrifying it was impossible to believe she was human, and not some demonic spirit from hell.

The people on the street were now also approaching our car, some smiling, and some deadly serious.

By now I could hardly breathe. I was shaking too violently to talk, and I knew my legs were too weak to take me out of the car to make a run for it.

Just as the first of the people reached our car, Jean-Claude slammed on the accelerator and we lunged forward, creating clouds of dust too thick for us to see anything outside.

"No really run out of petrol, *madame*. Just a joke to make you a leetle nervous."

It was a very long time before I could reply to him.

"Ah, Zanar. Why you afraid? Is only hocus-pocus nonsense."

But the power of the woman had a lasting effect on me. I was haunted by abysmal dreams of her for many nights afterwards, and, if truth be known, it took me a very long time to get back into my right mind after seeing that spectre of Satan.

Jean-Claude, however, continued to laugh and pooh-pooh the whole thing, saying that it was only a symptom of the ignorance in which the peasants live.

We drove back to Port-au-Prince, passing through a striking town called Gonaives. A harbour was filled with ships of all shapes and sizes. Very picturesque little fishing boats bobbed up and down side by side with grand vessels of the old school, painted beautifully with biblical scenes. People were jammed into the boats, mainly women and children with their animals scrunched into undersized bags.

There was an Elizabethan atmosphere about the town, a hustle-bustle that one imagines existed in Shakespeare's London. Comely wenches held baskets of goodly fare upon their heads and sang sweetly for custom. Bright-eyed children leant from the windows of the lop-sided wooden houses, or played by the brilliantly painted boats. Across the harbour stood a quaint little fishing village, aswarm with men in the huge Haitian straw hats, pulling large ropes, and sitting by the bay smoking pensive pipes.

Gonaives was so rich in charm, I felt it to be the perfect antidote to the devil woman and, after a hearty meal of mashed fish and rice, I could feel the old fighting spirit returning once again.

Jean-Claude had waited for me in a small café just outside the town.

"The smell is too awful when you get near the water," he complained.

When I returned to the car, I asked him if he had ever been to the Iron Market.

"But no! Of course not!"

I can't say I blamed him, but all the same, it did seem a trifle odd never to have visited an edifice that dominates your town in such a way as the Iron Market does.

On the way back from Gonaives, we stopped off at a little bar near a tiny village to buy a drink. No one seemed to sell water or tea, so I was forced to make do with fizzy drinks, and believe you me, there's nothing less refreshing on a hot summer's day than a warm Coca-Cola.

The village was composed of dainty little thatched cottages with Africanesque carvings on the walls. A few chickens clucked, and the odd bleat of a goat could be heard, but apart from that, there was no other sound, not even the usual wail of a baby.

"Where have all the people gone?" I asked Jean-Claude who sniffed in reply.

We snooped about, but still no sign of human life.

All of a sudden, from behind an ancient stone wall, there lurched an exceedingly tall man, clad in miserable strips of cloth. He stumbled towards us, his hand outstretched beseechingly. I made towards him to give him a dollar – and then caught sight of his eyes. The eyeballs were rolled up into his head, and the whites were so swollen as to be all but hanging from his face. Jean-Claude yelped, and galloped back to his car. I pressed a handful of notes into the unfortunate man's hand, and hot-footed it close on Jean-Claude's trail.

The diseased man lolloped onto the road side and murmured at us as we drove away. I did not turn back. The eyes were too dreadful to look into.

"So, there it is. You have seen one. Not bad, eh, for one day. A devil woman, and now a zombie."

"Zombie! Don't tell me he was a zombie."

"Of course not. Zombies do not exist."

"Then why do you tell me he was a zombie?"

"Because that is what the local people would call him. What the poor fellow really has is a disease of the eyes."

"But zombies *do* exist."

"You sometimes are as ignorant as a peasant."

Ignorant as a peasant or not, I shall always believe that the man I saw in that village was a zombie. The mystery, though, will never be explained, the same as the mystery over the missing Ricard.

On the way to the airport, I insisted that Jean-Claude drive me to the Iron Market once more so I could say goodbye. After having spent so long in Haiti, I was quite used to it, and had even grown fairly tolerant of the semi-fights that my presence seemed to cause. Everyone in the art section of the market seemed to remember me, and the tough woman who had sold me the paintings grabbed me once again. When she heard I was leaving, never again to buy one of her pictures, her expression soured, and there were no more smiles.

I could not make up my mind whether I was pleased or sorry to be leaving Haiti. Santo Domingo, with its jazzy, Latin American pzazz seemed a very long way away. Sometimes it seemed real, and Haiti a fantasy, and sometimes vice versa, but I could never connect the two.

Jean-Claude saw me off to the airport prattling advice to me all the while, the gist of it being that I should stop being nice to people. I told him that he had been very good to me, and he smiled, a lop-sided smile.

As I sat in the airport lounge, I mused that Haiti is like a sparkler, with explosions of energy shooting out in every direction, but never forming into any definite shape. There is so much power and intensity, that being in Haiti is like riding on the back of a monstrous, intriguing animal. But where is Haiti going?

The first thing that strikes the visitor on arrival is not the poverty, but the art. Haiti's art is not shut away in museums and galleries. It is alive in the streets, the villages, the homes of the people. I found I had developed a profound respect for Haiti for this reason above everything else.

High Times in the Dominican Republic

How odd to be back in the Dominican Republic, surrounded once more by the familiar car-hire men, jostling and shouting.
Was I really ever in Haiti?

I took a taxi back to the hotel, and flew up to my room to meet
Abbas, who I presumed would have some treat up his sleeve as a
welcome present. The room was empty, save for a bottle of wine and
three glasses.

"Have you seen my brother?" I asked the receptionist.

"Your brother gone out with Consuelo and Maria. He no say where.
He had good time since you away."

"How is his ankle?"

"He take nurse to help with the ankle, and nurse make him feel better. Every night nurse come, and now is no prob with foot."

I couldn't bear to hear any more, so I took the lift back up to the empty room and waited in vain for Abbas.

Early next morning the phone rang bright and clear. I picked it up whilst at the same time lighting a cigarette. Phone calls early in the morning or late at night can never be answered unless a cigarette is readily at hand.

"Ha ha ha ha! Ooooo! Don'ta do *that*!" Was this some kind of joke at my expense?

"Khallo? Khallo?"

"Hello, who is this!"

"Oooo! Stop it! Khallo! Ouch!"

"What do you want!"

"Mees Zenga?"

"Speaking."

"Thees reception 'ere. Abbas ees done stair. (Oooo! Abbas! It tickles!) 'E say come down now 'e 'as car for you, a khire car, an' 'e say come done stair now an' 'e – ow! – tek you khout." More sudden giggled expletives burst down the phone and I quickly hung up.

In the reception stood the beautiful receptionist flirting outrageously with Abbas.

"Shhh! Stop it. You seesta 'ere!"

"Hello, hello, hello! I've hired a car, and we're going for a short drive to a place called Constance. Look, you can see it on the map. I *was* hoping Rosiana could come instead, but when she told me you were back, I thought you may as well tag along – especially as they won't let poor Rosiana have the day off." The lovely Rosiana chortled winsomely.

Constance, advertised in the map as a tourist area, looked all set to be a lovely journey away, through mountains, across rivers, with little pictures of animals and trees.

"It's a tourist area," said Abbas. "The man at the bureau said that everybody goes there. It'll make a lovely day out."

Ah, welladay. If only I knew then what I was later to discover, I would have uttered a careless laugh and said something in the lines of, oh no, let's have a look around the shops instead. But, like happy-go-lucky flies flitting around a Venus fly trap, we jumped into the hired Mazda with joy in our hearts. The morning sun slanted over us. Our fates were sealed.

Leaving the vibrant Santo Domingo was easy enough. The roads became more bumpy, but that merely added to the fun. There were two roads to Constance, and we had chosen to use the scenic route on the way there, and come back by the main road. After a pleasant drive through hills which became higher and higher, we passed pretty little villages, which looked more Haitian than any villages I have seen outside of Africa. People rode on donkeys laden with produce, walking slowly towards their thatched huts.

Very soon, we drove upwards to a beautiful valley, a fabulous tropical island paradise. Limestone hills rose among the palms, pouring forth gentle waterfalls. Children ran from their tiny huts to wave hello. It was very noticeable that the poor people outside of Santo Domingo were considerably darker in complexion than the sleek city slickers.

Travelling uphill, the road became increasingly more rutted.

"Shall we turn back?"

"No," said Abbas, firmly.

Suddenly we came to a thundering river, about forty feet wide, roaring past dense vegetation. Our car stood poised atop a steep slope, and both Abbas and I saw to our concern that the bridge, a decayed wooden affair, had collapsed into the foaming torrent.

A lorry was making its way slowly down the slope to the river, accelerating rapidly, then whoosh! It rolled headlong into the waters with a mighty crash, sheets of water rising in great billows on either side, then, with a swoop, it swooshed up the other side.

"Go on, then, Abbas, you try that."

Not realising I was joking, Abbas shot the car down the slope at hair-raising speed, but unlike the lorry, our car got stuck half-way across the river. Again and again, Abbas tried to accelerate, but found the car would not move an inch. Then, in a sudden fit of goodwill, the little Mazda jolted forward out of the terrifying river, and edged slowly up the slope. We had made it. My emotions, by this time, were stunned. I felt neither fear nor joy. Maybe the shock of having experienced Haiti had dulled my senses. However, we crawled slowly up the mountain, hoping passionately that the car would not backslide into the raging torrent. Zig-zagging carefully, we arrived at the top of the hill and looked down the valley.

Several little girls ran from their houses to stare at us, galloping away like young deer when we tried to speak to them. By now it was about two-thirty, and we had not yet eaten. There was no indication on the map that there were going to be such impossible mountains and, looking around us, it was clear that the mountains were going to become even higher before we reached Constance. One thing was certain, we could not retrace our steps because of the river, so we travelled on in silence, marvelling at the magnificent landscape.

The mountains became ever steeper and, after two hours, a chilly mist surrounded us, swirling eerily around the car. Everything was covered in dew. I shivered slightly, and wound up the car windows. We were in the clouds. A few bedraggled people stood by their huts, gloomily eyeing our car. The villages, by now, were exactly like the villages in Haiti: compound huts topped by a thatch of thick straw, but here a cheerless desolation loomed in the mist.

By five o'clock the eddying mists had become so dense it was impossible to see the road. All we knew was that there was a precipice on either side of us. Bumping very gingerly over ruts two feet deep, we bounced forever upwards.

Where was this Constance? Did it actually exist? Six o'clock dusk fell, and the thick fog-like cloud mist was at its worst. Billowing swirls swept up from the depth of the earth, creating the spirit of hell. Peering through the windows, we realised that for the last hour we had seen no people, no plants, and no other sign of life; just bare rock stretching upwards into a furious swish of icy winds. Our car switchbacked constantly, travelling at the painful speed of twelve miles an hour.

And then, quite suddenly, we began to descend.

"We must be here!"

"Don't count your chickens," groaned Abbas.

Four hours later, we were still descending, until, in another instant, we found we were going up again, higher, if that's possible, than before. It was now pitch dark, freezing cold, and still, the area seemed totally lifeless.

The little Mazda did us proud. After a four-hour climb, we began, once again to descend, and descend, seeing no more in front of us than the haze around the light of the headlamps.

Lights shone on the horizon, creating a spate of unabated excitement in our jolting little car. Three hours later, the lights still shone, seemingly in the self same spot, coming and going, beckoning, but never moving. One or two blades of grass could now be seen, lit up in the glare of the headlights. Nature had replaced rocks, mists and wind. But still the air was creepy and cold. Somehow I didn't trust the inky blackness of the night.

"I'm sure there's going to be another huge river to cross," I jested thoughtlessly, "before we get to this Constance place."

The road was as rutted as ever. Here and there a hut could be seen in the darkness, made out only vaguely by a glimmering light filtering below a door.

"What's that noise?" I asked Abbas. A rumbling sound could be heard beneath us.

Steering delicately around a sharp bend, we beheld a sight that made Abbas gasp, and me laugh. Below us gushed a thunderous river, raging in the moonlight, with sheets of spray shooting upwards. Our car drove down to the great, foaming torrent, and stopped. Abbas gazed dumbly ahead of him, deciding in his own inimitable way what to do. I could not advise, because by now I was no longer sure whether this was an hallucination or a nightmare.

From a small, battered hut next to the river, came a squat, mustachioed man. Hailing our car in a resigned manner, he took off his shoes, and waded into the river up to the thigh.

Our car followed him up to an island in the middle of the water, and then he stopped, and banged on the window. Speaking in Spanish, but using extremely explicit sign language, he told us that he would only guide us further after we had paid him. Abbas pulled out his wallet and forked out a handful of notes. I'm not sure how much – about a hundred pounds or something, and the man pointed the way. We all but floated over the river, and made our way safely to the other side. After two and a half hours, we reached a village. Great chasms sank deep into the road, testing the car's endurance to the hilt.

Three quarters of an hour later, we saw a garage by the side of the street. A very friendly man cleaned the car, and filled up the petrol tank, smiling and chatting all the while.

"Which is the way back to Santo Domingo?" asked Abbas. The main road, judging by the map, which went straight to the capital, should not be too far away.

"Up there," said the mechanic, and pointed up the way we had come. Abbas and I caught our breaths. We had travelled an eleven-hour obstacle course up precipitous mountains and across seething rapids, and now the only way back was through this living hell.

"No," said Abbas, sternly, "there must be another way," and so saying, we ventured forth along the furrowed road, until we came to the ever elusive Constance.

Although the houses gave off a very poverty-stricken appearance, the village was a hubbub of life. Bonfires burnt brightly on the street corners with people gathered round them, throwing in sticks and frisking playfully. Bars and tacos shops were still open, although it was way past midnight.

Dominican food tasted sweet that night, which only goes to show the depth of starvation that Abbas and I had sunk to.

A swarthy man told us that the way back to Santo Domingo was the road ahead of us that the lorries were taking, so we dutifully followed the lorries around the winding, stony roads. Glowing lights lit up the sky ahead of us, strange multicoloured lights which almost appeared to be throbbing. I have never heard that the Caribbean has its version of the Northern Lights, and I have no idea what this uncanny phenomenon could have been.

After an hour's drive, following the lights of the lorry ahead of us around precarious bends, we finally hit the main road. Fwooop! In less than three hours we had arrived home and dry in the flashy heart of Santo Domingo.

"So, we've arrived unscathed, save for a flat tyre!"

"Flat tyre! The car is in perfect working condition. It's just the roads that bump, unevenly, not a puncture."

We drove back to the hotel by an unfamiliar route, and to my surprise, standing by a run-down market-place, was a tap-tap. I gawped. The market, in the half-light, could have been the Iron Market. What was a tap-tap doing in the middle of Santo Domingo?

"This is the Haitian quarter!" came a voice from outside the car. "Can I help you?"

A tall, strong black man peered through the car windows.

"Could you direct us to our hotel?" asked Abbas.

"Sure!" The man squared himself up as if he were about to climb into the car.

"Don't let him in," I said.

"Why?"

"Just don't, my spirit doesn't take to him."

"Why not, because he's Haitian?"

"No, not because he's Haitian. It's just that we've had so many near misses today, I feel that this man's presence will be the straw that broke the Mazda's back."

"Very well, sister."

With a shouted apology, Abbas began to drive away.

The man set up a roar, and chased our car a good long way down the road, shouting in a bellow that we owed him money, but we swerved round a corner, leaving the angry young man behind.

"Well, I hope that little trip has got Haiti out of your system," said Abbas, when we had reached the hotel.

"No," I replied, "nothing could do that, but what it has done is given me a poignant longing to leave Hispaniola, and travel to pastures new."

Abbas, who had never seen Haiti, said that the day had been the most dramatic of his life.

Carnival Cavalcades
DOMINICA

I was very much looking forward to staying in Dominica because I knew that the carnival would be in full swing by the time we arrived. It was all too exciting to be true. I hoped it would be a soothing carnival, quelling the nerves and resting the eye.

The journey over the windy Caribbean sea, however, made me forget about the carnival, and indeed about anything at all apart from staying alive.

We were in a four-seater plane, and it seemed as if a Force Eight gale was raging without. The plane swooped up and down with big dipper ferocity, throwing the passengers back and forth in their seats. Everyone laughed at my screaming at first, then they became bored and irritated, turning in their seats to give me dirty looks.

"How come they're not frightened?" I kept having to ask myself, before closing my eyes and yelling out to whom I hoped was a benevolent God.

Abbas sat complacently by the window cheerfully telling me to look out and admire the view. The view was a dot in the distance. As we approached, it turned into a mountainous island, green with lush vegetation.

Our little plane dived downward into the tiny airport, and we had arrived. I wobbled out on shaky legs and breathed in long and deep. The air was so much clearer and fresher than it had been in the Dominican Republic, with cool breezes.

The little calypso band of men dressed up in colourful costumes to welcome the tourists from the plane were wasted on me. Pretty young women danced and handed out carnival leaflets, but I was too much in a state of nerves to be able to appreciate the sweet gesture, so I stomped grumpily past them, hardly giving the musicians a second glance.

The first thought that struck me on stepping from the airport was, "England".

Cars drove on the proper side of the road, and the phone boxes were red with royal motifs. The accent of the cab driver was standard English but with a delightful lilt.

Rastafarians strolled around in the gloaming, eating fried chicken and dumplings. I saw more Rastas that one night in Roseau, than I had done in all my weeks in Jamaica. The idea of finding a Rasta in Haiti or Santo Domingo was totally unimaginable.

Our hotel, a Victorian timber building, was right in the centre of town.

"Welcome back to Dominica! I'm *so* glad you've chosen to stay in our hotel. You come back home for carnival?"

"We have come for the carnival, but Dominica is not our original home."

The hotel staff looked a little puzzled. If we were not from Dominica, what were we doing here? Only tourists came for a holiday, apart from visitors who were of Dominican extraction; and tourists were white.

All the hotel staff were friendly in the extreme, and I felt safe in the glow of their motherly care. I was home.

Proper food was being sold in the dining-room, good old-fashioned curried goat and rice, with "ital", or natural, juices. How good it was to hear English being spoken once again; to be able to listen in on other people's conversations and understand every word. Yes, I decided I liked Dominica, I liked it very much.

That night, Abbas lay abed phoning his girlfriends in London, and I set out alone to savour the fruits of the carnival.

Roseau struck me as being a very fine town, with wooden houses in the Creole style, and narrow streets ablaze with flowers and charm. Already a carnival mood invaded the air. Revellers dressed in all manner of costumes patched together wandered around, and the tiny bars poured loud soca music into the warm night air. Couples clicked fingers and twitched hips to the rhythms, all making their way to the Carnival King competition, to be held in a vast stadium.

As I came into the enormous stadium, it seemed to me that the whole of Roseau's 20,000 strong population had gathered there to elect the reigning monarch of calypso. I sat on the dry grass, wedged between two drunken old men.

Now Dominica has a very high class of drunken old men. Search the Caribbean from top to bottom, and their eloquence remains unequalled. Even after the show had started they refused to stop talking. Not that I minded.

All the songs the calypsonians belted out were richer in political content than they were in rhythmical swing.

For nearly five hours, I was preached to by very pretentious sounding calypsonians about the economic factors of the banana produce, taxes, investments, and Margaret Thatcher's involvement in the economic stranglehold that Britain has imposed upon Dominica. At first I tried to understand what was going on, but with swift alacrity I gave up the struggle, and settled down to chatting with the old men, eating spiced fish and drinking cold beer.

"So I spec' you be staying for the jumping tomorrow, little brown miss."

"Jumping?"

"Ehgn! See how she ignorant about her own isle. When floats come 'long down the roads, everybody follows them and jumps in the streets. Lord Jesus! Jus' because you live in England for a while, doesn't mean to say that you shouldn't – hic – learn 'bout the country that you are or-ig-in-ally from."

"But I am not or-ig-in-ally from Dominica."

"Oh, darlin'. Don't be so 'shame of your roots. Hear me now. You know what carnival is and why?"

"Yes."

"Tell me then."

"Something to do with Shrove Tuesday and Lent."

"Stupid. Stupid. Stupid this girl is. You think we should carry on talking to such a stupid person?"

His friend looked me up and down then shook his head, but the old man went on regardless.

"After Lent when all the fasting was going on, there was a big celebration and a masquerade, and all this partying was called carnival."

"That's what I just said!"

"Liar you liar! You said Christmas!"

A Rasta was singing a song addressed to Miss Charles, the Prime Minister, running down everything she'd ever done, but the chorus went, 'We love you, we adore you.'

"So how you like our music?"

"Too political by three quarters."

"You don't like politics?"

Before I had time to answer, the old man launched into a heavily involved speech about the pitiful state of Dominica's falling economy, blaming it all on Margaret Thatcher, but he loved, he said, the Queen.

"The Queen, hoh yeah! The Queen is good. I like the Queen plenty plenty, but old Thatcher, she hate black people like we, and she is doing her best to ruin the country. We sell all our bananas to England. All our cocoa crop goes to England too, but when the cocoa comes back to us as Milo, we pay something like ten times more than what we sold it for – heh, Danny –"

"Yes man."

"Ten times more isn't it?"

"Yes man."

"See. You come from a rich land of sookooyas, y'know, vampires, and I come from a poor land of honest people who can't make decent livings because of the greed of a far-off nation. What do you make of that? Come round to my house tonight, meet my wife, and I'll educate you good and proper. You strike me as being a little bit simple."

"Thanks awfully for the offer, but I have a sick brother waiting at the hotel who needs me."

"Well, meet me another time, and we can talk."

I thanked him and made to leave. I had imagined there would be dancing at the concert, but found instead a bored audience, who very often did not applaud when the songs had reached an end. I was more than a bit miffed at being called simple, and needed to pore over an improving book to restore my faith in my little grey cells. Besides, I was powerfully tired, and more than a little tipsy.

On the way home I stopped for a long time to gaze in wonder at the pretty little river that ran through the town. Not a soul passed me without greeting me in some way. I suddenly felt so happy I thought

I was going to explode, but at the same time I also felt the burden of guilt that happiness always seems to bestow. 'What have I done to deserve this?' I kept thinking. Maybe it was the contrast to Haiti and the Dominican Republic that shocked me into an unnatural state of giddy pleasure. My faith in the Caribbean was restored.

The next day I saw a startling sight. Policemen were ambling about the streets *without* carrying guns! I had forgotten that that breed of police existed, and it was gratifying to remember that they did.

The Islamic world has a belief that nothing should be perfect. An intricately woven carpet that has taken years to complete will be purposefully flawed by the weaver, because it is thought that a man-made object that is ideal in every way is an offence to Allah, who alone should be the creator of the perfect. Mankind the world over seems wilfully to mar the good and the beautiful, whether man- or God-made, and the Dominicans are no exception. It did not take me long to discover Dominica's one flaw – tourists.

The tourist industry is the blight of any country. Apart from the ugly hotels and the ruined landscapes that inevitably accompany the tourist trade, there is also the problem that everyone in the country who has any truck with tourists tends to become phoney, because people always imagine that tourists cannot appreciate the genuine attributes of their country. The English become laughably cockney or Bertie Woosterish when American tourists are anywhere around, thinking that that is what the Americans like, and the sad fact is that it actually *is* what they like. In Zimbabwe, the false "African Villages" that are built for the tourists are chock-a-block with clucking Europeans and clicking cameras, whereas the *real* African villages are totally ignored as if they didn't exist. This practice of the locals establishing the sham to please the tourists is upheld all over the globe.

Although I tried to steer clear of the tourist areas, to do so in Dominica was a near impossibility.

Sitting in one of the smart hotels by the beach, Abbas and I were quite shocked by the arrogant way in which the tourists treated the local people, and I am sorry to say the worst culprits were the English. Waitresses, almost reduced to tears, were mercilessly shouted at by harsh-voiced men and women complaining about such piffling details as a pin-size stain on the table cloth. This disagreeable state of affairs was worsened by the grovelling attitude that the Dominicans adopted towards their European customers.

None of the tourists liked me at all. First they would ask me what part of Dominica I was from, and when it transpired that I was a tourist just as they were, I would be looked upon with mistrustful eyes. Black people were here to provide a dash of local colour, and serve them rum punches, not sit among them as equals. It was all wrong.

Unfortunately, because there were no cars to hire owing to the number of carnival tourists, Abbas and I were forced to take excursion tours around the island.

Dominica is the hilliest island in the Caribbean, with 365 rivers, one for each day of the year, and there is nowhere in the world that can match its loveliness. It is impossible not to fall under the spell of this beautiful island.

Trafalgar Falls, with its two large waterfalls, was a splendid sight. Tiny little boys "guided" us in a very intelligent fashion, naming all the plants that abounded around the falls, occasionally pressing their fingers into various shrubs to demonstrate how the leaves folded up.

"That is the woman falls, and that is the man," said an eager little boy.

"Why is one the woman, and one the man?"

The child blushed prettily: "Because the woman is fatter." He was right. One stream of water gushing downwards was short and fat, and the other was long and skinny, but both were staggering in their beauty.

Another beauty spot Abbas and I visited was the Emerald Pool. Set in the splendour of a primeval forest, a strange eerie mood is created around the turquoise pool. Tarzan-like creepers wend and twine around the ancient rocks, and one is aware of the wood spirits who lurk in the steamy air. Sadly, however, once we reached the Emerald Pool itself, the water was so full of French tourists washing their hair in the waterfall, that the sight was completely ruined.

The beaches were aswarm with locals and tourists alike, swimming in the clear sea. Many tiny fishing boats bobbed up and down alongside the opulent yachts in which the tourists had sailed into the harbour. "Professional Rastas" (as Little Mannie had called them) were helping the tourists anchor the boats; many of them were being treated to a rum punch in return for their favours.

One of the Rastas, a tall skinny fellow with very dark skin and gingery hair, hung around Abbas and me telling us to pay his friend to take us around the island.

"Let my friend take you around, man, c'mon, don' be shy."

"No," I joked, "we just want to sit in the hotel for three weeks, we don't want to see the island."

"Oh c'mon, man, you can't jus' sit in the hotel! That does be boring, get around, man, an' see all the sights. You been anywhere yet?"

"No."

"You naw been to Trafalgar Falls or Emerald Pool or anywhere else?"

"No, and we don't want to go either. It's much better just to stay in the hotel, and not go out at all."

The young man shook his head in disgust. Abbas sat drinking coconut water feeling very embarrassed, wondering how I could allow myself to appear such a dim-witted tourist.

"You naw even want to go and see the Indian Reserve?"

"Nope."

"Where you from, England?"

"Yep."

The Rasta shot me a meaningful look, as though to say, 'typical!'

He then dived into the water and swam over to one of the yachts, and next thing I knew he was leaning over the railings of the vessel with a rum punch in one hand, and a sausage on a stick in the other.

After our drink we walked to the local school to get a good nose around.

Blaring from the school hall was loud soca music, and faint shadowy figures were visible from behind the thick curtains.

"It is the boys having their own little carnival in there. When carnival comes around, all the boys dress up as girls, and we all have plenty fun," said a young child.

The child then said it would be all right for us to have a look around the classrooms.

Written on the blackboard in the first class we entered was, "It's party time, it's boogie time!"

Ah, that was more like it, I thought, remembering with a shudder the ominous maths in the Haitian school. The Dominican teachers obviously had a more advanced idea of what school was all about.

"Morning, boys!" I intoned austerely at a group of boys kicking a ball about in the playground.

"Morning, ma'am," they chorused, stopping their game to salute me.

Just as I became rather frightened by a group of young boys who didn't jeer behind my back, a series of muffled sneers could be heard as I turned through the gate.

"Serves you right for thinking you're Joyce Grenfell," laughed Abbas. Abbas was going to the carnival that night with a shy young girl called Rita. Tonight was his last in the West Indies, and he was determined to finish his trip by stepping high, wide and plentiful.

After a sumptuous meal at a posh hotel where Jean Rhys once lived, Abbas and I went our separate ways.

The little streets were hung with bunting and flowers, and floats of all kinds paraded up and down, each one vibrating with addictive harmonies. Carnival Queens, dressed in brilliant flouncy costumes, simpered coyly beneath the shadow of extravagant flowery hats. An impressive Gulliver's Travels float edged its way slowly through the heaving crowds, displaying a gigantic Gulliver model strapped to the bottom of the lorry, with gaudily dressed Lilliputians jigging around him. More and more floats squeezed through the revellers, each one more fanciful than the next.

Everyone danced with furious abandon, some waving their arms in the air in ecstasy. "What have they got to be so joyous about?" I kept asking myself. Then, all of a sudden, I was infected with the spirit of joy that had possessed the rest of the throng. The crowds were so thick, that once caught among them, it was impossible to leave without a struggle, but, instead of the atmosphere becoming claustrophobic, it became headily exciting, and one felt drunk with pleasure at being a part of this whirlpool of revelry.

Some of the people dressed as gladiators, some as Harlequins, but the popular pet was the devil. In ancient folklore, music and dancing were thought to be Satan's work, so no Carnival can be complete without the Prince of Darkness keeping an eye on things. Red tights and horns were the order of the night, and many a handsome devil could be caught bumping and grinding till dawn.

Grannies, old men, and children alike, all partook of the celebrations, and the way some of the old folk danced with one another, made you wonder whether life did not begin at seventy.

"Hey, let me dance with you."

A squat, red-eyed young man grabbed me round the waist, and danced in the Dominican style, where the man stands behind the woman holding on for dear life, and they both shimmy with a frantic whirling of hips.

"You know why I like you? It is your complexion. I only like black people, and I only like people of your colour. You naw know how I wish I was your complexion."

"Hey, what have you been smoking?"

"Only tobacco. It's true! Do you think I like being so dark? No, no, no. I want to have your gold colour."

"Well, isn't that strange. I would love to be darker, so it only goes to show we're never satisfied with what we're born with."

A thin mist of rain, that falls constantly in forested Dominica, was descending gently, so I used that as an excuse to leave the dissatisfied man and have a drink at a local bar.

A young woman asked me for my hat and sun-glasses, and gave me two cans of beer in exchange. She spoke in a sing-song voice of her hatred of English politics, and her love of Dominica.

"I been to London once, it crowded, ugly and smelly. All the people are rude, and nobody helps anyone else. A woman could be lying naked in the streets, and the people will just walk past her pretending they haven't seen. Everything is money, money, money. Beauty and kindness they have all forgotten. I blame the government. Bad, isn't it, ehng?"

"None too hot," I replied.

Her friend introduced himself as Colbert, and insisted I dance with him.

"Why do you waste your time gossiping with women at a carnival where the people are supposed to jump?"

We danced behind the floats for hours on end. Every now and again, he would pull me aside, saying, "Let's get away. There's white people here, and I don't like to be around them."

The white people looked very self-conscious, but glowed with pride as if they were thinking, 'How exciting to be among all these blacks. Wait till I tell the folks back home!'

Maybe I misjudged them, but I can't say I was over-enamoured by any of the tourists I met.

"Do you like white people?" asked Colbert, eyeing me gravely.

"Some of them are all right. My mother's really nice."

"Your mother's w- oh, sorry, sorry, sorry. I- I- I- didn –"

"That's all right, just so long as it never happens again."

Although Colbert bowed his head and swore he would rather cut out his tongue than offend me, he continued his habit of dragging me away from the white people. I myself had the sneaking suspicion, that if I lived in Dominica, and the self-satisfied tourists were the only whites I encountered, I too would have developed an aversion for white people, and I can guarantee that most *white people* travelling the West Indies would feel the same.

Colbert was very drunk. At midnight he proposed to me, and because I had also had one over the eight, I accepted him.

"I just want to spend the rest of my life with you. Can we marry?"

"Oh, all right then, if I mushed."

"I have to go see my friend now. Meet me at the Beehive Club at one in the morning, then we can talk about the de-*tails* of the wedding."

"Will do."

I lurched back to the hotel in a shameful state of debauchery. A muscular Rasta waved an enormous python at my face when I reached the steps of the hotel. Women screamed in panic, but I wearily brushed both man and snake aside. Colbert would have to find another fiancée that night. I was going *straight* to bed.

"It's *you!*" said a startled voice behind me. "I thought you said you weren't going out of your hotel, not even to the carnival."

I turned, and through bleary eyes made out the form of the Rasta at the beach.

"I changed my mind."

"Well, you can't go to your bed now. Come back and join the carnival."

"Sorry, I'm going to die in a minute."

"You'll only die if you sleep. If you dance you'll live."

"Will I?"

"Eh hehng."

We threw ourselves back into the crowds, and "jumped" for a long time. The Rasta, whose name was Halbert, was right: I lived.

Many of the dancers had crippling deformities. Some of their legs were so bandy as to resemble sideways Vs. Whether they suffered from rickets or not, they joined in the fun, and sang along to the records.

The atmosphere, by now, had become extraordinarily sexual. Couples "wined" so intimately they seemed only a step away from making love. (The rub-a-dub-dub of London blues parties had nothing on the winings and grindings of the Dominica carnival.) Hips were thrust against one another in the most suggestive manner, and a teenage girl was doing something rather shocking to the wheels of a lorry. She turned to shout at Halbert telling him he was too rough for me. Halbert laughed loudly, and gabbled a stream of patois to her.

Dominican patois is a form of broken French with a few English and African words thrown in. The population, as in Jamaica, is bilingual.

A hand gripped my arm, and I wheeled round to see the gripper, and encountered a pair of tortured eyes. The eyes belonged to my "fiancé", Colbert.

For a moment we stood hypnotised, then Colbert stared unbelievingly at Halbert.

I couldn't explain Halbert away as my brother, and I certainly could not explain why I was in the streets, and not at the Beehive, so I did the next best thing.

With a cheery wave to Col and Halbert, I sprang over a muddy wall, and ran pell-mell back to the hotel, as fast as my weakened legs could carry me.

I burst into the hotel, crashing into the receptionist who held me by the shoulders in a motherly embrace, and asked, "Who you running from?"

"I've er – seen a snake."

"A snake?"

I peered out of the hotel into the crowds to see if there was any sign of the seething Colbert.

Halbert was lurking by the steps of the front porch, looking at me sadly, with large, luminous eyes.

"Why you run so?"

"Sorry about that, I suddenly remembered I'd left something on the stove."

"I know why you ran so. You met that guy and you remembered you s'posed to meet him tonight. But I know the guy, he's from country, he won't hurt you. Let's go to the Beehive."

"I can't!"

"Listen, man, if he's there, jus' say, 'cool out, man'."

"Sorry, no can do."

"Well, come to another club with me."

"Where?"

"Not too far, we'll get a lift or a bus."

I agreed.

Roseau is like a village, with everyone knowing everyone else, so it was easy for Halbert and me to sponge a lift off the first passer-by who was lucky enough to own a car.

"Firs' we go to my house, where you can chill out, irie?"

Halbert lived about a mile away from the town centre, and in the moonless night, it was impossible to see more than an inch ahead. The night seemed dramatically still and quiet, save for the tropical insect noises, and the faint swish of an unseen sea.

Halbert held my hand, leading me downwards into his village. I could make out rocks and sand with my feet, and every so often would step on a goat, or a bad-tempered sleeping dog. Gingerly I picked my way downwards. How Halbert knew his way in the blackness was impossible to fathom.

A dull thud resounded, and I realised that a door had been pushed open.

"Ben' your head low, now, because the ceiling it plenty, plenty low."

I bent almost double, and remained rooted to the spot until Halbert lit a kerosene lamp, and instantly we were swathed in a warm, amber light.

I looked around to find myself in a shanty shack, with a hard mud floor, wooden walls, corrugated iron roof, and a plenty, plenty low ceiling.

There was no furniture except a bed made from foam rubber scraps, with just an old army coat for covering. In the corner was a besom made from a bundle of sticks, and a plastic carrier bag lying in the middle of the room contained Halbert's clothes and other worldly possessions. I was quite amazed. Halbert cut so fine a figure, it was hard to believe he was so poor. His clothes were trendy in the Rasta style, khaki shorts, a neatly pressed Hawaian shirt, and a red, green and gold band tying back his pale locks.

Halbert smiled a twinkly grin at me, and at that moment, two things occurred to me. One was how unbearably handsome he was, and the other was maybe I shouldn't have agreed so glibly to come to his house in the middle of the night.

I cleared my throat.

"Lovely pictures you have on the wall . . ."

The walls were entirely covered with large prints of Haile Selassie and the Lion of Judah, with snippets of the Rasta doctrine all in curly writing.

"So you really are a true Rasta, those are not just designer locks."

"I and I a true Rasta. I worship Haile Selassie. I have no dealings at all with Babylon or artificial ways of life. Everyting in me life is 'ital', an' me don' never touch meat. I and I a peaceful man, descended from the Israelites, like all me black brethren, an' me tribe is the tribe of Levi. Jah Ras Tafari, King of Kings."

I didn't think it fitting that I should ask him why his accent had become Jamaican all of a sudden, so I merely nodded and tried to look sage.

"Do you smoke ganja?"

"I smoke the weed of wisdom, yes."

"Ah."

"Come over to my mother's house, first, and we can watch a bit of TV, then we can go over to the club."

Back up the inky steps we trod, until we found ourselves on the street. Halbert began to sing an improvised rapping song about the carnival, and we both snapped our fingers in time to the rhythm.

His mother's house was a squalid block of flats a half-an-hour's walk away.

The interior, though, was neat and cosy. As so often happens, the dwellers had defied the evil schemes of the architect, and had actually succeeded in making the hideous design of the building look reasonably decent, inside at least.

The floors were covered in sparkling white lino, and on one of the formica divans lay a long, sleeping body of a man.

"My brother, that. My mother, sister and her two kids are sleeping in the next room. Don't scream when you see any more cockroaches, 'cause you'll wake them all up. No matter if you wake my brother up."

The brother grunted in his sleep.

"You wanna cuppa tea?"

"Yes, please."

I switched on the TV and stared at an American cop series in a sort of coma.

Halbert came back into the room with a mug of steaming brew. I took a sip, and spluttered into the cup. Not that I meant to be rude, but my taste-buds were deeply offended. When you're expecting an honest to goodness cuppa tea, and you receive a watery mixture tasting of chocolate and chemical, good manners go the way of all flesh.

"What's the matter, ehng? You don't like tea?"

"I love it, but this . . ."

And then, of course, I remembered in a flash. In the West Indies all hot drinks are called tea, and worse still, they are plied with as much sugar as a cup can hold. This particular tea was chocolate Nesquick tea, made with tepid water.

Halbert and I sat chatting about his lazy brother. We were both sure his brother was really awake, despite the loud snores, so our snide comments about him became more and more outrageous in their character. It ended up with Halbert criticising the top of the hapless man's head, at which point the brother awoke, eyes ablaze. Halbert and I darted from the room, and ran into the hot night.

"My brother wants me to cut off my locks, he don't like my religion, but I would sooner dead than loose my faith in Selassie I. Once I eat meat, I'm as good as done."

After a fairly long walk we reached the club, or should I say we reached a tiny room with no lights or customers. I'm not sure if it had staff, I can't remember. However, there was very loud music playing from an amplifier on the bar: old-fashioned Jamaican reggae.

Halbert and I sat in the corner sipping beer from dented cans.

The door suddenly burst open, and a glassy-eyed man threw himself into the room, and shook Halbert by the arms.

"Captain Hook a coming!"

Halbert dived behind the bar, and Mr Glassy-eyes flattened himself against the wall.

A car screeched past the club, and the sound of its engine was soon fading into the distance.

Two white eyes peeped over the top of the bar swivelling right and left. The newcomer cautiously vacated his wall, and both men drifted back to my table.

We sat for a short while without speaking.

"So – er – what was all that about?"

"What about?" came the reply, fifteen minutes later.

"That 'Captain Hook' business."

"Captain Hook don't like we, and if he see us here he may try to kill we."

"But who's Captain Hook?"

"A detective. He don't like Rastaman. If he caught us here drinking in an illegal club like this, he would beat we like he did last time. The man is wicked. He is evil. Do you know what him do to my friend here? He took a long stick and he jab him in the neck with it. Still he has the scars. George, George, man, show her the scar."

George swept back his locks, unbuttoned his shirt front and pointed to his neck. I peered in the darkness, but could only vaguely make out the gleam of his gold chain.

"See the marks? That's the type of man we're dealing with."

George took a deep swig of my beer, and said, "And if he see that we sit here with a tourist he'll get all the more vex. He love tourist girls, and it'll make him mad to see we chatting to one. That's why I come to warn Halbert."

Halbert clasped George's hand in gratitude.

Maybe I had been mistaken about Dominica's benevolent police force.

Halbert and I took a mini-bus back to my hotel and arranged to meet the next day, early in the morning.

The carnival was still raging away, but although the street was throbbing with "jumpers" I only had eyes for Halbert, as his skinny figure swung away through the dancers.

At half past four in the morning, Abbas woke me up to tell me he was leaving.

"How was Rita?"

A smile that almost amounted to a leer crossed his lips.

"I see, say no more. Give my regards to England, and remember to tell Mamushka how well I looked after you."

"Abbas! Hurry up, darlin', or you'll miss your plane. It gone four thirty already, man," came a sweet purry voice from outside the door.

I lay back in the bed and groaned. Abbas jauntily picked up his suitcase and made for the door. At least he could have looked suitably embarrassed!

"Farewell, sister, and remember, steer clear of the Yacoubs!" And with that he was gone.

It was only after the door had slammed that I realised how much I was going to miss him. Although he had not been with me for much of the time, his very presence had become a rock of security for me. Now he was going, and I was all alone.

The next day was Valentine's day. I stood on the balcony watching the floats go by. Little children, looking very sweet, as children always do when they're all dressed up, stood on the lorries wearing white frilly dresses.

"Tea Tray Fantasy", "Mrs Winsten presents Powder Puffs on Parade", and an advertisement for a brand of soap were just a few of the impressive titles the floats had on offer.

I walked to the town, soaking up the carnival spirit and missing Abbas. A little mini-bus took me to the beach where I had arranged to meet Halbert, and as I stepped off the bus, there he was, chatting to two American tourists.

Halbert furtively threw me a sideways glance, and continued his talk with the tourists, turning his back to me.

'He hates me now,' I thought miserably, 'now that he sees me in the cold light of day.'

"So why don' you let my friend show you round the island, man?"

"No, I kinda wanna take a little stroll around town first."

"But surely you wanna see all the nice spots."

"No, no, we're OK for the while."

Halbert continued to pester them, guiding them out of the sun which he said was bad for them. The Americans said that they *liked* the sun. The sun, they said, was the only reason that they came to the island in the first place. I could see that Halbert was getting on their nerves, so I retreated onto the beach, and sat by some rocks.

A moody Halbert joined me a few minutes later, standing behind me, gazing out into the lovely sea.

I had a sinking feeling that he wasn't going to talk to me, and was, in fact, hoping that I would go away.

"You look like a tourist," he said at last.

I was wearing a wide-brimmed hat and a white spotted suit.

"Oh well, never mind, eh. What shall we do today?" I tried to sound as cheerful as possible.

Halbert pointed to a Carib-looking man in a tiny canoe.

"We're going to Pointe Michel and Soufrière Bay in my friend's boat. Then we're having lunch at my mother's house. If you worry about anything at all today, I shall know that my whole life has been wasted."

"That's a bit dramatic for someone who didn't even greet me when they saw me just now."

"As yet I don't understand you, and you don't understand me, but in time, you'll know why I'm like this. Climb in the boat now, man."

We waded into the sea, and sat in the boat. Our rower sat hunched and silent.

"Put the English flag up, John, we have a English girl on board!"

A tiny Union Jack was held aloft before I battered it down.

Flying fish in black swarms leapt from the sea as we rolled over the waves. Dominica looked fabulous, rising from the ocean like green cake-icing, in giant peaks.

When we reached Pointe Michel, we climbed out of the rocking boat into the sea, and waded to shore.

Pointe Michel is a tall skinny hill, covered in sharp rocks. Can't say it was up my street.

"C'mon, and walk up the hill, now, man. When you reach the top you can see Martinique."

"Tell you what, you walk, I'll watch."

Halbert was horrified, and began a fearsome diatribe concerning my sophisticated ways. Why, he asked, did I wear tight skirts and high heels?

"A-what you mean, to look posh! Posh! What the use o' looking posh if you climbing a mountain, man? Anyway you should always be natural, ital living is the way to be, not lipstick and eye black! Now move up the hill."

I took a step forward, then twisted a pointed heel on a stone.

Halbert looked pitifully at me, then, in one move, he strolled towards me, swooped me up in his arms, and carried me up the hill. I was sure his slender limbs would snap under the strain of my buxom weight, but instead he managed his burden with an easy swagger, and very shortly we were at the very peak of the hill, looking out at a grey blob that was Martinique.

Far down below, I saw that we were between two seas. The Caribbean was blue and peaceful, but the Atlantic, a rusty grey, raged and frothed furiously. Why that should be, is a complete mystery, but, in all the Caribbean islands, there is a marked difference between the cool Caribbean , and the bad-tempered Atlantic.

Halbert was the strong, silent type. A moody broody 'Rasta without a cause'. The stuff film stars are made of, with high cheekbones, full pouting lips, and eyes that quickened the heart, but slowed everything else.

We walked down the hill, and proceeded in our boat to Soufrière Bay, an idyllic little fishing village. Halbert sat on one side of me, and the Carib sailor slouched on the other as we sat 'neath a palm, drinking sour sop juice.

On the way back, the boat began to sway slightly, then all of a sudden, we rocked furiously, as if someone was frantically tugging the canoe. 'Sharks!' I thought, wildly, 'a shark has caught our boat, and tomorrow morning in *The Times*, there'll be a tiny paragraph saying, "Three people, including one Brit, were eaten by mad shark off coast of Dominica."'

For some reason, as water began to pour into the heaving vessel, my one and only thought was to save my hat, so instead of clinging onto the side of the boat, both hands shot up to my head, and clamped on for dear life. My panic had blinded me to the fact that my two companions, far from looking frightened, were in an uproarious state of excitement.

"We done it, we done it, man!"

"Awoah! Yeah, heh! We catch one!"

"A big one too! Wooo!"

"Gentle, now, ease up, now, man, it come! Naw, it back in again."

The boat swished and plunged.

Suddenly the largest fish I have ever seen made a guest appearance near the side of the boat. I screamed at the top of my lungs. We were all going to die.

"Zinga, man, cool out, and move down the end of the boat, sit here and hold on. See the nice fish we catch!"

I goggled. I had no idea there was a fishing rod anywhere around, and here was this monstrous fish being dragged on board. At least four feet long, it gleamed in the sun, lying at the bottom of the canoe with such serenity, it looked unreal, as if it was made of mother of pearl. Only the eye revealed that life was seething in its veins. It stared up at us as if to say, "Could it be possible that you don't know who I am?"

The poor fish had every reason to feel gravely affronted. Next minute, the sailor began beating its head with a rock. The fish shook in violent convulsions quivering the boat and soaking us all with sea water. It looked a bit like my brother Lancelot always does when he sees a magpie.

As the vicious man murdered the fish, bright red blood spurted from its head, and drenched my skirt. After a few minutes, the luckless sea creature expired, leaving the legacy of a ruined suit in its wake.

"It dead!" the sailor grinned, picturing in his mind succulent fish suppers for the next few days, although how he could have eaten that fish which had contained so much blood, was quite beyond me. I had made up my mind I would never eat fish again.

We floated on to Halbert's village, which tumbled down to the sea in a jumble of wood and corrugated iron. Seeing it in the light of day, I was struck by the camaraderie of the place, and the proud movements of its dwellers. Each shack was piled upon the other in intricate confusion.

Raising a hand to my head, I realised for the first time my hat had blown off, and my hair hung in salty snarls about my neck. Halbert laughed, saying that I looked more like a Rasta than he did.

When we reached Halbert's home, after saying goodbye to the sailor (and paying him), Halbert lent me a pair of his cut-off shorts and a tee shirt with a design of ganja leaves. I removed my shoes and sat outside to watch Halbert scrubbing my suit on a washboard at a tap near his house. A woman from the house balanced above his called me up to show me her five-day-old baby. Her husband sat in the corner giving the child devoted looks, with so soppy an expression in his misted eyes, it was difficult not to laugh.

While the suit was hanging up to dry, Halbert and I walked to his mother's house for lunch.

His sister, an extremely shy girl, and her two children, sat in front of the telly, and didn't look up when we entered the room.

I stood in the kitchen watching Halbert heat up the food.

"You see, Zinga, you too soft. You should be like me, always go your own way. No one tells me what to do, and I am afraid of no man or woman. See how you cry out on the boat! Don't do that again. Always be strong – like me."

My eyes glazed over. I don't like lectures very much, and anyway, Halbert had asked me to make juice, so I was struggling with a grapefruit and a bowl.

"Can't you make juice?" he asked, horrified at my attempt. Taking the grapefruit from me, he squeezed out the juice, added water and sugar, then poured it into a jug.

The two little girls watched us with round eyes as we ate our meal of rice and black-eyed peas, thick with tomato ketchup. No one spoke, except for Halbert saying I could eat as much rice as I liked because he had cooked it.

Just as the atmosphere became totally sterile – BANG! An enormous mother burst into the room, and stood glaring at us, hands on hips. She began to yell at Halbert in patois, while I stared at the telly, pretending not to notice. Halbert caught my eye and smiled sheepishly, which made the mother even worse. After a few minutes of this, I stood up to say hello, and she gave me a pshaw of disgust. I looked down at myself; raggedy old shorts, ganja leaves on the chest, no shoes on my dirty feet, all set off by wild Rastary looking hair.

"You an' your blast-ted Rasta friends!" she said in English.

"I'm not a Ras –"

"Take yourself and your Rasta friends away!"

Halbert tried to look tough, but failed ignominiously, like a naughty schoolboy caught drawing rude pictures in the headmaster's study.

"An' who say," continued the mother, "that you can eat all the food I cook up?"

Seeing the Gorgon march towards our table, I realised that it was our cue to leave, so we stumbled out of the flat, followed by the mother, who stood in the doorway waving the grapefruit skin that I'd left on the floor.

"She was only joking," soothed Halbert as we wandered away through the woods.

"Oh yes, I'm sure she was." I made a mental note never to drop in on the mother again.

As we walked, the woods became more and more jungly, and soon we noticed brilliantly coloured humming-birds fluttering around the undergrowth, hovering over the wild flowers.

Halbert picked the fruits and berries from the trees, pointing out the poisonous and the nutritious.

"You can only eat the seeds of this one, 'cause if you eat the flesh, it'll sicken you plenty, plenty. Just eat the white part of this one, 'cause the rind makes you froth at the mouth. This one'll kill you if you even have a pin prick of the juice, so just eat the skin."

Needless to say, I didn't partake.

Soon we came to a crystal pool in the forest, with a tinkling waterfall. I sat on the rock, and wondered whether I wasn't in the Garden of

Eden. Turning to look for Halbert, I realised I *was*, for he stood in the pool stripped naked as Adam. I averted my blushing face quickly, but not before I had time to see that he had the most enormous amount of energy – the man was a very good swimmer.

"Come inside, Zinga, man."

But no amount of persuading could get me into that pool. Whatever else I may be, I am no child of nature.

"Come on, man, why you so styly, styly and a wily, wily? Forget the false ways and values, and have a bath. See how you dirty up, so."

I would love to have swum in that cool blue pool with Adam, but modesty forbade.

On the way back to his house, Halbert complained of a headache, and wanted to lie down, so I said I would meet him at the hotel that night at eight. Unfortunately it was not to be.

We bade a tender farewell outside his house, standing in the way of a fat old woman balancing a number of sheets on a scarf-bound head.

Everyone in the hotel bar was making a loud rumpus over the Carnival Queen competition. The wrong queen had carried away the title, and the drinkers in the bar were none too happy about it.

A short, stocky, jovial man asked me in very soft tones who I thought should have won. I replied that I knew nothing about it. The man giggled softly, then asked me quietly if I wanted a drink. When I refused, he asked in a whisper whether I knew Abbas.

"Yes, he's my brother."

"A very nice man, I met him yesterday. We all went out together, with my cousin, Rita."

This came as no great surprise. Nothing could happen in Roseau without everyone knowing all about it within the next few minutes. The man, Albert, came across as so shy and sweet that when Halbert failed to turn up I accepted his invite to the infamous Beehive Club. In hushed mumbles he told me all about his ex-wife and kids, whom he adored, and described in the boringest detail, every second of a dull trip he took to New York. Between yawns I nodded politely, wondering how anyone could be so dull and yet still be alive.

"What do you do for a living?"

We were inside the Beehive, an intimate little night spot, boasting of only a few more customers than Halbert's club.

Albert mumbled a muffled reply.

"Pardon?"

"Detective."

"Really?"

"Yes."

"You wouldn't by any chance know a fiend in human shape called Captain Hook?"

"Yes," he sniggered.

"Is he as bad as they say?"

"What do you think?"

"Don't know the blighter."

"Yes you do, I am Captain Hook, Captain Albert Hook."

I reeled back. Captain Hook ducked his head and chuckled softly, then asked me for a dance. How could Halbert and his friends live in mortal terror of this bashful, unassuming man? Looking around, however, it became noticeable that the dancers in the club treated him with awe-filled respect, and were supplying him with free drinks. The man obviously had hidden depths, but why hide them under a façade of such utter boringness?

Roseau had many swish night clubs to offer, and in each of these could be found, at one time or another, Captain Hook and myself. Much of the evening was spent in the bar, listening to the Captain's endless anecdotes. By four in the morning, I made my way back to the hotel.

"I will call for you in one hour's time," said Captain Hook, as we stood on the front porch. "You must come to see the wedding masquerade, and all the plays that start very early on in the day. You look tired, but all the same you will have to wake at five. I have noticed that you have been yawning all evening."

I apologised and returned to my room for a welcome rest.

It was impossible to believe that the carnival music raging from without was not blaring from inside the room, but after a few seconds, the pounding beat lulled me into a heavy sleep.

A loud hammering at the door shattered the dreams. A bang, bang, bang that blended rather beautifully with the soca.

"Zenga!" came the voice of Captain Hook, "come outside!" I slipped on a dressing gown and poked my head through the door. "It six thirty now, an' I tink I ought to tell you that you've missed all the good shows. The wedding, the plays, and all the masquerades."

"Thanks for waking me up to tell me that. Thanks a blinking bunch."

"That's all right, no problem. See you later, right."

'Curse your tripes,' I thought as I watched his squat form plod down the stairs.

Seeing that I was up so early with the whole day hanging heavily on my hands, I decided to go to see the Caribbean's only Carib reservation.

Travelling there by tourist coach, it was quite apparent that the Carib population has intermarried with the neighbouring folk on a grand scale. When a woman from the community marries an outsider, she is sent away, by Carib law, but a man can keep his wife to live with him on the reserve. In ancient times, Caribs were a warlike people, but now they are understandably rather bitter.

Many of the thousand or so inhabitants on the reserve live in the traditional Carib style of hut, made from leaves and branches. Their dug-out canoes, hollowed out from the trunk of a rubber tree, are to be seen all over Dominica. I can't think of a more humiliating experience for any person to endure than to have gaping tourists swishing past in a gleaming coach, pointing and laughing at everything you do.

"They didn't want a main road through their reservation, they preferred living in the forest, but we built one all the same, and now the reservation is one of Dominica's main tourist attractions."

The coach driver smirked as though to say, "That's got them on the jugular!"

Carib men and women stood outside their neat little huts to stare resentfully at us.

"I feel sorry for these kids, it must be awful to have to be Dominica's main tourist attraction, when all you want to do is play around in peace."

"Don't waste your pity on any one of 'em. They can't do anything but get drunk and be violent. They're still very savage, you know."

We stopped off at a craft shop to coo over some very expensive wood carvings. The tourists, mainly Swedes and English, were aggressively unimpressed, and tried to cajole the assistant into letting them have a wooden vase for almost nothing.

"No," the Carib man kept repeating, become tenser by the second.

Travelling around Dominica, one becomes almost stunned by the spectacular beauty, especially by the rivers which run between lush green foliage.

"But the rivers are always overflowing, y'know, and many people get drowned, or lose all their possessions."

The driver was a very friendly chap, sharing his fruit and rum punch with his passengers. The windward side of the island, unfortunately, was scrubby and grey. We sat by the Atlantic, looking at some washerwomen drying their clothes on the pebbles. Staring into the murky Atlantic, I began to worry about Halbert. What had happened to him? Why did he not turn up last night? I made up my mind to pay him a social call as soon as I returned to Roseau. Besides, he still had my white suit.

The door to Halbert's mother's flat stood slightly ajar. I knocked politely, and receiving no reply, called, "Hello!" I could hear the telly blaring away, and soft voices coming from within, but still no answer. I knocked again.

Halbert's niece came to the door after a few minutes and lisped:

"Granma says that if you don't leave her door right now she gon' fetch police. She also tol' me to say that she armed."

"Oh, thank you very much for the message. *Do* give her my regards."

With that I trotted down the stone steps, and headed towards Halbert's side of town. I thought I would never be able to find Halbert's home, but I needn't have worried. I had forgotten the character of Roseau. The first person I asked knew exactly who Halbert was, where he lived, and (at this a hand rose to her mouth conspiratorially) a woman's suit was hanging outside his door to dry.

Halbert did not reply when I banged upon the wooden door. Maybe answering doors was a hereditary phobia, passed on from the maternal side. It was beginning to rain, so I picked up my suit, and was just about to leave, when a weak cry was heard from inside the house.

"Halbert?"

"Errrrr."

I pushed open the door and stepped into the dank darkness. Halbert was lying on his makeshift bed, covered with a coat and looking very lacklustre.

"What on earth is wrong with you?"

"I sick."

When my eyes got used to the dark, I saw that indeed his face did look a little grey, with a thin sheet of perspiration covering his whole body. He shivered slightly, and threw me a highly accusatory look.

"I lie here sick, an' you go off with – Captain Hook."

"How was I supposed to know you were ill, and, more to the point, how did you know that I was with Captain Hook?"

"Everyone told me. Is that the respect you have for Rastaman?"

Smudgy circles ringed his yellowy eyes. He lay back on his bed, and coughed hoarsely.

"Well, now I'm here, would you like me to get you anything?"

"It late now, an' it plenty, plenty dark, otherwise you could go to bush an' carry back some herb, but not now. What I'd like for you to do is stay with me an' keep my company."

I did just that. After daubing his forehead with a rag dampened by the rain, I sat in his shack and read to him. The only book he kept was the Bible, so I read out passages from the Old Testament, being interrupted every so often by him saying, "Jah, Rastafari!"

It occurred to me that the shanty town was extraordinarily quiet. Even the upstairs baby was not making a sound. Only the insects made their presence felt, hullabalooing all night long.

Halbert admired my star of David, telling me that far from being the Jewish symbol, it was, in truth, the Rasta symbol so was therefore rightfully his. An emaciated arm protruded from the greasy coat, and he touched the pendant softly.

"You'll let me have it, ehng?"

Something about Halbert had changed. Maybe it was that when he wasn't looking, his Jamaican Rasta accent slipped into the soft, Frenchified sound of Dominican. France and Britain had battled over control of the island until 1805, when the French, after a settlement of £12,000, yielded Dominica to Britain, then razed Roseau to the ground out of spite. However, a French influence remains very apparent in Dominica, mainly in the patois and in the Catholic church.

Whilst I sat upon the damp floor, and Halbert lay in bed, we became very confiding with one another. He told me about his ambition of becoming a sailor, and moving to Antigua where he would float tourists about on boats. I told him jokingly, that I had taken a photograph of him, with a concealed camera, whilst he was bathing in the pool, and was going to print it on the front page of every English newspaper.

"The headline will be, 'Dominica – the naked truth!'"

Halbert closed his eyes wearily, indicating that he, for one, did not hold with such unseemly jests.

The night wore on.

At what point I fell asleep, I do not know, but it seemed as if two seconds later, I was being awakened by a startling stream of sunlight pouring upon my face. The outside world was alive with a deafening din. Hens clucked, dogs roared like lions, and evil-tempered goats made the sort of noises that evil-tempered goats do in early morning Roseau. A baby wailed dismally, and a woman bawled in patois. She bawled for hours on end, rattling metal objects, and clanking something that sounded like chains.

Halbert lay motionless with his eyes fixed on the ceiling. His face had taken on a waxy quality, and his chest showed no sign of respiratory action. Maybe he was . . . I spat three times in the air to ward off any evil spirits who may have heard my thoughts, and shook him.

"Errrr."

"Halbert, thank goodness you're alive! How are you?"

"Who say I'm alive?"

"Me."

"Well I glad you tell me, 'cause I would never 'ave known. Now go to bush where we went for the bath, and pick me the herb."

"What herb?"

"When you go you'll see a mauve flower growing on a tree. By the side of the tree you'll see a small bluey-green plant. Pick the leaves of the plant, go over to Mummy's house and boil them up for about twenty minutes, then bring it round to me and let me drink it."

"Bluey-green you say."

"Eh hehng."

"Near a mauve flower tree."

"Eh hehng."

"Can't you make do with an aspirin?"

"Aspirin? I and I don't deal in Babylon remedies."

"But can't you just for today? I really don't think I can be trusted to know which plant is which."

Actually, it was not the fear of not being able to locate the plant which unnerved me. Finding the herb would be a doddle. No, it was the "going to Mummy's house" bit, that shook me to the quick. For all I knew, this herb was the bad stuff, and I did not relish the idea of waltzing into his mother's house brandishing ganja leaves.

"This herb isn't sensi, by any chance?"

"Nooor."

I could not abandon him in this sorry state, so I did the decent thing. After leaving a large mug of water by his side, I set out on the quest for the mysterious herb. I would be lying if I said that I did not feel like one of the knights of old, searching gallantly into unknown parts to fetch magic potions for a dying man.

On the way I bought a couple of spicy patties from a tumble-down store, and, with the day's meal in my hand, I walked deep into the forest. Trees with flowers of every colour in the rainbow, thickened the dark, sultry rain forest. Blue, red, orange, vivid pink, even multi-coloured, but mauve was nowhere to be seen. For three hours I searched, drinking water from the little streams that flowed between the vines, but no mauve flower did I behold. After a while, I sat upon the upraised roots of an ancient tree, and ate a pattie. Dear Halbert was lying sick, and I was impotent to do aught but search fruitlessly. I cursed aloud to the four winds.

"Who scream so?" sounded a voice from behind the tree. Looking round I saw an old lady gathering sticks.

"You man lef' you?"

"No, worse. A friend of mine is sick, and asked for some herbs, but I can't find the herb he means."

"Is why he don' get a doctor?"

"He's a Rasta, and doesn't trust them."

The woman snorted at the word Rasta, but I continued.

"He says they're to be found near some mauve flowers."

"I know dem. But how he does expect you to find flowers when it not the season for dem? Come, sweetheart, an' I show you where they to be found."

We walked through the tangle of vegetation, until we came to a slight clearing, aswarm with shimmering humming-birds. The woman bent double, and picked some leaves.

"Tek dem to your frien', but boil dem firs'."

The leaves were thick and fibrous, coloured a dull turquoise.

"Thank you, *madame*, what are they called?"

"Don't know what you call them in English."

I gave her a pattie, which she accepted with a gappy smile.

It was easy to find the way back, because I had been following the one and only pathway cut out through the trees.

On reaching the mother's house, I was most relieved to find that the dragoness was not at home, leaving me with the simple task of dealing with the silent sister. I showed her the herbs to check if they were the right ones, and she nodded.

"Your brother's sick."

"Ahhoh."

"Are you coming to see him?"

She shook her head and glued her eyes to the telly. She was watching a ridiculously violent American film, about a man who drags people out of cars and hacks them up with a meat cleaver. Her two children gazed at me as I boiled up the brew.

"I'm a witch," I whispered softly, so their mother wouldn't hear, "and when I have boiled this, you'll both turn into frogs. Hah hah haaaah!"

"Em, ectually we won't turn into frogs," said the eldest child, a wan seven-year-old, "because the plant you are boiling is beneficial for flus and common colds."

The five-year-old looked seriously at me.

"Why do you tell lies?"

Children such as these have a way of flummoxing one, so I found I was spilling hot herb juice all over myself, before I finally put it in a jug, and legged it out of the house.

Halbert was sitting up in bed, sipping water. As soon as he saw me, he lay back and gurgled.

"What take you so long?"

"You look much better, now drink it up, and I'm going."

"You can't go! How can you leave me when I sick?" He took a long draught of the bitter brew, and heaved a deep sigh.

"Well, whether you're sick or not, I'm going somewhere to enjoy myself. I am on holiday, you know."

"Why you so wicked?"

"Wicked! After all I've d –"

"Read to me."

I read the Bible to him for a long time. He explained that he could not read or write because he had had to look after a blind grandfather from the age of six. Illiteracy in the Caribbean is far more rampant among men than women, so I came to discover.

"You need a nice man," he told me, "someone who can buy you good things, like a goat, a few fowls, and a boat."

Ah! How sweet you are, I thought. A goat, chickens and a boat would not go down too well in Brixton, but I didn't have the heart to say so.

After a while, he fell asleep, breathing evenly. He had stopped shivering and a healthy sheen had returned to his cheeks. My heart was so stirred by the sight of this lonesome Adonis, that I made the ultimate sacrifice. I removed the star of David and hung it round his neck while he slept. Then I tiptoed from the house, and made my way back to my hotel.

Captain Hook was in the bar.

"Heh, I've been waiting for you all day. Can I drive you somewhere?"

I agreed. Anything to get away from the hotel staff who raised shocked eyebrows at the sight of me. Word had got around that I had stayed at Halbert's house the night before, and now mutterings and giggled cooings followed me from lounge to bar. How could I explain the purity and innocence of our passion?

Captain Hook drove me far out of town to an overwhelmingly posh hotel. I have never held with posh hotels. Those characterless clean places, where tinkly music plays from nowhere. You could be anywhere in the world, especially America.

Captain Hook said he was hungry. We sat at a gleaming table and I watched as he worked his way through the priciest items on the menu. All the while I was told leaden stories of Captain Hook's life and loves. When the bill came, Captain Hook wiped his chubby little face with a linen napkin, and looked the other way. I forked out bitterly.

The white manager of the hotel was shouting at a Dominican barman in front of the customers.

"When a gentleman asks you for cocktails, you use the shakers," he was telling him, "you don't use a fork to stir it with! I hired you as a cocktail waiter, not a road mechanic, now do your job properly, or not at all!"

The customers who had apparently made the complaint laughed as the manager flipped them a wink. The barman slunk away to find the shaker.

"Let's go."

"Soon, soon. First I would like some of those cocktails." Captain Hook scampered towards the bar, and studied the wine list. Had he really beaten Halbert up?

"What do you think of Rastas?"

"Rastas! They are terrible people! They start all the trouble here, but luckily I am doing my best to eliminate them."

"Eliminate them?"

Captain Hook giggled.

"Sorry about the cocktails, Captain Hook, but I'm going now."

Captain Hook began to sulk, but I was adamant. Marcia once told me about her assertiveness training. "If," she said, "you want to do something that other people disagree with, you don't apologise or plead. You just look at them coldly, and say, 'I am going to do this or that,' and repeat it over and over again without giving any excuses." That technique always works. Until, that is, I tried it out on Captain Hook.

"I want to go now."

"But I want to have cocktails first."

"I want to go."

"But I don't want to go."

"I want to go."

"I don't."

This went on for a long, long time, with Captain Hook ordering the cocktails while we spoke. Maybe he had taken the same assertiveness classes as Marcia. Anyway, he won the day, and as my travellers' cheques were waved in the faces of the barmen, Captain Hook sucked down pink and yellow sticky drinks.

The next day I looked over my balcony to see that the carnival was over. People took down flags and bunting in the rain, and what a dismal sight it was.

This was my last day in Dominica, and I was determined to enjoy myself, or should I say, I was determined to steer clear of Captain Hook.

"There you are!" A car pulled up beside me, and Captain Hook opened the door. "Where shall we have breakfast? I know a very nice hotel on the other side of town."

I stared glumly at him. Then, in a flash I remembered Sammy. I knew exactly how the Eureka man felt, all those years ago. Sammy is a friend of mine, whose vocabulary extends to two words. "Is" and "it". The "is it" approach works so much better than years of assertiveness training, I have noticed, and I was right.

"We'll go to a hotel where you can get a fine American breakfast of steak and French fries."

"Is it," I said, walking towards Halbert's house.

"Get into the car, and we'll go there now."

"Is it."

"What's the matter? You don't want to go?"

"Is it."

I stepped into a mini-bus, and sped away from the injured Captain. Thank you, Sammy.

Halbert gave me a look of reproach mingled with quiet devotion. He was sitting on the bed looking pale and tired. All around him were the noises of raucous family life. A group of teenage girls giggled in loud shrieks as they followed me to Halbert's door.

"Is real gold?" Halbert touched the star of David with a bony finger. I nodded. He turned to the wall and lay motionless for a few moments, then reached over the bed and opened his bag of personal possessions.

"Take this," and he handed me a photograph of himself, "and this, and this, and this."

Soon I was holding a whole pile of treasures from the carrier bag. A bead necklace, a brass bangle, and a tee-shirt with Haile Selassie's face staring out in red, green and gold.

"What else can I give you?"

"A lock of hair."

"I man could never sever no hair from my head."

"Very well, Halbert. I shall treasure your gifts until the day I die."
Halbert turned away, and collapsed on the bed.

"Is what you do las' night?"

"Went to bed."

"You sure, Zanga?"

"Yep."

"You didn't go out anywhere, with Captain Hook for instance?"

"Of course not!"

"My sister cooking you lunch today. You got to be there by twelve."

I was leaving Dominica that day, and I felt my heart would burst. Leaving Halbert would prove an agonising experience.

"So you're better today?"

"Eh hehng."

The room smelt of illness, and the pungent brew I had made.

"Halbert."

"What?"

"Did you know it's leap year?"

"I did."

"And did you know that on a leap year, a woman can propose to a man?"

"But the man doesn't have to accept, does he?"

Halbert leapt from the bed, and backed against the wall, his eyes red with terror.

"Not if they don't want to."

Halbert stared at me like a male spider caught in a web while his female spouse creeps towards him. Then he breathed a sigh, but remained in his defensive position.

"Let's go to my mother's house now, I don't feel too comfortable in here any more."

To put his mind at rest, I told him I was catching a boat to Guadeloupe in a few hours.

"Well, when you finish your lunch, I come with you to your hotel, and carry your bags to *le port*."

Could anyone in the world be as wonderful as Halbert? Ah me. If only I could stay with him for ever, or take him with me where e'er I roam. But it was not to be.

His sister served me a huge plateful of chicken, lentils, rice and cabbage, swathed in lashings of tomato ketchup. Halbert ate a few lentils, and nobody spoke.

Just as we were leaving, the mother walked up the stairs and blocked our exit.

"You not leaving till you cut off the locks, boy."

"Listen, Mummy —"

"You think I joke, I don't joke."

"But, Mummy, losing my hair means I lose my religion, and losing my religion means losing my life."

"Cut 'em off!"

"But —"

"Louise, fetch the scissors."

"Yes, Mummy."

"And you, whoever you are," (to me) "hold him down!"

"Certainly not!"

"Mummy, leave me be!" Halbert twisted himself from her grip, and pulled away. Then he stood on the steps and chanted, "Jah, Rastafari. Selassie I. King of Kings. Lord of Lords. Conquering lion in the tribe of Judah. Ever loving. Ever faithful. Selassie I. Rastafari!"

Whilst the neighbours clustered round to laugh, the mother slammed the door in a fit of embarrassed temper. We galloped down the steps, and cantered down the road.

The chambermaids at the hotel had very kindly allowed me to wash my clothes in a metal bucket in the yard. They had laughed heartily, sneaking away from their duties to witness this eccentric tourist scrubbing her own clothes with a brush. Now the clothes shone in the sunshine. I gathered them up, and away we went, to *le port*.

Halbert and I sat in a rickety shack in the harbour, drinking syrupy cane juice, and eating saltfish and tomato ketchup sandwiches. All of the other passengers were Guadeloupan, speaking astonishingly rapid French.

One woman sat alone at the bar, drinking bottled water in a most majestic fashion. Her enormous almond-shaped eyes focused into the distance and she sat so perfectly poised it was easy to imagine her to be a waxwork. Her skin, the colour of ripe cashew nuts, seemed to glow, as if an amber candle shone beneath the surface. Seldom have I encountered any woman possessing such extraordinary beauty and serenity.

"Heh." Halbert nudged her, and wiped a smear of ketchup from his lips. Then he spoke to her for a long time in French, with the woman glancing regally in my direction every now and again.

"What was all that about?" I asked sulkily when the conversation had finished.

"I ask her if she take care of you in Guadeloupe and she say she will. I told her you were much too trusting an' couldn't speak French, an' she say she make sure you keep out of trouble."

"What do you mean, 'much too trusting'?"

"Well, you just do whatever people tell you like a madwoman. Look how you went out with Captain Hook las' night."

"How did you know?"

"*He* tol' me." Halbert pointed to a young man with nose studs and cropped hair. I was sure I had seen the man somewhere before. Was it Santo Domingo, Haiti, or both?

"So she say she take plenty care of you, don' worry."

The woman and I smiled unsurely at one another. She flicked a stray wisp of thick reddish hair from her face, and raised her glass to me.

"She's very attractive, isn't she," I mumbled.

"She's a sharbeen."

"What's that?"

"Light-skinned black person with red hair. Come, Zinga, give me your bag. Your boat's about to leave."

This was it. I was saying goodbye to Halbert, and maybe I would never see him again.

"Stop crying, and get into the boat before it leaves you behind. You can always return. My mother would be *most* pleased for you to stay with her."

I could not reply.

"One thing before you go. Please don't publish the photos you took of me." No amount of explaining could convince dear Halbert that I had not committed so vile a trick.

"Take this." Halbert cut off a lock of his hair with a penknife. "Keep it and don't forget me."

I stood on the deck in the golden sunshine, and we said our last farewell. As the boat floated away from the beautiful island of Dominica, I felt that this journey had no more meaning for me. My happiness lay shattered at the foot of a precipice. Halbert grew smaller and smaller as we chugged away. As I waved, the lock of his hair blew out of my hand and into the sea. An omen, a definite omen. There was no star of David to protect me now, and Guadeloupe awaited. The calm blue ocean twinkled innocently. I was sailing into the unknown, and the waving speck of Halbert was now no more.

Vive l'Afrique!
GUADELOUPE

*H*albert had disappeared for ever. The sparkling waters blurred with tears.

The woman whose wing Halbert had persuaded to take me under was somewhere downstairs in the cabin. I deliberated for a while over whether or not to join her. It seemed likely that she had only told Halbert she would help me out of politeness, and so would regard my presence as an embarrassment. I needn't have worried. A bejewelled finger tapped my elbow.

"Please, mademoiselle, if you desire, I would like your company for a drink."

I tried to look pleased and well-mannered, but my heart was ready to break.

Dominica's mountainous greenery rose up by the side of the ship – if you could call it a ship. A very slipshod affair if you ask me, with creaking planks and lengths of old rope tying various bits and pieces together.

"You would enjoy *une* glass of wine?"

"Thank you."

Although there was not a cloud in the sky, it was very heavy weather conversation-wise. Her English was broken and she spoke softly in a low-pitched voice. It was only when we got onto the subject of names that she unfurled like a rare blossom in sunlight.

"But you have *un* name from *l'Afrique*!"

"Yes."

Her clear brown eyes gazed upon me with all the reverence of an astrologer discovering a new star.

"You are from *l'Afrique*?"

"My father is, yes."

"You have *been* to *l'Afrique*?"

"Yes."

"Ahhhhhh!" she pressed my hand warmly, "then we are real sisters, true sisters. My name is Estelle Lekain, but you must know that is, err, er, not proper name. My proper name is from *l'Afrique* like you. The only diff'ronce between you and me, is you come from direct and me, my family come to this island in a slave boat many years ago."

"Well, I didn't come direct from Africa, as such, I was born in –"

"You ze first ladee from *l'Afrique* I ever meet. You know to cook le fud, and make the cloths in authentic?"

"Yes, but you need the right ingredients and materials and things like –"

"So you would like to come to *mon apart-ment* and show me how, if you, er, err, what is word?"

"I'd love to."

The ship had begun to sway, and I could feel the heavy afternoon's lunch rising and falling.

"*L'Afrique* is my home, but it eez home I know vewy leetle of." She chattered brightly on, asking me question after question about every detail of Nigerian lifestyle and customs, especially the haute coiffure and costumes. 'If I concentrate on the beauty spot by her right temple,' I told myself, 'then maybe I can force myself not to be sick all over her Yves St Laurent blouse.'

"I 'ave read in ze oracle zat Guadeloupe is not long for this world. Ze volcano at La Soufrière is likely to erupt at any day, and all ze people they die like le Pompéi."

At that point, *I* seemed to erupt. I dashed upstairs just in time to see the lunch, cane juice and tomato ketchup sandwiches cascade overboard. Clinging to the railings, I was sprayed from head to foot with great torrents of water. The vessel climbed up and up, then *ker-sploosh!* It thundered downwards into the foaming Sargasso. The other passengers on board had Indian/African faces, burnt and salty from the sun and sea. They all looked so seaworthy, regarding me with crinkly eyes and twisted smiles.

After a while, I looked over the side of the ship to see that we had not yet left the Dominican coast.

"*Bienvenue à Guadeloupe, madame,*" came the voice of a saucy seaman.

I couldn't make it out at all. How could we have reached Guadeloupe before leaving Dominica?

I staggered downstairs to find Estelle deftly packing away her belongings in a smart beige case.

"Ah, there you are my friend. Enzhoy ze cwossing? Full of exciting, non? Ah, you poor little mongoose. You have not yet learn to be good boat-woman!"

I was drenched from head to foot, and still gasping from the horror of it all.

"Come, we shall go to *mon apart-ment* and you shange you cloth."

Gathering our luggage together, we stepped off the ship. I gazed around with unbelieving eyes.

The Dominican harbour had been a rough and ready jumble of shacks and corrugated cafés. The people had a homespun appearance, and the roads were pot-holed, with battered old cars and vans. Now here I was in the "first world". Perfect roads, with people bedecked in the latest from Paris, many of them parading snowy-white Fi Fis on jewelled leashes. Glistening shops lined the streets selling every luxury Westernisation has on offer. I felt dizzy with culture shock. After a twenty-mile journey I had landed in France.

Estelle parked me in a pâtisserie while she collected her zippy little Renault. Sipping a *café au lait* and nibbling on a French fancy I watched the fair-skinned population strolling past, wondering whether this was not a dream.

"Helloo!" Estelle pulled up her car, and in a trice we were whizzing through the narrow streets of Basse-Terre. Every shop was a marvel of crystals, jewels, designer clothes and perfumes.

Guadeloupe is a department of France, but it looked as if the people were restless for a change of government. Political slogans such as "Blacks back to Africa" daubed the walls. African costume, with a Parisian twang, was the in-thing to be seen in, and the Rastas were swathed in designer Ethiopian regalia. From all appearances, the lighter the skin colour, the more the people wanted to proclaim their African heritage.

Estelle's flat was unbearably tasteful. Reproductions of Renoirs and Monets blended subtly with African objets d'art, and books, mainly French literature, lined a wall.

"My brother iz away at the moment, but he weel be back so soon. 'E shares ze apart-mont wiz me, but when he come back, you must be kind to him, because I zink 'e iz a leetle shy, especially wiz ladys, you understand. Zis ees hiz bedwoom, you can sleep 'ere until he comes home."

She opened the door and a whoosh of aftershave hit me in the face. Above the plush double-bed were photos of the shy young brother in different poses, some at parties surrounded by girls, some on the beach with bikini-clad lovelies rubbing suntan lotion on his back, but the one taking pride of place was of him with a voluptuous woman on his knee. The brother was of darker complexion than Estelle, square of face with swaggering, insolent, upturned mustachios. In many of the photographs his black hair was slicked back and greased in waves. I judged him to be slightly younger than his 34-year-old sister. His expression in the large black-and-white prints recalled the cartoon wolves of the forties.

"He will be happy for you to sleep in his room while he is away, so do not worry for his feelings."

At risk of sounding selfish, it was not for his feelings that I worried, but for my safety, lest he return one steamy night!

"His name is Henri and he plays music in the hotels, so he is often away, but he would love to see you, I know. He has the intwest in l'Afrique."

Before we went out to eat, I plaited Estelle's hair in cane row, which pleased her enormously. She was, she told me, a schoolteacher, but since she divorced her husband, she only worked part time. A photograph of her black grandmother hung above the mantel shelf, piercing me with austere eyes. In her nineteen-thirties' straw hat, the grandmother seemed to be the only reminder that we were in the West Indies.

Estelle phoned up a number of her friends to arrange to meet for dinner that evening. I could not understand what was being said, but every now and then she turned towards me with a fond smile, and said, "... l'Afrique ..."

I would be most grateful if someone could explain to me why the French have turned the art of eating into a semi-religion. Where an

English housewife will bung a couple of eggs and a streaky rasher into a pan of grease, splatter it on a plate and call it breakfast, the French will whisk the eggs into the fluffiest of omelettes, chop up the bacon and do artistic things with it, then serve it on a table laden with breads, bottled waters and flowers. The meal will last for a long time, and it is very important the guests sit over bottles of wine and chatter wittily away.

I never expected Guadeloupe would go in for this food rigmarole in such a big way, but I was in for a surprise. Whilst Estelle and her little party sat on wicker chairs in a snug little bistro overlooking the harbour, a hapless table groaned with all manner of Frenchification. Although very few of the company could speak English well enough for me to understand, I realised I was in the midst of Guadeloupe's intelligentsia. Odd phrases from the genteel chit-chat floated to my ears: "*l'idéologie nègre*" and "*l'impérialisme de la France*", to quote but a couple.

And then the bombshell dropped over the lobster à la couch chón chón. Estelle suddenly announced to her guests:

"I forgot to tell you, my friend here is from *l'Afrique*."

After a breathless silence all heads turned towards me in expectation. The Indian couple in the grey tunics gaped in open-mouthed astonishment. The Guadeloupan lecturers clattered their cutlery noisily to their plates – an unforgivable sin in the eyes of the French food etiquette. The Rastafarian writer removed his gold-rimmed spectacles, then replaced them slowly, tilting his head back to get a better look. What could I do? I smirked.

"Where exactly are you from?" asked the writer, spellbound with admiration.

"Oh, a little village near Worthing."

"Worthing?" asked one of the lecturers, "which part of Africa is Worthing?"

"Em –" At that point I happened to catch the eye of my hostess, Estelle, and in that one meaningful glance I knew it would be too, too cruel to give the game away.

"Nigeria," I mumbled softly.

From that moment on I could do no wrong. Béarnaise sauce was eased over to my plate by obliging hands, cream was poured unsparingly into my tea, and my lead crystal glass was never empty of fine red claret. By now, a lot of attention had shifted towards Estelle, who hinted darkly that she had met me in Africa, and could speak numerous West African languages.

I could feel the sweat pouring from my brow in reams. Seldom have I felt so uncomfortable, apart from, that is, the time when, at the tender age of fourteen, I told a man in a train I was a lion tamer. For two and a half hours I was quizzed by the fascinated man on the finer points of taming lions, because he himself worked with the benighted beasts in a zoo.

However, Estelle was most pleased with the way the evening was turning out, beaming at me from the top of her glass, and showing off her new hairstyle.

"Yes, you may have seen it before, my dear, but not styled by a *genuine* African!"

If only I was back in Dominica, I kept thinking, sitting on the beach with Halbert, looking at the moon.

As hot gusts of air blew through the open windows, I concentrated my mind on the imminent visit to Martinique. Ah! Martinique. Something magical would happen there I knew. The very name Martinique conjured up images of beauty and mystery.

"But Martinique is too French in its culture," said the Rasta, sipping a glass of Beaujolais, "Guadeloupe is far richer culturally."

"But Martinique is more famous."

"How more famous?"

"Well, it's produced films and literature and Napoleon's Josephine."

"But my dear young lady, what of *our* films and literature?"

"Yes, of course, that is to say – em –"

I struggled to think of anything of note that Guadeloupe had ever come up with, but my mind remained a blank. However, so grateful was I that he had ceased begging me to teach him Yoruba and Hausa, that I was glad to talk of anything else. Jamaica surged into my mind, where I had promised to send for everyone, and here I was promising to post various African curios to one and all when I returned "back home". Deep in the back of my mind I promised myself a trip to Brixton market where I would buy as many African artefacts as were required. Only the postmark presented a slight problem, but I would cross that bridge when I came to it.

Estelle's high spirits had in no way been dampened by the time we reached her flat. She bubbled and giggled and fluttered around like a beautiful bird.

"Tomowwow we dwive awound Basse-Terre, and I show you ze sight. We see all ze nice beaches, yes?"

Guadeloupe is a butterfly shaped island, with Basse-Terre making up the left wing, Grande-Terre the right.

Basse-Terre proved to be somewhat of a disappointment after the dramatic loveliness of the other islands. It is scrubby and arid, resembling one of the more boring parts of Essex. Everyone seemed to look grumpy, slouching the roads with bowed heads, glaring up at the world every once in a while. Wine was the main commodity in all the supermarkets, and bijou little wine shops were dotted around. It was very easy to see that we were in French territory.

"We would be much better off if we weren't under the France. Not with money, naturalment, the France puts much money into Guadeloupe, and Guadeloupe does not produce too much of its own, but at least we could 'ave ze pride national."

If Guadeloupe really did not produce much for itself, then someone was pouring vast amounts of money into this island. The houses, the roads, and the shops were all in immaculate condition.

Although we went to many beaches, and visited a grand aquarium, I found Basse-Terre somewhat lacklustre. Only the food grabbed the attention and stuck in the memory. Crayfish, and other local delicacies, deliciously cooked, preceded by an exquisite *hors d'oeuvre* called *beignets*, a savoury fish fritter. Everything else about Basse-Terre appeared to be rather sterile. Even the air has lost the dense humidity of the tropics, the sun glowed sullenly behind greying clouds, refusing to lend its sparkle on the wrinkled colourless sea.

Grande-Terre, however, uplifted the spirits on the following day. It was a sight to behold. Waterfalls cascaded in rainbows of wonderment, gushing in the midst of tangled forests and hot sulphur springs. Hibiscus, purple bougainvillea and flame trees spread in glorious profusion, humming-birds fluttering from bloom to bloom. The people grew flowers in their gardens for purely aesthetic purposes, an uncommon sight in the West Indies where gardens are there to grow food. For honeymoon couples, Guadeloupe is the perfect place to be. With its deserted beaches and mountainous beauty, it is the world's most romantic country. But, and maybe this was because I was not part of a honeymoon twosome, it left me rather cold.

That night, Estelle persuaded me to cook a genuine African meal for fifteen of her friends. After the exhilarating Guadeloupan fare, I was sure that anything I cooked would ruin the party but, luckily, all went smoothly, food-wise at least. After the guests had filled up on foo foo and egusi soup, we sat around politely smiling at one another, and talked of how African we all were. I could not imagine a less African setting than people dressed in French attire, listening to discreet classical music, drinking wine.

Estelle was a little sad because her brother had not yet arrived home.
"I don't know what keep him. But I think maybe iz good he iz not
'ere, because I sink the party would 'ave made him a leetle nervous."

Every time the door opened, I glanced around in fear in case it was
the nervous brother making a guest appearance.

Over the weekend, in return for being African, Estelle took me to
a group of islands I had never heard of, called Isles des Saintes. Estelle,
who was on holiday, took great pleasure in showing off her gorgeous
country to me.

The Isles des Saintes, she told me, were populated by French settlers
of Brittany, and they are very proud of their culture. We sat on the
boat for the five-mile crossing, waves foaming furiously all around us,
but by now I had acquired my sea legs. Estelle sat straight and calmly
poised, telling me about the marvellous champagnes that were to be
found on the Islands. Holiday-makers of all nationalities crammed into
the tiny sailing vessel, craning their necks to get a better look at my
stunning companion. Ignoring the attention she was receiving, Estelle
talked in a low voice of the lack of trade between the Caribbean Islands,
and the fact that the peoples of the Caribbean identify not with the
other islanders, but with the European countries who had enslaved
them.

"Even if we gain our independence, we still will not be, er, free from
ze er, er –"

"Shackles?" I suggested.

"*Oui, oui*, ze shack-elles."

Landing at Isles des Saintes, we walked straight to the hotel, but not
before I had taken a good look at the Isles des Saintians. What must
Brittany have been like in 1648 when these people first established themselves on the islands? Wild blond hair in thick matted locks waved in the
sun as the half-naked people stomped the streets. Thick dark skins and
bright blue eyes. For the first time in the West Indies I saw yobs, wild-
eyed young men in strange, flowing attire, marching down the narrow
streets swigging beer and singing discordant songs deriving from the
dawn of time. Some of the men emitted eerie bat-like shrieks and threw
themselves around, whirling in a mysterious, primeval dance.

The town was very prettily laid out, with dinky little squares fringed
with tall palm-trees, their tops bent by the weight of coconuts. After
a heavy, champagne-soaked meal, Estelle insisted we go to a night-club.
I knew we were making a grave mistake. "Let these ancient Bretons
loose in a night club," I told myself, "and we may see the end of
civilisation as we know it."

The club was situated at the edge of town, a large open space. Estelle and I crouched in the corner, whilst the men and women leapt and jumped on the scrubby grass, as strange, fluted music blared out. Bare-footed, snaggle-toothed, they performed strange, Isles des Saintanic rites. Beer bottles waved high in the air, and the wild women threw themselves around in screaming abandon.

Neither Estelle or myself wished to admit that we were not enjoying every second of our night out, but luckily we both pleaded illness at the same time, and finally escaped from the den of horror.

The next day we went on a tour of the island in a coach, the local people stopping in their tracks to watch the bus go by. Some sat squatting on their haunches in doorways, sharpening iron-age tools. Children played with enormous iguanas, some even larger than the children whose pets they were. The children had a troll-like aspect, snub noses, deep brown skins, and blond hair resembling Rasta locks.

Back in Basse-Terre there was a surprise awaiting us. As Estelle fumbled with the lock, the door swung open to reveal a life-size version of the brother. A short, square man with hair greased down the middle and curling moustaches. He smiled slowly, showing a set of yellow teeth with a gap in the centre.

"Hullo, *bébe*."

Henri grabbed my hand and began to kiss it almost up to the elbow before I wrenched it from his grasp. Something about his over lecherous manner terrified me to the quick.

Estelle took him by the arm and led him into the living room, and they spoke for a long time in French, Henri pausing every now and then to give me a long, lecherous leer.

"I hope you do not mind me using your bedroom," I said, not catching his eye.

Henri whispered something in a soft voice and re-grasped my clammy hand.

"What did he say?" I asked Estelle.

"'E say non problem. 'E say you sleep there, and 'e sleep on the floor in his woom."

Henri gave me a look of such undiluted carnality that I shuddered. There and then, I made up my mind that I had had enough of Guadeloupe. Beautiful it may be, but after all, beauty is only skin deep, but the fear I held for the brother went right down to the core.

"There is no need for Henri to do without his bed tonight."

Henri's eyes glistened when the sentence had been translated. "Because I am leaving for Martinique tonight."

"Tonight!"

"Yes, I'm afraid."

Henri grinned in an oily manner, refusing to release my hand.

Adamantly I refused all offers of lifts to the airport. With my small bag already packed, I caught a taxi.

Estelle was sorry to see me go, and begged me to send her African batik materials when I returned.

"You must not be put off by my brother's quiet, reserved way about him. He really does not mind you sleep in his woom."

"No, no. Your brother seems awfully nice, it's just that I've got a plane to catch, I've suddenly remembered that it leaves in about two minutes."

"Two minutes! Then you 'ave alweady missed it."

"Did I say two minutes? I meant two hours."

"Ah, I see. Well it was so nice to 'ave you with me. You welcome any time. Maybe I spend a leetle time wiz you in *l'Afrique?*"

"I will give you the address of my family there, and I know they would be pleased to let you stay."

"Thank you, thank you," she cried brokenly, and waved me cheerfully out of sight as the taxi zoomed away.

No plane was leaving for Martinique until eleven the next morning, but I spent a comfortable night curled up on one of the benches in Guadeloupe's ultra modernised airport.

A wave of guilt passed over me when I thought of my hurried exit, but then I anticipated my time in Martinique, and quivered with pleasure.

A Narrow Escape
from Fort-de-France
MARTINIQUE

So trembling with excitement was I actually to be flying to Martinique, I clean forgot to be frightened by the plane journey. Martinique! The magical isle of songs, films and books. The music of Martinique is an exquisite blend of jazz and Latin American with a unique flavour all of its own – the music from the nineteen twenties, that is. I had no idea what great strides modern Martinique had made musically, but I was only too keen to find out.

Misted grey mountain peaks could be seen far down below. The plane angled downwards and swept noisily into the airport. I was here. I had actually arrived in the one country that I had wanted passionately to visit from the age of seven, when I read a short story based on the Creole childhood of Napoleon's Josephine.

A humid breeze hit me as I climbed from the plane. In my elation, I began to sing an old Martiniquais song I had heard: "La Belle Amélie". I had no idea what it was all about, but I sang loud and clear, oblivious to the ratty glances I received. A magical glow abounded, I could tell, a glow which said, "something special and wonderful is going to happen to you here, something that you have been missing out on all these years."

Reaching the terminal, I was first surprised to see that it cost ten francs for the honour of using a trolley. Surprise number two was discovering how rude the airport officials were. They openly sneered at my Frenchless tongue, and refused to believe that I had come alone with no one in the country to stay with. In the end, after savage glances and banging fists, I said I was staying with an aunt in Fort-de-France, then I breezed out of the airport to look for a taxi. Then, with a gasp, I realised I only had five francs left, so I beetled to the nearest bank.

A sullen bank clerk told me, with tightened lips, that she was not going to change my dollars, because of orders from above.

"Oh, well, never mind, eh. Do you know where I can change my dollars so I can take a taxi to town?"

"*Non*."

"But –"

"*Eh vous*," and she proceeded to serve the next customer, a billowy American tourist.

Undaunted, I caught a taxi, asking the driver, a young man of Indian extraction, to drive me to a nice, cheap hotel. The driver looked me up and down then nodded without a word. Just as we were pulling out, an old man lurched towards us and swung open the cab door.

"*L'hôpital*," he groaned, wedging himself beside me, throwing me a furious glance. I wanted to tell him that whatever was wrong with him was not my fault, but I couldn't express it in French.

Martinique seemed even more prosperous than Guadeloupe, with large white colonial-style houses lining the streets, hidden behind the scarlet blooms of the bougainvillea. The Martiniquais dressed in even posher clothes than their Guadeloupan cousins, only here there was no African garb, and most of the women had relaxed their hair. Gone were the wooden stalls selling jelly coconut and sky juice. France had arrived in the West Indies good and proper this time, scattering a trail of wine bars and pâtisseries in its wake.

The hospital was a gleaming building with nurses and doctors scurrying around in white coats, reeking of calm and efficiency.

In the casualty ward where the old man directed us, I was horrified to see that everyone had a broken leg. A little girl wobbled slowly with a splint, a young boy slouched miserably in a wheelchair, yet another man swung jauntily on crutches, and a doleful man was being pushed painfully into a car wearing a full-sized leg plaster. It all said a lot for the Martiniquais drivers.

The old man climbed out of the car looking very sad.

As soon as we had the cab all to ourselves, the driver began to tell me of his friend who lived in London. I wasn't in the least bit interested, and wished he'd keep quiet so I could look at Martinique. A strength and vibrancy existed here, nothing like the dreamy romantic Guadeloupe. Fort-de-France, the capital, was much more attractive than Guadeloupe's Pointe-à-Pitre, with straight grid streets and little Creole-style houses. I wasn't sure that I liked the sophisticated atmosphere, but, well after all, I hadn't given it a chance yet.

In the centre of Fort-de-France, a building of staggering beauty made me catch my breath. Gold twines and spires, the edifice shone like an Indian temple in rich blues and greens. Looking closer at it as the cab swung towards it, I saw it was the Bibliothèque Schoelcher. Across the street a vivid green sea nestled between graceful mountains, and a harbour sparkled in the sun, filled with luxurious sailing boats.

The driver chattered on constantly about Highgate or somewhere, but I had long since stopped even pretending to listen. Fort-de-France was indeed a lovely town.

"Here is a 'otel. Nice an' sheep."

We had stopped by a promenade lined with souvenir shops and waving palms. The driver pointed above a pâtisserie in which sat languid American tourists.

"Zoh, you want to go on tour of ze island?"

"I don't know, I'll think about it."

"I take you."

"We'll see."

"Let me show you round."

"Give me your number and I'll call you."

He gave me his number, then said, "So, lunchtime. We go for lunch. I meet you here at one."

"Meet me for lunch?" I had an awful vision of him sitting before a plateful of something expensive, talking about his friend in London, while I footed the bill.

"No, thank you, I don't eat lunch. I'll see you soon, goodbye." I paid him in dollars and walked away in search of the hotel which didn't appear to exist. Everyone I asked shook their heads grumpily and moved away. Then, looking in between two shops, I saw winding stone steps on which sat a pile of refuse boxes and great stacks of dustbin liners overflowing with fetid rubbish. A pretty brownskin boy with green eyes cantered down the steps giving me an enquiring look.

"*Esker une 'otel here, monsieur?*"

"*Oui, là-bas.*"

I picked my way through the rubbish, and climbed up the steep steps, becoming more and more exhausted. I had forgotten my luggage was so heavy.

Upon reaching the second landing, a tiny light-skinned black woman with a kerchief tied around her head asked me what I wanted.

"*Avez vous une room in ça 'otel, madame?*"

"*Ou-ou-i,*" she said slowly, her black, hollow eyes running me quickly up and down.

"*Oh, merci bookoo.* Can je avez une room for two days?"

Her sharp little eyes continued to dart over me swiftly and she produced a pen and paper, and wrote 200 francs.

"*Ça est 200 francs par nuit?*"

"*Oui, deux cents par jour.*"

A bit steep, but I accepted without quarrel. I was tired and in need of cigarettes, and there would be no time to buy any if I spent my time arguing with this woman who wouldn't be able to understand me anyway.

My room was squalid, with peeling walls and rotting floor boards. I placed my bags down and heaved a deep sigh.

"Well, well, well, Madame la Martinique," I said aloud. "You have a lot of work in store for you before you can redeem yourself after this."

The door trembled slightly, and turning, I saw the concierge framed in the doorway, her lips twisted into a smirk. I started, and the door swung to with a clatter.

Walking around Fort-de-France I was struck by the bright-eyed vivacity of the town's folk. I walked back to the sumptuous

Bibliothèque, and past the white marble statue of the Empress Josephine. A gaggle of American tourists rudely pushed me out of the way, as they posed each one of their gang in turn to be photographed beneath Josephine's serene, stony figure. After I had changed some money, and walked around a craft market, marvelling at the prices, I felt hot, tired and miserable, so I went for lunch in a smart-looking outside café.

Customers and assistants alike gave me resentful stares.

"*Une petite fromage sandwich, s'il vous plaît, madame,*" I said, in a pure, sweet French.

The assistant eyed me snappily, then told me the price in a French so rapid, I could not understand.

"*Pardon, madame?*"

She gabbled something which sounded like, "*Deux millions trois cents.*"

"*Je ne vous comprends pas!*"

A look of bright malice crossed her face, and, taking my purse, she picked out a hundred franc note, and gave me about three francs change.

"*Mais madame! C'est une not so cher,* surely?"

"*Oui, oui – et vous!*" and she served the next customer with alacrity, giving me a blazing glance out of the corner of her eye.

What could I do, except stagger out of the fromage sandwich shop with a heavy heart, and a light purse.

Fort-de-France has buildings of New Orleanian charm, with wrought-iron balconies spilling over with baskets of ferns and flowers. Elegant shops, containing everything that can be acquired in the shops of Paris, were alive with thrilled American tourists. Although the faces of the people were not as open as they had been in Guadeloupe, the atmosphere was one of bustling buoyancy. But still I felt ill at ease. Everyone seemed to be staring at me in a hostile manner. I began to wonder whether my dress was split; but no, it was *me* they resented. As an actress, it is always easy to tell if you are going to be a hit as soon as you step on the stage. By a certain buzz as you make your entrance, you can tell if the audience is going to be with you all the way or whether they will sit in stony silence as you desperately try to make them laugh. In Martinique, I knew I was going to be a flop. I felt infinitely depressed.

To cheer myself up, I took my films to a developers, so I could at least see the photos I had taken of Halbert in Dominica and indulge in waves of sweet nostalgia. I had already written to him half-a-dozen times, so I thought it would be nice to send him the photographs I had taken of his timeless beauty. When she saw me come to collect the prints, the young assistant's eyes lit up with an evil intelligence. She snatched the receipt out of my hand and began to ring up the cost – 100, 200 and 200 –

"*Cinq cents.*"

"*Cinq cents!* That's fifty quid!"

"*Oui,*" she smiled.

"*Non, trop cher.*"

"*Eh bien – non photos – et vous –*"

Well, the long and the short is I did get them out. What else could I do? They were even very badly developed with dark smudges where Halbert's face ought to be.

Pushing past the heaps of rubbish back at the hotel I walked up the four flights of the rickety staircase, which wound up into blackness. As I climbed up into the dark, I saw two glowing lights, glimmering out at me. These were the eyes of the concierge as she stood in wait, like a spider.

"Pay ze money *maintenant.*"

I forked out the full amount, and asked her, in perfect phrase book French, for a receipt.

"*Moment,*" she muttered and slithered off into the darkness, throwing me a horrible smile. I shuddered.

From my window I could see the azure harbour. Watching the sky change from ice pink to indigo blue, I felt lonely and drifting, like a ghost. By eight at night, the streets became devoid of human life, save for darting little French cars. I comforted myself with the thought that maybe it wasn't done for women to walk the streets of Fort-de-France alone at night. With this excuse, I settled down to writing self-pitying letters home, then read a good book. A tried and tested book that I had read many times before. I felt I could not cope with a new experience which might have proved a disappointment. Very early in the evening, as the sea birds crowed mournfully, I fell into a fitful sleep.

I dreamed I was Christopher Columbus, sailing around the island in 1493, but being too frightened of the inhabitants to land. Apparently the Caribs who had settled on the island after massacring the peaceful Arawaks were so warlike that for hundreds of years after Columbus first landed, the Europeans did not dare set foot in Martinique. Thinking how the concierge's eyes had glowed like hot coals, I began to wonder whether anything had changed.

I was no happier next morning. The bugs in the bed had been merciless to me that night, and when I awoke my skin was alive with itchy pain. Passing the concierge, I twisted my ankle painfully on a jutting floorboard. Soft, sneering laughter could be heard from amongst the shadows.

The only thing to do was to get away from the villainous town of Fort-de-France, and travel deep into the heart of the country, and there discover its innermost soul.

A travel agent was situated very near to the hotel, so I walked timidly in, and sat on a chair in front of a dark-skinned assistant dressed in American-style clothes.

"*Excuse em moi –*"

He brushed me away as if I was a blue-tail fly, and dialled a number on the telephone. I waited patiently for half-an-hour, sitting before him, looking at the posters of France that covered the walls. At last he replaced the receiver and glanced at his watch.

"*Er, excuse em moi –*"

He took out a book with an ostentatious flourish, and began to read, his eyes flicking in my direction every now and again, relishing the effect his ill manners were having on me.

"*Monsieur!*"

"*Oui.*" He scanned me insolently, tapping his long fingers on the book.

"*Je voudrais to allons on a tour de Martinique.*"

"I've lived in New York for three years, lady, so there's no need to speak that style of French to me." So saying he reburied his nose into his book.

"Oh, in that case, could you tell me how I can take a tour around the island?"

"What?"

"I would like to see your beautiful country," I smarmed, unctuously.

"You want to go on a tour of Martinique?"

"Yes."

His mouth twisted into a bitter expression, as if he were thinking, 'well, that's too bad for Martinique.'

"Could you tell me how I'd go about it?"

"Go about what?"

"Seeing Martinique."

"Why look at me, I can't arrange tours."

"But I thought you were a travel agent."

"I am."

"So –"

He breathed deeply, demonstrating that I had offended everything in him that could possibly be offended.

"There are no tours around the island, or if there are, I don't know about them."

"Do you know how I could find out?"

"No."

Utterly defeated I walked out of the agents, clinging onto the last vestige of dignity I had left. I turned left into a cobbled street and walked blindly forward unaware of anything that happened around me. The grim Victorian cathedral towered above, but I noticed it not. A few men grouped around the grounds of a large government building shouted out crude comments to me in French. I swore back fiercely in English, telling them that they could all go to the Bald Devil of Kiev. Delighted, they followed me down the street, waving their arms and cat-calling in unseemly tones.

Halbert had warned me of this. He had said that the people of Martinique would approach me and smile, and he smiled a hideous smile, "An' when deh smile so, deh'll seh – *'Bonjour ma soeur, comment allez-vous?'* An' den deh tek all your money, an' you'll be plenty, plenty stuck!"

"If anyone gave me a smile like that," I had replied, "I'd run so fast they wouldn't have time to take a penny!"

But uncannily Halbert was right. The treacherous smile he imitated was the exact Martinique smile. Oh, would I had heeded Halbert's wise words when he said, "Don't go a Martinique alone, man. Awoah! It plenty, plenty rrrrough!"

Ah, Halbert, so clever, so inimitable.

I had roamed into the back streets of Fort-de-France, and was now in dire need of refreshment. I could not help but marvel at the number of young men who hung around the street corners, dressed immaculately, with nothing to do but stand on one leg idly watching the world go by. One man, short and square with a beard, dark glasses, and precious few teeth threw me a pleasant smile which I found most engaging. He asked me something in French, and when I couldn't understand, began to count out the words very slowly on his fingers, counting, *"Où-all-ez-vous?"* then he said, *"quatre – savah."* Somehow he thought it would help me to understand. It didn't, but we had a conversation of sorts, with my atrocious French, and his counting French.

He told me of how he loved Paris which is where he would like to live if only he could afford it.

Miming that he could do with some chicken and chips, he directed me to a fast food café. The woman serving was so rude my hair all but stood on end, refusing to serve me, and glaring with too much venom to be true. Wrapping it up in greasy paper, she tossed the food vaguely in my direction, then leaned with her elbows on the desk, poking her head forward and grimacing evilly, grinding her teeth. Just as I was about to ask my bearded friend what was wrong with the woman, I noticed he had gone. I ran into the street to look for him, and saw that he was skulking behind the café, gorging on the chicken I had bought him. Had he said, "*Merci*"? Had he even bestowed upon me a smile? Nay. No word nor look of kindness had I received. When he saw I was looking at him from afar, he darted down a dark alleyway, like a sewer rat escaping a predatory cat.

As a lost soul in timeless Hades, I trod with dismal step to the beach, and there sat in a soothing corner amongst dirt and pebbles. I threw a stone into the polluted waters and dwelt upon the injustices of life.

"*Une cigarette, s'il vous plaît,*" asked an emaciated little white man. I handed him a Silk Cut mechanically. I had been sitting and staring like a half-witted halibut for a very long time.

When the man spoke to me again, I ignored him, not being bothered to tell him I couldn't understand a word he said.

"You are American?"

"Might be, might not be." I chucked a dog-end into the sea. If Martinique, I reasoned, is not going to be nice to me, then there is no reason why I should be nice to it.

"So you speak English?"

"Could do."

"See the unemployed we have in this country. Thirty-five per cent of all the people have no work. I have nothing. May I have ten francs."

"Nope."

With a sigh, the poor, skinny man rejoined his friends and soon their little party were throwing me unsavoury looks. I was past caring. As long as I could sit alone on the beach in peace, then I felt I could vaguely stomach this wretched state of affairs.

"*Hé, madame! Madame!*" A man dressed in uniform, looking a bit like a postman, hurried towards me, and told me in spicy sign language to move along.

"But why?"

"*Trop sale, ici, trop, trop sale.*"

With a long stick, the seakeeper, or whoever he was, prodded me in the back, and pushed me away.

I could not even sit by the sea without being butted by a seakeeper. Was there any hope left? Feeling utterly jaded, a cynical smile playing about my lips, I walked back to the hotel. The chambermaids had not touched my room which smelt of stale soap and dry rot. Night fell with strange, chirpy noises.

'Martinique is outside these dingy walls,' said a little voice from inside my head. 'How can you just sit inside and let it escape you?' But I found to my surprise that I could do just that, and quite easily.

A bold rap at the door interrupted my reveries. Before I had time to say "go away", the concierge had stepped into the room, tiny eyes alight with defiance.

"You pay money, *maintenant*."

"Pay money! But, *madame*. I have already paid you!"

"*Non*." Her shoulders were tensed, as if fully prepared for the battle to follow, and, what's worse, determined to win.

"*Oui!* Je payer vous yesterjour."

"*Non*. I receive nothing. Give me money."

"But I gave vous six hundred francs!"

"*Non*. You owe six 'undred francs. Please give."

She stood by my bed, her wizened face searching mine, spite radiating from every pore.

"Unless I get money this minute, I call *la police*."

A quick wit was needed here.

"Didn't I pay you?" I scratched my head in perplexity. "I thought I did! How strange. Well, I have no money on me at the moment. Could I pay you tomorrow?"

The concierge scanned me carefully for any sign of trickery, but, evidently satisfied, she nodded, and stole silently from the room.

I settled back to my seat by the window and continued to stare outside wondering what to do. The next morning, the concierge would be waiting for her money, the money she had already received, and I would be powerless to do aught but pay her again. All night long I tried to think up some plan of action, but nothing came to mind. The dark webs of despair had closed in.

The next day I awoke with a mind as clear as Caribbean skies. The only thing to do was to go far away from Martinique quicker than a wink. Taking all the money I owned in a tiny holdall, I went to the travel agents, and enquired about planes to St Lucia.

The man who had served me before with the tours, told me gleefully that I could not get a plane to St Lucia. He didn't actually add, 'not even for ready money,' but there was that sort of look in his eye.

"Listen, Mister." I was in no mood for slack behaviour. "I want to go to St Lucia, and I want to go today, and if you are unable to book me a plane, let me speak to someone more competent." I had meant my voice to be low and controlled, but I am afraid the last few words of the sentence exploded in a shrill screech. But it did the trick. A plane was ordered for me that evening at seven o'clock. The agent even managed a smile that looked passably genuine as I left the office, firmly clutching in my sweaty hand a ticket to St Lucia.

To fill in the time before my plane left, I decided to take a trip to Trois Ilets where the Empress Josephine was born. Trois Ilets is a tiny town south of Fort-de-France. To get there, one must take a ferry across the water, from a pier, and one must sit amongst hordes of tourists from all over the world for a very long time because the ferry is always late.

It was already firmly lodged in my brain that along with Martiniquais, tourists didn't like me, so I sat aloof, reading a newspaper.

"It says in the guide book," said a middle-aged American man in a very loud voice, "that the local women have a good dress sense, but look at the way that one's dressed! Red skirt with a pink top! We Americans could teach these people a thing or two when it comes to style!" He pointed a stubby finger at me.

I carried on reading the paper.

"But a lot of the girls here sure are pretty," said his wife, sweetly. "But," she continued, looking blandly at me, "you do always get exceptions."

I rustled the newspaper in a marked manner.

By the time the ferry arrived I had lost all interest in Trois Ilets. The only thing that kept me from throwing myself in the sea were the screaming tourists, who kicked up a powerful din whenever the boat rocked to and fro. I laughed heartily as we were all sprayed with water, and terrified young girls screeched like banshees. The more the tourists screamed, the funnier it seemed. I could now see why people always laughed at me when I flew into panics. It does seem very amusing.

When I reached Trois Ilets, I didn't know quite what to do, so I wandered in the direction of La Pagerie, where Josephine was born. I couldn't find the place for love nor money, so I sat on a bench in front of some little shops, and eyed up all the handsome young men as they strolled past. The Martinique men are quite the handsomest I have ever seen, but the ones who came over to talk to me became so frustrated by my lack of French, they au revoired in a flash.

Trois Ilets is a fussy little town, full of Creole restaurants, bars and hotels, with a lovely palm-fringed, sandy beach by the bay. Probably it is perfectly enchanting, but I felt too anxious about *La Concierge* to fully appreciate it. For all I knew, that ogress had done away with my bags, and let my room to some other hapless tourist. There and then I decided to return to the hotel, and work out an escape plan.

As the ferry back to Fort-de-France left in an hour, I went into a bar and ordered a beer so I could sit near the pier to wait for the boat. The woman serving me did so with undisguised reluctance, dragging her feet theatrically, and banging down the beer bottle. Looking into the glass she gave me, I saw that a thick film of grease lined the interior, on which clung dense clusters of black flies.

"May I have another glass, please?"

The woman looked blankly at me, not understanding what I was saying.

"Glass – look."

I held the glass to the woman's face, but she pointedly refused to look, and after a few minutes, about five women stood behind the bar and gazed at me through cold eyes as I tried to ask them in French for another glass.

"*Une autre tasse,*" one of them said at last, "*pourquoi?*"

"*Parce que this glass est très sale.*"

"*Très sale!*" they chorused in unison, clutching at beer bottles in their rage.

I backed away defensively, hoping they weren't going to beat me up. I could always jump over the balcony into the sea, I thought, if they try any funny business.

"*Très sale,*" they said again, and glared.

Damn your diaphragms, I told them in my mind, what have you all got to be so snooty about?

One of the women banged down a fresh glass on my table with such ferocity it nearly broke. I did my best to match her glare, spite for spite, but with all her years of practice, she won hands down.

Come on, ferry, I pleaded, unless you come within the next two seconds I shall be torn to pieces by these female vultures.

After what seemed like an eternity of giving and receiving dirty looks, the ferry finally arrived.

Running to the hotel, I saw a shifty figure dressed in a Cab Calloway-style zoot suit, leaning against a news-stand, idly smoking a cigarette. On closer inspection I observed that the man's hair was sleeked back in an oily Marcel wave, and parted evenly down the centre. No, surely it couldn't be . . .

"*Ah! Ma chérie! Comment allez-vous?* 'Ow ya doing, huh?" It was Henri, the "shy" brother of Estelle.

I gave him a cursory nod, and quickly darted away, down a side street. Running like mad, past shops and prettily painted houses, I reached the outskirts of town. Soon I came to a small river, where men and women in curly straw hats lugged baskets of fish from little boats to the shore. Behind them rose misted mountains. The sun peered out from between the peaks at a slant, sending a golden glow on the workers as they sang in unison, throwing the baskets skilfully to one another. This was more like it. A Martinique I will never discover. Not the flashy, crooked façade of Fort-de-France, but a mellow, gentle Martinique. I walked into a tiny café bar, where a vivacious, light-skinned woman began to chat to me in an animated French. Advising me on the type of Coca-Cola I should drink, she sat down at my table, and began talking earnestly about her life. The first Martiniquais to be relaxed and friendly. I liked her so much I felt like weeping on her shoulder.

An old man wearing torn ragged clothing and a big straw hat stomped in and gave the girl an enormous crab.

The girl offered to show me the crab which was tied up in a string bag, but I developed an attack of the jitters, so with a laugh, she put it behind the counter and, rejoining me at my table, told me in detail how to prepare the crab. The crab was not dead, she said in an easily understandable French, it was only sleeping, "and tomorrow I make a feast – please come." Tomorrow I would be far away, but I would have given the world to have been able to join her.

Next minute, a troop of old fishermen walked in and began to chuckle with one another, chatting in a good-humoured fashion. They found it highly comical that I couldn't speak French, although they didn't quite believe me and continued to talk in a rapid tongue. I laughed in all the right places, and for the first time in Martinique, I felt at ease. This is how it should always be, I thought. Sitting in this little café surrounded by crabs and paintings of fish on the walls in a cosy, dingy atmosphere, laughing with fishermen and talking to this sprightly woman. Maybe this was the real Martinique, and the chilling hostility of Fort-de-France was but a mere veneer.

We sat for a long time, until dusk fell.

Realising it must be nearly six, I dashed out of the café, waving sad goodbyes to the wonderful people, and made my way back to the hotel.

I still had not thought up a plan concerning my escape. I knew it would be impossible to sneak out of the hotel with my bags without being seen by the concierge, who would stop me, demand the money, then call the police if I did not pay up. And what if she said I owed her for two weeks' board – or three weeks' board? The horrific possibilities were endless.

Pushing past the piles of refuse I glanced quickly around to see if Henri was still on the prowl, and seeing that he wasn't I raced up the stairs.

"You pay me money now."

The concierge sat in her little dark corner on the second landing.

"My son, 'e get upset. 'E don't like ze people who try rob and – er – er –"

"Tak advantage of ze orld leddy," boomed a masculine voice.

Out of the blackness stepped an enormous man, at least six foot seven in his stockinged feet, wearing a black beret, a leather cat suit, and slit black glasses. Something suspiciously metallic glinted in the faint light.

"But of course I'll pay you the money, I'll just dash into my room and get it for you now." So saying I ran into my room, locked the door, and stood in the middle of the floor. Suddenly everything began to sway, and for a moment I thought someone had put the bed upside down. Several moments later, when I recovered, I staggered to the window and threw it open, in the vain hope that the fresh air would clear the mind. Loosening the jaw, I stuck my head out of the window and fell into a sort of trance.

Cars beeped, the sea swished, and someone was shouting "Hullo, hullo, hullo," but no noise from without could shake me from the coma I had lapsed into.

A tiny pebble landing just above my right eyebrow shook me into consciousness. Looking down into the street I saw the portly figure of Henri waving frantically at me.

"*Hullo, hullo! Ça va, ma chère?*"

"Henri! What are you doing here?"

"I play music in ze bar! You come down for ze drink? I 'ave three hours before I start."

The time was ten past six, and my plane was due to leave in fifty minutes. Henri's face glowed like molten gold in the sunlight.

"Yes, I shall come down, but I tell you what. Could you do me a favour?"

"*Mais oui!*"

"I am leaving the hotel today, and I have some heavy luggage to carry downstairs. If I throw my bags out of the window, could you look after them until I get down?"

"But of course!"

"Fabulous – catch!" And a suitcase hurtled down into the street below, landing a few yards from Henri's feet.

"I'll be down in just a mo'."

Grabbing my handbag, I flew out of the room, turning just once to take a last look at the squalor of it all. Then I crept warily down the steps.

"*Eh! Madame!*"

Two shady figures lurked in the shadows.

"Oh, hello, I was looking for you. I thought you would rather have the money in cash, so I'm just nipping out to a bureau de change."

"*Bureau de change?*"

"*Oui.*"

The son stood silently, exchanging glances with his mother. The mother looked down at my hands and noted with evident satisfaction that I was not carrying any luggage. She nodded to the son, who tilted his head back as though to give his assent. I clattered down the steps like a mighty rhinoceros. Reaching Henri, who stood smirking and primping his twirly mustachios, I grabbed the case and hailed a passing taxi.

"The airport!"

"But, madame! You are not coming with me for the drink."

"Not on your nelly!"

"What? I do not understand." The taxi moved slowly away.

"But, madame! There are two people calling you from the hotel!"

The taxi driver started to slow down.

Turning round, I saw to my mounting horror, the concierge and son racing towards the taxi, waving their fists in the air.

"Step on it!" I yelled.

"You wish to stop?" asked the dim-witted driver.

"No! Quick! Move!"

With a jerk, the taxi whizzed forward, and, when I realised we were well and truly out of harm's way, I turned to give the three angry people a cheery wave.

How graceful and elegant Fort-de-France seemed as I was leaving. Maybe I did not give it a fair chance. All the same, I can't say I was sorry to see the back of it.

When I had time to get back into my right head, I asked the driver if he thought Martinique would soon gain its independence.

"Of course, and very soon. We are not happy here under France. So much prejudice there is in this country. If you are white or light-skinned, then you get all the fine jobs, but if you black like me, there is nothing."

"But Martinique would not be better off financially if you ceased to be a department of France."

"Money? What is money! I spit on money! What we need is our own flag!"

What a collective mind the man had. To me it doesn't matter what sort of flag England has. I don't care a fig. The Union Jack has become a National Front symbol anyway, and, as I'm not allowed to be English in the true sense of the word, it seems strange to think of a flag stirring up strong emotions.

I was quite surprised when the driver asked for a very large tip. I reminded him that he spat upon money, but it didn't do much good. My plane was leaving in a quarter of an hour's time, but still I could not relax. What if the concierge, the son and Henri had followed me in another taxi, and were somewhere in the airport? But fortunately they must have given the whole thing up as a bad job.

I boarded the plane and sank gratefully in my seat.

St Lucia, here I come.

The Land Where the Jumbies Live

ST LUCIA

*P*eering downwards from the window of the tiny aircraft which boggled away towards St Lucia, I noticed that even from high above, Martinique looked very bad-tempered. Querulous mountains elbowed snivelling rivers out of the way, and the whole island was tinted in a deep, satanic grey. Usually, I liked to wave a secret goodbye to the country I was leaving behind, or blow a surreptitious kiss, but not to Martinique. Besides, the ten-seater plane had not yet begun to swoop, so I was clinging to my crucifix and praying.

"How did you enjoy Martinique?"

I turned round in my seat to see a startlingly glamorous woman sitting behind me, wearing an extravagantly feathered hat, and a baggy silk suit.

"Martinique was interesting," came the guarded reply.

"Well, I assure you, sweetheart, you won't like St Lucia half as much. I know, because I am St Lucian, but I come to Martinique every month to do my shopping. Martinique has no dirty market-places like we have, and everyone in Martinique dresses up nice and neat, whereas in St Lucia, oh my dear! You see some people dressed up in rags. It's disgusting!"

"Well, I expect St Lucia is a lot poorer."

"Even so, that's no excuse for looking dirty and scruffy. How long are you staying in St Lucia?"

"About ten days."

"Whereabouts?"

"I can't remember the name of the hotel, but it's in La Toc – or something."

"La Toc!" The lady's eyes lit up with a deep admiration for me. "La Toc is the best hotel in the island! It is so nice and clean, and you don't get any ragamuffin people staying there, only the respectable ones."

My heart sank. I was hoping that the hotel I had booked into was one of the cosy, sleezy, seven-pound-a-night ones.

The woman I was talking to had a very pretty accent, with slow Frenchified vowels.

Although the English were the first European settlers on the island in 1605, the French took over in 1635 after the British were fought off by the Caribs. Then, for nearly two hundred years the French and the British battled over ascendancy of St Lucia, and, after the country had changed hands fourteen times, the British finally gained control over it in 1814, after having murdered the Caribs. However, the fine features of the Caribs are still apparent in the handsome population of St Lucia where many of the black people have Carib ancestry.

As we approached St Lucia, my friend behind me told me that I was welcome to her house any time.

"There is La Toc hotel," she said, pointing to an enormous pink edifice nestling between the hills and the sea.

I began to laugh.

"Oh no, I'm not staying *there*. The place I am staying is a small hotel in La Toc Road."

"Oh! You must mean," and she pulled her rouged lips downwards as if the words were too frightful to be voiced, "the Mini Trop Hotel."

"Yes, that's the one."

"Eyech! That's not a nice hotel at all. I thought you were staying in the big one."

"Oh no. So, when would it be convenient for me to come and pay you a visit?"

She stared down at the huge hotel I was not staying in.

"Well, I shall be busy for a long while." Taking out a glossy woman's magazine, she indicated that the friendship between us had come to an abrupt end.

Very smoothly we landed in Castries airport.

A beautiful cool breeze blew on my face as I walked out of the small airport building and into the wide, dusty street. A friendly taxi driver pulled up and very politely placed my luggage in his cab, chatting easily all the while. Ah! This was more like it! A lovely mellowness hung in the air. Everyone moved with an easy-going slowness, and it was rare to see a face that did not possess a gentle expression. The women, with their relaxed hair and modest clothes looked sweet and beautiful. Poverty was rife. Tin shacks had been erected on the outskirts of Castries, and although vendors sold sugar cane, oranges, bananas and green coconuts on makeshift stalls on the side of the streets, the general appearance was one of quiet sobriety.

Castries itself is a town totally lacking in charm. Because of numerous earthquakes and hurricanes, most of the older buildings have been destroyed. A terrible fire in 1948 swept through the capital, and razed four-fifths of the old wooden buildings to the ground. As a result, Castries is a somewhat ugly town made up of grey concrete houses.

My hotel was a sprawling flat-roofed building set atop a steep hill. A bowed little old man came to greet me, his face falling slightly at the sight of me.

"You sure you book in here? It was an English lady who phone up."

"I am from England."

"Oh!" He looked none too convinced.

Unpacking my luggage I could hear loud American accents coming from next door. The hotel was obviously full. It was late afternoon, so the thing to do was to stroll back into town before the sun went down, which it does very quickly in the Caribbean, blackening the sky in seconds.

Down the bottom of the hill where my hotel was situated was a ramshackle bar-cum-shop, with a large wooden table outside on which

sat talkative young men and women, drinking beer and playing dominoes in a sedate manner. How different from Jamaica, where domino
playing involves loud whoops and shrieks, as the dominoes are
slammed with Herculean force upon the table. I wanted to join the
little crowd, and make merry, but the nerve failed me. Instead I walked
about a mile into town, past a harbour abob with fishing boats. Over
the sea loomed a hill covered with brick and shanty houses. Women
sat outside, bathing their children in tin tubs, and plaiting one another's
hair, and a few men wearing cut-off shorts sat around with radios
listening to pounding Jamaican music.

Not knowing how to get around the island, I decided for the first
time on this trip to take guided tours, and see the sights. The women
in the tourist office were friendly in the extreme, talking in pretty
voices and giggling shyly. The pen cannot describe my joy at seeing
genuine smiles again. After Martinique I had almost come to believe
that the only time a person smiles is when he has seen some terrible
disaster.

The one lovely building in Castries is the cathedral. Inside, the most
beautiful scenes of biblical life are painted on the wall, depicting all
the characters to be of African extraction (which I believe they were).
A large sign outside the cathedral says, 'Do not enter into the house
of God unless you are dressed modestly.' Modesty in all things is the
order of the day in St Lucia. With rosaries in hand, devout worshippers
sat in the pews and mumbled soft prayers.

There is not much in the way of cafés in Castries, which deprived
me of my usual pleasure of sitting rooted to the spot for a number of
hours drinking tea. The only place I found to eat was a dark little room
in the backstreets of town, where *rôti* was served by a middle-aged
lady of Indian extraction. As I took a large bite, a shiny black bug
crawled out from the inmost recesses of the *rôti*, and made its wiggly
way down my chin. I stroked the bug's black back with tender fingers,
so happy was I to see it. That bug said I was no longer in Martinique,
so I cherished it, and almost felt like keeping it in a matchbox as a
souvenir. The rest of the *rôti* was eaten with relish.

I returned to the hotel, having cadged a lift off two young men who
refused to accept a penny for their pains. St Lucia is very much a
young person's country, with a soaring population rate, and nearly
everyone you see seems to be under thirty.

Walking past the bar at the bottom of the hill on which my hotel
was situated, a slightly built man with a pleasant, boyish face, pulled
away from his game of dominoes, and ran up towards me.

"*Excusez-moi, Mademoiselle –*"

"I'm sorry, I don't speak French or patois."

"Oh, *do* excuse me, I thought you were French."

"French?"

"Yes. You see my father is French, so I speak it."

"Your father's French?"

"Yes."

"Pure French?"

"Yes." He wiped a sheet of perspiration from his brow and hit at a mosquito that had settled on his neatly pressed shirt. I noticed that his lips were trembling, and realised that his nerves were so acute as to be almost like a physical pain. If I am making the poor man so nervous, I thought, then it's best I leave him to "chill out", as they say in Jamaica.

"Excuse me." I turned to see him biting his lip anxiously. "Would you like to come to the barbecue tomorrow. We are having it here."

"That's very kind of you."

"It going to be all different type of fish that my brother catch. If you come around one thirty I'll be so happy. My name is Lionel, and you're Miss –"

"Zenga."

"Please to meet you Miss Zenga." And he kissed my hand.

Turning away speedily, he was gone. I was surprised he could have a French father with so dark a complexion, although by now my own skin had become so dark, I found myself looking at various limbs of mine and not recognising them.

Next morning at breakfast, a group of American tourists sat at a large table, being waited on by the proprietress, a full-figured old lady wearing a flowery scarf pulled tightly around her head. She fussed and grinned and hurried to and from the kitchens laden with tropical fruits, hot buttered toast, and collations of every other nicety the Americans required. With her full cheeks quivering and puffing, she shouted harsh orders to her daughters, who scurried around the Americans, filling up their coffee cups and pouring cream. I sat at a little table at the end of the room, feebly putting up my hand whenever one of the waitresses walked past. The young girls ignored me, but the old woman shouted a snappy "Wait!" whenever she caught my eye.

After a while, a cracked plate with a piece of stale bread, and a slice of spam with jam and butter on top clattered onto my table, startling me out of my wits.

"Thank you," I said, looking up from my book.

"Hey, are you from England?" A cheerful American girl from the next table pulled her chair towards me and pressed her face close to mine. She seemed to be composed entirely of freckles and teeth.

"Yes."

"Hi. My name's Evelyn, I'm from Washington DC. We're Christians, and we want to share with you the word of Gard."

"Oh. Ah."

"What bookarya reading?"

"Gogol."

"Yeah? Well I'm reading something a whole lot bedda than that." And she pulled out a Bible.

"Ah."

"You wanna trade your book in for the book of Gard?"

"I – em –" Luckily I was saved by a waitress clanking down a metal pot of stewed tea.

The barbecue in Lionel's brother's bar proved to be a very delightful event indeed. Lionel's tiny nieces and nephews ran about laughing and teasing one another, indicating that the next generation of St Lucians will be a far more mischievous bunch than the present. I was introduced to sisters, brothers and the cat, Meg. Sitting beneath an almond tree with a paper plate of delicious parrot fish on my lap, I chatted to Lionel about his life and aspirations. He was a 21-year-old sailor who was at present unemployed, but he had sailed on cargo ships many times before.

"And that's where I met Jamaicans. They really are rough, aren't they?"

"No, my brother-in-law's Jamaican, and all his family are adorable."

"Sorry, sorry, sorry. I didn't mean they're *all* rough, only the – er – the rough ones. They use the most terrible language, Miss Zenga, they really do."

"What type of terrible language?"

A cool breeze blew in from the sea, and a boat let forth a dismal wail of a horn. Lionel blushed.

"Well, you know, like (in a whisper) swearing!"

"They don't! I don't believe you!"

"They do! Honestly! When I get to know you better, I tell you of something really terrible I hear a Jamaican say."

A three-year-old child stumbled up and wrenched the bottle of hot pepper sauce out of my hand.

"You take any more pepper sauce, I going to beat you, lady!"

"Chantelle!" said Lionel, with an anxious frown. "Don' be rude to Miss Zenga!"

"But God going to punish her for wearing those earings!" Lionel only began to laugh after I smiled, but the other people in the bar were desperately embarrassed, dragging the child away and smacking her. However, she bounced up again like indiarubber, and began to chant rude words in patois at me. I knew then and there that the child and I would soon become bosom buddies, and I was right. Nothing gladdens the heart so much as a naughty child. Lionel fetched me a basket of fruit he had bought in the market, mangoes, bananas, oranges, jelly coconuts and tamarind sweets.

"Please accept them Miss Zenga as a token of my gratitude."

"But Master Lionel? What have you got to be grateful for?"

"Your company." His skin reddened deeply and he looked away towards the hills up above. I bought him a lot of beer and cigarettes in the hope of soothing his shyness, but nothing seemed to work. I looked at him, so small, sweaty and shy, and I thought of my Halbert, so brash, tall and confident. St Lucia with its quiet, gentle beauty and Dominica with primeval forests and density.

I suddenly felt totally at home, as if this was where I was always meant to be. The white ships gleaming in the sun, the children running in and out of the fishermen's cottages which lined the sea-front, and the old ladies sitting in doorways, plaited hair beneath faded scarves; everything looked so familiar and pleasant almost as if I had grown up amongst these surroundings.

Castries at night is a lifeless place. Few people walk the streets, only a handful of bars are open, and the ones that are have no customers.

Lionel suggested we go to the Kentucky Fried Chicken, and glad am I that we did. It is *the* hot spot of Castries, only here it was a *slow* food place, with neat little queues of well-mannered people stretching down the road.

As we sat and ate the tasteless fare, Lionel and I talked in soft voices about the "jumbies", or drug addicts, whom we had seen on the way to the centre of town. It appeared that there was a plague of drug addicts who take a drug called "rock", which apparently sends the user completely potty. A group of young men had sat upon a wall screaming wildly at passers-by, occasionally punching one another, their bodies contorted in wild spasms. No one took any notice of them, and Lionel's sense of propriety forbade him to mention them in any detail.

Just as I had begun to congratulate Lionel on his vast accumulation of friends, and was marvelling over the fact that everyone in Castries knew him by name, a wild-eyed Rasta plonked himself on our table and grabbed a piece of chicken from my hand.

"Yes, *do* help yourself."

He stared at me with eyes so mad and red I was forced to look away. Dressed in tatters, with a dirty woollen cap pulled low over his face he began to speak to me in French.

"I'm not French."

"When we say French here, we mean Martinique, fool girl. Where you from?"

"England."

"England! Heh! Mind if I finish your chips?"

"Be my guest."

"We're just going," said Lionel stiffly.

"So, from London – what's happening there now?"

"Oh, it's big with lots of shops and things like that."

"No! I mean how are the vibes?"

"All right I s'pose, as vibes go."

"Melting pot, eh? Brixton. The riots."

"Yep, I live in Brixton."

"Come, Miss Zenga, let's go!"

"Heh! You live in Brixton! What were you doing during the riots?"

"Watching the flames from my bedroom window."

"Wouch! I'm going to Addis Ababa. Back to Ethiopia. My name is Zion. I and I a dread."

"My name is Zenga. I and I hungry because you and you have eaten all my –"

"Heh!" His eyes bulged so far out of his head I had an awful feeling they would become unstuck. "Zenga! African name? What it mean?"

"I'll wait for you outside."

"No, Lionel, wait for me!"

"I and I want to go to Ethiopia, but first I want to go to see Babylon. France, Germany, England, Spain, Babylon."

"Why do you say that's Babylon?"

"How you talk so, sister? You don' understand. Babylon is where they deal in pure iniquity and in England they –"

Lionel began to walk out. I was dying to talk to Zion for hours on end, and was most reluctant to leave.

"Give me a buck – or two bucks," asked Zion once we were outside in the steamy night.

I gave him two dollars.

"Zenga man," and we gently tapped fists.

On the way back to the hotel, Lionel told me very primly that I must not associate with people like that.

Once we reached the outskirts of town, and had passed the uproari-ous jumbies, the shanties became alive with reggae, laughing and brawling. Everyone he passed shouted greetings to Lionel. A constant background noise of crickets and chirpings continued ceaselessly. "Toowee tooweet!"

"That a clack-clack. If a clack-clack come in your house you miserable for the whole night. You can never find them, but you can hear them."

Although it was late at night, Lionel took me to the hospital to see his brother's girlfriend who was suffering from dysentery. The hospital was wonderfully clean and neat with cheerful sympathetic nurses who even went so far as to read to their patients. However, they made short work of hustling me and Lionel out of the way, and shooed us back into the street quicker than a wink.

The next day was the first of the tours. A mini-bus picked me up at the hotel, and when the driver saw me, he immediately began to shout that I should have waited down the bottom of the hill.

"How you expect me to go all the way up here with all the passengers?"

The group of English tourists stared balefully at me.

St Lucia's beauty is so exquisite as to be perfectly dreamlike. The guide, an Indian woman called Margaret, began to talk in a stilted voice about how long a banana tree takes to grow, but, as with all guided tours, one ceases to listen to the guides, and just stares out of the window admiring the view.

We were on a rain forest tour, and I bitterly hated every second of the long walk. Down a narrow, muddy lane we trekked, dense jungle on either side. Every now and again, Margaret stopped and began to talk in her bad actress voice about some tree or other. I could not look up, only down in case I slipped into the squelchy mud. I made spasmodic conversation with the guide, who told me that she had relatives in Wembley.

"I hear it nice and clean in Wembley, with no unpleasant Jamaican people spoiling things for everyone. They really give black people a bad name in England, don't they?"

"Have you ever met a Jamaican?"

"Oh never!" Then she gave me a long sideways glance and tittered slightly. I think it had suddenly occurred to her that I was Jamaican, and the thought evidently tickled her pink.

Hearing a fluttering overhead, I glanced up to see the green parrot of St Lucia spreading its enormous wings. Although a beautiful bird, it failed to shake me from my depression. Everybody knows that talipots live in rain forests, so the journey proved one of nightmarish horror. How much more lovely were the rain forests of Dominica.

Lionel was sitting beneath the almond tree at his brother's bar when I arrived back.

"Come for dinner, Miss Zenga, if you would like, and then we can go to the cinema."

We climbed through the thickets to his little cottage, with Lionel pointing out all the trees on the way.

"That's tamarind, that's akee, that's mango, and this –" and he touched a small fernlike plant whose leaves instantly folded up, "is Lazy Mary."

By the time we reached his pretty green cottage, I was an expert in St Lucian botany.

Lionel shared the upstairs part of the house with his sister and brother, the downstairs being occupied by his two cousins and their wives. Although very poor, their cottage was very clean and neat, with Madonnas and other Catholic artefacts ornamenting the room.

"Christina!" called Lionel timidly.

"Yaas," came a voice from a room partitioned off with a delicate lace curtain.

"Meet my dear friend, Miss Zenga."

A big bossy woman strode out from behind the curtain, and shook my hand in a businesslike fashion.

"Hello, Miss Zenga, nice to meet you."

"Nice to meet you too, Miss Christina. Are you coming to the movies tonight?" I asked, for want of anything better to say.

"The what?"

"The movies, you know, the pictures."

"The movies! But I am a Christian! I would never go to a place like that! The only film I would see is one that is showing at my church on Sunday. You must come along."

"Love to. Which church do you belong to?"

"Pentecostal, and the film showing is called *Flames of Hell*."

"Mmmm, yes. It sounds really good! Lionel – want to come on Sunday?"

"No."

"Lionel isn't a Christian, he still a Catholic, but you'll come won't you?"

"Well, only if Lionel can come."

"I won't come."

"He never goes anywhere decent, but I hope to see *you* at the church on Sunday. Lionel will give you the address."

I nodded, and the sister pushed back the lace curtain with a purposeful sweep, and disappeared into her room.

On the small plastic table was a cotton cloth covering something that smelt dreamily delicious. Unfortunately, Lionel and I were being so polite to one another, that none of us could actually mention food. It would have seemed too vulgar somehow. Every time Lionel coughed, he would leave the room with an apologetic "excuse me please". After a while Lionel's elder brother walked in, after knocking on the door, and uncovered the bill of fare. A veritable feast! Macaroni, spiced baked chicken, "Irish" potatoes, and kidney beans boiled with pigs' tails.

"Please help yourself, Miss Zenga, to as much as you like."

"It looks lovely!" I slavered. "Who's the chef?"

"I am," said the brother, and ducked his head bashfully.

Now when someone tells me to help myself, I take them at their word. Piling my plate to a dizzy height, I embarked upon an onslaught of gluttony, smacking my lips loudly and gnawing at the bones. Turning to raise my glass of sour sop juice to the chef, I noticed that Lionel had not touched his meal, and, along with his brother, was staring at me with rounded eyes. I had made a big mistake. In St Lucia, a "lady" should not display overt emotions, whether of greed or otherwise, so I finished the meal as daintily as possible, and even asked to use the bathroom for the purpose of washing my hands, hoping to impress them.

"The bathroom!" gasped Lionel.

"The bathroom!" wheezed the brother, and they turned to face each other, mouths agape with confusion.

"Miss Zenga," whispered Lionel, pulling me aside. "Let me tell you something. I hope you will understand. You see – oh, I'm so ashamed."

"Of course I'll understand, my dear Master Lionel."

"Well," his eyes had turned moist with anxiety. "You see the thing is, we don't actually have a bathroom. Only a cess pit, and a tap in the yard. Miss Zenga – please speak. Are you really so shocked."

"Lionel. If you could see where I live in London, it would be you who would be shocked. The only feeling I have concerning you is friendship. Now please show me where the tap is and stop being so stupid."

Lionel almost collapsed with pleasure at my not being disgusted by his lack of a proper bathroom. So pleased was he, that his appetite returned, and he began to eat a few mouthfuls of food.

Daintily wiping the corner of his lips with a napkin, Lionel crossed himself to give thanks to the Lord.

"*Sa ces tout*, Miss Zenga, *un nous allez.*"

"I beg your pardon?"

"Oh, I'm so, so sorry, I was saying that's all, let's go."

I looked at him with a good deal of admiration. Bilingual people never fail to inspire me with awe, and most of the Caribbean population speak two languages, the official one, and the "people's'" one. St Lucian patois, or patwa as it is sometimes spelt, sounds like French, but has a deep West African feel to it. The r's are never pronounced, so cigarette becomes "cigawette".

After a good deal of shaking of hands, and genteel parting civilities with the family, Lionel and I walked down the pitch black hill. Mothers breastfeeding their babies gossiped quietly in the night, shouting: "*Sa ou fait*" to Lionel as we passed them. After about a mile walk, we came to the cinema. A neat procession of people queued outside, hands folded primly in front of them. Tonight, the feature film was *The Curse of the Mummy's Tomb.*

"Would you like some chocolate to eat during the film, Miss Zenga?"

"Oh yes, what a nice idea –" CRASH! A rock whizzed past my head at the speed of light, smashing into a shop window next to the cinema, shattering it into a thousand pieces. Everyone screamed and ran for cover. Next minute, another boulder followed suit, and if I hadn't ducked, I would not be alive to tell this tale. More rocks hurtled towards us, and soon it seemed as if Castries had been transformed into a mighty avalanche. Two jumbies were having a bloody fight. One was armed with a lethal-looking club, and was waving it about in the air, in the vague direction of the other jumbie's head. The other was hurling large stones with brute force. The air was alive with screamed curses in patois.

Lionel steered me away to another cinema where a stultifyingly boring film was being shown, about a man and a woman who go to Greece, and get up to dull escapades. Lionel insisted we sit up in the gods so as not to associate with the roughnecks down in the stalls.

"Yes," I joked, "it's not good to mix with the riff-raff."

"What's riff-raff?"

"Ragamuffins."

"What a wonderful word! Riff-raff. Write it down for me so I can say it. How right you are! Never deal with people like that. Some people really don't know how to behave, do they? They let their children play outside in the streets, and they make all kind of nasty talk."

The "riff-raff" downstairs were screaming and cat calling out of boredom. Every time the noise got too loud, a lighted sign flashed up on the screen saying "Please Keep Quiet", but no one took the blindest bit of notice. Because he was suffering from an overdeveloped attack of decorumitis, Lionel refused to comment on the jumbie fight, and the subject was never discussed.

After the show, Lionel suggested we go to Gros Islet, a sleepy little fishing village north of the island.

We packed into a tiny mini-bus in which tuneful calypso music played. Nothing was visible outside the bus, only the occasional shimmer of a river as the moon spilled upon it.

Gros Islet, which by day is immersed in a dreamy stillness, is by night a hotbed of revelry, thick with barbecue stands selling beef, lamb, and crayfish kebabs. Soca music and laughing filled the streets as locals and tourists alike swarmed and buzzed like so many wasps. Lionel and I sat in a cool bar called the Psychedelic Garden, a Rasta club. Drug-crazed Rastafarians sat with their white girlfriends, while bug-eyed white tourists looked on.

"Why do the white ladies like Rastas so?" asked Lionel.

"Similar to the poem Mary had a little lamb. Why, Rastas like white women, you know."

"But why do they like each other?"

"I don't know. Why don't you become a Rasta, and see?"

"Me! My dear Miss Zenga, don't make me laugh!" Lionel covered his face with his hands and giggled excitedly.

Much against my will, Lionel took me to a club frequented by tourists of all nationalities, with German being the predominant sect. The music was lively calypso, but there was no "wining" for Lionel and me. Whenever we touched accidentally during the dance, Lionel would pull quickly away with a mumbled "*do* excuse me!"

"Lionel," I said after a few hours, "let's go, it's nearly four in the morning. You can stand these late nights, you're young, but I'm pushing it a bit, and I can't take the pace."

"Pushing it! How old are you?"

"Somewhere around my mid-twenties."

"Mid-twenties! Oh Lord! You *are* getting on, aren't you! Sorry to keep you out so late!"

That was, of course, the wrong answer, but a handsome twenty-one-year-old boy can be excused anything.

Twining our way through the street parties, I stopped for a second to laugh at some of the English tourists. Where the St Lucians were dancing with a natural ease and grace, the English were throwing their bodies around in frenzied convulsions. One woman almost crashed into a liquor stall in her manic glee.

"You mustn't laugh at them, Miss Zenga, it is very impolite. You see you are African English, so you dance like a West Indian."

"Funny you should say that, 'cause so do you."

"Thank you very much."

So, revelling in the joy of the give and take of compliments, we joggled back to Castries in a little mini-bus.

"How would you like to come on a tour of the island with me tomorrow, Master Lionel?" I had been unbearably lonely on the previous tour, and felt that Lionel's sweet personality was the perfect antidote to the ill-effects of the disdainful tourists.

"Oh, Miss Zenga, do you really mean it? You honestly want me to come?"

"Let us meet outside your house at seven tomorrow morning."

"Oh, Miss Zenga, I would love to thank you, but my tongue cannot express the happiness you have caused me."

The sulphur springs, south of the island, are advertised as being the world's one and only drive-in volcano. As I, Lionel, and a group of English and American tourists trooped towards it, the smell of sulphur became positively abominable. The young guide complained that after months of working there, his sense of smell had become badly impaired.

"Even when my food burn up, I sit nice and comfy an' don't smell a thing."

A whiff of Hades surrounded the whole area. Great craters of boiling bubbling hotness seethed ominously. This is where the Carib Indians performed human sacrifices in days of yore. Even to this present day, people have fallen into the craters to meet an untimely death. A more terrifying sight I ne'er have beheld.

From there we entered the gates of heaven as we approached the Diamond Falls. A waterfall tinkled in a shady bower, surrounded by fragrant red and purple flowers. There is something about a true and perfect beauty that is almost unbearable, so strong is its power.

During the lunch in a smart hotel, the tourists ganged together and refused to create a space for Lionel and myself. A middle-aged English woman rested her bag with apparent mindlessness onto her seat just as I was about to sit down, and an American, wearing the regulation

American uniform of white cap, bush shirt and shorts, told Lionel with a smile that the seat was taken. So Lionel and I sat with the guides and tour managers on another table far away from the white people, and ate a very inferior lunch to the rest of the tourists.

"I wanted to marry an Englishman once," said the guide, laughing between mouthfuls of rice and christophine.

"But I decided not to because the culture was too different."

"That wouldn't have mattered. After all, true love conquers all."

"Not in this case. I mean the man wasn't even coloured!"

"In England," I couldn't help saying, "the word coloured is considered derogatory."

"But I *am* coloured! I'm not black."

Lionel began to choke on his food from nerves, and the subject was closed.

The tour lasted all day, through picturesque fishing villages and quaint towns made up of colonial wooden houses. Schoolchildren, of Indian and African descent, stared at the tourists as though they were creatures from outer space.

Taking a stroll through a very pretty village, with a sea-front strewn with gaily painted fishing boats, a tall man dressed in a snazzy outfit asked me if I had told the other tourists about the coral.

"What about the coral?"

"That there's a 5,000 dollar fine if you take it out of the country. I have coral for sale, and I want to sell it to these people."

"But why should *I* have told them?"

"You *are* a guide, aren't you?"

"'Course not! I'm a tourist."

"What! Aren't you ashamed of yourself going on a tourist trip! A black woman like you! You should be seeing the real culture of St Lucia, not going on coaches."

"Well, my friend here *is* St Lucian, and he's going about on coaches."

The man's heavy hooded eyes surveyed us both with scorn.

"You all should be shame." And with that he was gone.

"Oh, Miss Zenga, the man is selling illegal coral. Do you think we should inform the police?"

I shook my head. Lionel dashed towards a group of friendly American tourists, and passionately warned them of the imminent dangers of buying coral. Laughing, the Americans clapped an arm about Lionel's shoulders, and informed him that never in a million years would they so much as touch the coral. Lionel breathed freely.

"How dreadful it would be if someone fell into trouble!"

That night, Lionel and I sat on his front porch drinking home-made ginger beer. His brother had taught me to cook every type of St Lucian cuisine, from sausage chow mein to salt fish and dumplings, so we were recovering from a heavy meal that I had prepared for the eleven-strong family. Fireflies winked out here and there, and the moon reflected on the water of the harbour in a silver glow. Christina's gospel music intermingled with the thumping reggae the brothers were playing downstairs. Chantelle, Lionel's three-year-old niece, struck sexy poses in front of the mirror.

"Lots of boyfriends I have, lady. That's because I so nice to look at, you know."

"Yes, Chantelle, you're beautiful."

"Monsieur! I know that!"

"What is it like in England?" asked Lionel unexpectedly.

"People sneer, they sneer at anything and everything, and they don't stop sneering until you are driven right down to the ground. Anything you care to mention, nothing is sacred, everything is to be sneered at."

"Would they sneer at me?"

"'*Course* they would!"

"Do they sneer at you?"

"Without pausing for breath."

"Oh, dear. That's not very nice. That's not very nice at all! Why do they do that?"

"Maybe the gloom of the weather has something to do with it, but it's more likely that riches breed suspicion and bad will. Anyway, I think it's better we stop this conversation here and now, because for the first time in my life I'm developing the full-blown symptoms of Englanditis."

Englanditis is a very severe disease to develop, especially if you happen to live there.

On Sunday I went to church, to purge myself of the bitter and evil feelings festering in my heart.

Catholic services are particularly moving because of all the rituals involved. The paintings in the cathedral looked all the more lovely during the service. No pews were available. Hundreds of people stood at the back of the cathedral, and spilled outside in the street. With reverently bowed heads, the worshippers dressed in solemn black, and lace veils fell over the faces of many of the women.

Just as I was thinking how religious the St Lucians are, an old man standing next to me at the back of the cathedral began to chat me up, asking me my name, age, and whether I would drink rum with him that night.

"Shhhh. Let me listen to the mass."

"But you have sexy legs!"

"How dare you!"

"Don' be shy! Let's leave this service, it's boring. Come to my place and let me give you something nice."

I pushed my way forward, and tried to resume a pious expression. Strange that the first person I had met in St Lucia to utter indignities, should do so in a church, but there you are.

Lionel's father, a grumpy old Martiniquais, allowed Lionel to take me around the island in his little fishing boat. Every day, for the next week, we sailed around the island, anchoring at idyllic secluded bays, swimming in the water amongst brightly coloured fish. Man and nature in perfect harmony.

On one occasion we anchored near a hill, and climbed up through a pathway entangled with vines, guava and banana trees (called fig trees in St Lucia).

A formidable grey building loomed before us, and I noticed that on one side of the wall, men stared out from behind impenetrable iron bars. Most were shouting in garbled screams, but one man, wearing a Martinique-style hat, gazed out at the world through the saddest eyes I have ever seen.

"Miss, Miss," yelled one of the men, "give me a dollar to buy a cake!"

"Don't give the man nothing," whispered Lionel, "this is the mental home, and these men will just take all your money if you give one of them something."

We walked around to the women's section, where women sat around in a complete mêlée. A few young boys stood outside offering them food and canned drinks.

Walking back past the men's court, a man shouted something out in patois.

"Heh, heh! Don't you speak to people like me, Antoinette?" I turned to him, and saw a woebegone man dressed in a soiled white suit.

"Of course I speak to you."

"Français?"

"No, Anglais."

"No, no, you're French. You Antoinette!"

I began to walk away, as the man stretched his arms out through the iron grid, shouting out something in patois in a hoarse voice, and continued shouting until we were far away down the winding lane.

"What did he say, Lionel?"

"He say you're his widowed wife from Pointe-à-Pitre, Guadeloupe."

"His widow." I tingled all over.

"Most of the inmates have lived in England for a long time and the one who shouted at you is a very intelligent man who used to work in Buckingham Palace. But now his mind is shot away."

England, with its hollow promises of riches and happiness must very easily drive outsiders to madness.

The day before I left, Lionel's sister-in-law's aunt took sick, leaving no one to run the store for the day. I offered to do so, after hearing that all it involved was making sandwiches, and selling bottles of beer and tins of food. The shop was a small shack standing half-way up a hill overlooking the fishermen's cottages by the harbour.

World-weary fishermen came in and stood by the counter drinking beer and smoking. Whenever someone entered the shop who looked especially poor, I would buy him drinks and food, and so the long day wore on. Much of my time was spent sitting on a rock in the shade, outside the shop, staring into space and feeling very Caribbean. Occasionally I played cards with the men, losing money at an alarming rate, on a game called "Chase the Spotted Lady". I never grew to understand the rules. The gist of the game seemed to be, I put a lot of money down, the men put a few cards down, then my money was taken up and pocketed equally between the men. A highly unnerving game which I hope never to play again.

On our last night together, Lionel and I went out to some of the local bars for a goodbye drink.

It had occurred to me that although I had been in the Caribbean for a number of weeks, I had not drunk nearly enough rum. As the old song goes:

> Rum more rum rum, for a festival.
> Rum for a wedding or a funeral.
> Rum with your friends, doesn't matter who,
> Rum with your foes – have yourself a-two.

I was endeavouring to teach Lionel this merry ditty as we walked the long road to a wooden bar in an area called Fulasha.

Lionel ordered the drinks, while I sat at a table stroking a fluffy tabby cat, who purred gently on my lap.

Lionel joined me a few minutes later with a smug smile upon his face.

"Here you are, Miss, a nice bottle of whisky to set you up and please your soul before you fly off to this Trinidad place Lionel was telling me about," said the barman, setting the bottle and glasses upon the table.

"Whisky!"

"Eh heh! Lionel knew you'd be pleased."

It's times like this when you wish you were a child again, so you can throw an enormous tantrum and not be thought of as mad.

"But Lionel," I muttered in a strangled whisper, "you *know* I wanted rum."

Lionel smirked. "Yes, but I thought that you being so highbrow would prefer whisky. Isn't it what all the highbrow people drink?"

I took a sip, instantly pacified. No one has ever called me highbrow before, and I rather enjoyed the experience.

Two men sitting at the next table struck up conversation, and soon Lionel was telling them in impassioned patois about his cat, Meg. The barman replied that he treasures the love of a good cat above all else.

"'' nurse the cat from kittenhood to womanhood, and she never played me false yet!"

Soon everyone in the bar was relating stories of cats they had known and loved, and one man even took the floor, and gave a powerful and moving demonstration of how his cat played with his daughter's rag doll in the gloaming.

"I prefer dogs," I said innocently, trying to muscle in on the conversation. The barman froze. The two men sitting at the next table blinked unbelievingly. Lionel giggled nervously. Even the tabby on my lap stopped purring. A split second later the barman continued his tale of how he found his cat abandoned by the beach, and my unfortunate remark was indulgently swept aside.

As I watched them waving their arms about, animatedly topping the next person's cat story, I wondered what I would think they were talking about if I could not hear them. In England the subject would most certainly be sport. In Jamaica, such exuberance of speech could only mean gossip of the woman down the road. In Martinique, such sprightly, uproarious conversation would probably be about mass murders or something like that, but, in soft, dreamlike St Lucia, it was cats. A great warmth for the country surged within my breast. How sweet life would be if I could live here until the end of my days. At one point I almost felt like ensuring my future in St Lucia by asking

Lionel to marry me, but I had an awful feeling that, unlike Halbert, he might accept!

"I sell souvenirs, Miss. Sit there for a while and I will bring them out to you," said the barman, moving swiftly into a back room. He emerged a few minutes later holding a tray on which sat an array of birds made out of coconut shells. They were prettily crafted, with feathers cleverly done out of coconut fur.

"Yes, they're very beautiful. Did you make them?"

"I did."

"Good grief, you're a genius! Unfortunately I haven't got any money to buy them with."

"That's no problem. Take whatever you want, and send the money when you reach Trinidad."

Such blind trust! If too many tourists come to St Lucia and betray that trust, as they obviously will, then men with honest hearts such as the barman's will become tragically corrupted.

I took three of the birds, wrote down the man's address, and with a shake of the hand, Lionel and I departed.

On the way back, Lionel picked a long brown pod from a tree and began to shake it, producing a rhythmical beat sounding rather like a maracas.

"It call a shack-shack. When we were kids we used to have shack-shack bands, and you would have love to hear some of the tunes we made."

The moon cast a silver glow upon his sweet, childlike face. This was the last time I would see dear Lionel, who had proved a godsend to me. I fought back the tears.

Lionel made me a gift of the shack-shack, and, in return, I gave him two of the coconut birds, and, planting a modest kiss on my cheek, he wove his way up through the trees to his little green cottage in the woods.

None of the original members of the black population had come to St Lucia by choice, and yet, out of slavery, a very high, cultured civilisation has arisen. The art in the churches, the music and dancing, and the gentle, affectionate lifestyle of the people combine to make up one of the most blissful societies on earth.

The next morning, I left the spam with jam and butter on top untouched. My plane left early in the morning, and the tears in my throat made swallowing too difficult an action to perform.

When the taxi finally arrived, I threw in my luggage, and away we clattered down the steep hill.

Down at the bottom of the hill, sitting beneath a flourishing almond tree, was Lionel, waving frantically as our taxi swung round the corner and along the dusty road.

Goodbye, St Lucia, ethereal St Lucia with your calming serenity and your kind, if somewhat prissy people. St Lucia, I shall cherish every memory of you with a deep tenderness, for you are truly the queen of the West Indies.

Bacchanal Aunties
TRINIDAD

Aunty Sweets, with whom I was to stay in Trinidad, had told me but three things about her country. One was that tarantulas live in bananas, and jump out at you just as you are about to peel them, another was that vampire bats make their home in the cinemas, sucking your blood during the film, and the third pearl of wisdom was that most houses are haunted by a Largabless, a vampiress, who floats through windows attacking you while you sleep. You can always tell a Largabless, she told me, because her feet face the wrong way, so she cannot be mistaken for a common or garden vampire. Aunty Sweets told me all these things when I was six years old, and I had not seen her since. For ever afterwards I have nurtured a recondite fear of Trinidad; a fear that was only slightly dispelled by the chatter of a good natured Englishman on the plane, who informed me that Trinidad was his second home, and is, in his words, "a most marvellous country".

The first stop en route was brown old Barbados, looking arid and scrubby from the air. St Vincent, our next stop, was far more intriguing. Mysterious hills stood wreathed in mist, and the few houses that could be seen from an aerial view were pleasantly old-fashioned, if rather sad and haunted.

"You should have stayed here," the hills of St Vincent seemed to whisper to me, "but you have missed your chance."

Grenada, our last stop before Trinidad, was a most pathetic spectacle, from the airport at least. American fighter planes crowded onto the hot tarmac. How evil they looked, with their pointed noses and sharp angles, so obviously designed for death.

And then we flew over a massive island, hazy with steam which hung fog-like over the dense rain forests. Concrete buildings gleamed grey and off-white in the glow of the midday sun. Miniature cars wove in and out of the clusters of houses. This was Trinidad, my last stop, home of Aunty Sweets.

Although we are not related by blood, Aunty Sweets had been a friend of our family's for years before I was even born. The last visit she made to England was twenty years ago, when she came to attend the wedding of her younger brother. She had stayed with us in the Sussex village where we lived, and I can remember her spending all her time plaiting the hair of myself and my sisters. A burning pain still tingles around my scalp whenever I so much as think about that agonising coiffure. While my head was tightly gripped between her knees, strands of hair were pulled and twisted by ruthless fingers. Morbid though the medieval imagination may have been, it is curious to note that none of their tortures could rival the horrors of "hair plaiting by Aunty Sweets".

A blanket of sweat enveloped my entire body as soon as I stepped off the plane. Everything seemed to sag. The cloth of my dress drooped, my hair sulked, and even the straw hat upon my head wilted, as if it were telling me that it could not bear the heat. It was early March, and Trinidad was humid to an extreme. Would I be able to breathe this moist air for the two-week stay?

By the time I reached the immigration official's desk, I felt thoroughly filleted.

"Welcome to Trinidad. Welcome to Trinidad. Welcome to Trinidad," the airport official was repeating mechanically to the other tourists as they filtered through the foreign section.

"Welcome home," he said to me.

"Trinidad," I said, "is not where I'm from."

"Then you are a tourist?"

"I am."

"Well, in that case, welcome home, tourist miss."

I'm not going to understand Trinidad, I thought on hearing that remark. Some countries you go to, and you only have to walk through the customs and you say to yourself, 'a-ha, I can understand this place,' but other places, like the Dominican Republic and Trinidad, baffle the brain and befuddle the soul.

By the time I had stepped out of the airport, my mind was so bunged up by the sticky atmosphere, I could hardly remember which country I was in, or how I came to be there. All I knew was that I must get a taxi to Aunty Sweets', and when I got to Aunty Sweets' I must lie down in a darkened room with something cold on my forehead.

The taxi, a long blue American car, took us past endless fields of sugar-cane. The taxi driver was the type I was so familiar with in London. He did not stop talking. In his lilting voice he told me about every Englishman and American person who had ever graced the seats of his cab.

". . . and there was this one coloured girl from Miami, she look jus' like you" – he gave me a sidelong glance – "only she slim" – he looked me full in the face – "and pretty."

My clothes stuck uncomfortably to my skin.

On the one side of the wide street loomed dark ominous mountains. On the other stood fruit stands, bedecked with tinsel and fairy lights, selling paw paws, swollen melons, bananas and tangerines. Tired Indians sat behind the stalls, waiting, waiting, forever waiting.

There's no getting around it. Port of Spain is no oil painting. At first the indescribable ugliness of the concrete seems but a mirage, then, driving deeper into the heart of the capital, the hideousness becomes all too real, shimmering slightly in the heat. Yet the vibrancy and *joie de vivre* of the population more than compensates for the architectural failings.

Whereas the St Lucians walk in slow motion rather like astronauts, the Trinidadians stride with bustling step, shoulders back, chests way out. Calypso music is everywhere, sweet voices and complicated rhythms blaring from cars and houses. The men and women dress with a sharpness unmatched by the other islanders, and many of the Indian women wear make-up, the amount of which only their Dominican sisters could equal.

Reaching downtown Port of Spain, we got stuck in a fumy traffic jam. Drab hovels thick with filth stood before smart office blocks. A pack of motley pooches stood upon a dustbin and tipped it over, scattering the fetid contents upon a naked toddler who was lying asleep in the sun. With a sudden jerk we lunged forward, spasmodically moving onwards until we came to a leafy suburb just outside Port of Spain.

We stopped by an elegant suburban house with a wrought-iron gate and gleaming white pillars.

"I not going inside with your luggage, chile, 'cause there going to be dog in a house like that, and I very much afraid."

I took out my bags and stood by the locked gate, not quite knowing what to do.

"That you, chile?" An old lady poked her head through the bars on the window and pursed her lips at me.

"Aunty Sweets? Is it really you?"

"Stop your nonsense, now girl. 'Course it me. Who you think it is. Ambrose! Ambrose! Come nah! Let the woman in the house, nah. She look sick."

The main door swung open, and a skinny, hollow, haunted-looking young man with sunken cheeks and a plaintive countenance appeared, and walked towards me.

"Seventy dollar," whispered the taxi driver, his eyes darting towards the young man. I paid up the equivalent of nine pounds, startled at the deftness at which the driver sprang into his car, and whizzed down the road.

"Hello, Zenga. It good to see you. My name is Ambrose, Aunty Sweets' nephew."

"Then you and I are cousins."

Ambrose smiled a wan smile, and carried my luggage into the house.

The living-room which we had walked into was plush to a dizzy extreme. Shag pile red carpets with Turkish rugs glared out in a multitude of heady colours. Divans set at angles to one another were furbished in thick velvet, and all around the room were wooden tables and what-nots covered in twirly bits and pieces. Every inch of the walls was covered with paintings and African carvings.

An Indian man on the television, wearing a white dhoti and a thick pair of glasses, was talking at full blast about the recession in oil prices. The radio blared David Rudder, Trinidad's most honoured calypsonian's hit, "Bacchanal Woman". The noise was so all-invading it was impossible to hear what was being thought.

Two old ladies sat on the divan. One was smiling pleasantly at me, and the other sucked in her cheeks and threw me a highly disapproving glare. Which one was Aunty Sweets? The cross one spoke.

"I am, chile. Well, you no going to kiss Aunty?"

"Aunty Sweets! How wonderful to see you! Thank you ever so much for letting me stay with you, I really don't know what I would do without you!"

"Eh ehh! What trouble is this? Haven't change, have you, with all your damn foolishness, ay yi yi yi yi! Woooo! Heh heeeh!" and she threw back her head and emitted a shrill cackle that ended in a loud belch.

"Now come into your room, it jus' there, so. Let me carry your bags."

"Oh no, Aunty Sweets, I'll carry them."

Slap! A horny hand whacked my arm.

"I thought I tell you not to mamaguy me! Now let me carry de damn tings into your room, chile, and shut up de nise."

I smiled helplessly at the other old lady, who grinned back shyly.

"You met me cousin Maudy? Maudy, this is em – er – the niece I tell you about who staying for a good long while."

"How do," said Maudy, ducking her head and giggling, "your hat is very pretty."

"What you mean her hat pretty! Don't put more conceit into the chile than she already have! Now come into your room and unpack de ting."

I followed the swaying figure of Aunty Sweets into a cosy bedroom, furnished with dark mahogany furniture, and a lavish dressing table carved from Congolese teak.

"Now unpack an' make yourself very much at home."

"Aunty Sweets, I have a few things for you."

"Pass dem to me, nah."

"Some petticoats, a nightie, and a pair of shoes." The shoes I had bought in London, and I was especially proud of them.

Aunty Sweets picked up the articles and gave me a vinegary smile.

"This all you got? The petticoats are OK, the nightie is far too lacey for an old lady like me, and the shoes – ow! Dey don' fit me foot one small bit! What else you got?"

"A bird made from coconut shells."

I parted sorrowfully with the bird. It had been a special present for my brother-in-law.

"A bird. Yes, dat alright. OK, unpack den come an' eat up the food.

Whoops!" and she belched so loudly that if I had not witnessed with my own eyes the source of the abominable noise, I would have thought I was hearing a lion's roar.

Ten minutes later I was seated at the table eating sloppy beef curry with rice and christophines. Ambrose, having cooked the lunch, had gone off to work.

"He work hard, you know. From six-thirty till nine at night de chile work an' work. In the hospital in de morning, an' de restaurant at night."

"De restaurant at night," repeated Maudy.

"Never does he stop. De chile power-packed!"

"Power-packed!"

The food was very spicy compared with the blander fare of the other islands.

Maudy slobbered over her meal, picking at the bones with her toothless gums, and hawking the gristle back on the plate. I looked away discreetly.

"So how your family doing? Heh heeh! I remember your uncle, that fat ugly one! What a man he was, an' how he could talk. That man put shit in your mouth, call it sugar and expec' you to swallow it! African men are crazy."

"I happen to be particularly fond of my uncle."

"What! That damn ignorant nigger-man? Don' look so shock up, sweetheart. I'm not saying that *you're* a nigger. You're a negro, an' that's another different ting. A negro is just part of a race, but your uncle, now he was a nigger, you understand me nah, chile. An' what a dutty nigger bwai he was."

"Aunty Sweets. I hate the term negro, and I detest the word nigger, so please don't use them."

Aunty Sweets threw back her head and laughed so loudly she began to choke on her curry.

"Eh heeh! Aye yi yi! What damn trouble is this! You hear de chile, Maudy! Heh heeeh! She say she *detest* the word negro. So what you tink you are? You one of those bake niggers who tink dey white?"

"Who tink dey white!" repeated Maudy.

"No, I would call myself black."

"Black! Wooooo! You a red skin negro, so don't try to pretend otherwise. You as bad as my cousin. He marry a Indian woman who tink she sweeter than honey an' better than money jus' because she got long straight hair and custard-coloured skin. So now my cousin tink he sweet because he married the Indian girl. What they don' know is that she just a damn meddlesome Coolie bitch."

"Coolie bitch," Maudy chuckled.

"Please stop talking like that!"

"Heh heeh! You mad – heh! – Wait! – Listen! Is a bacchanal going on outside. Come, sweetheart, quick! Let we go pick pigeon peas from de tree an' see what going on."

Grabbing me by the hand, Aunty Sweets pulled me outside into the garden. A young woman across the road was shouting at a man who looked like her father. Because of the garden's thick foliage, it was impossible to see them clearly, but the curses came over loud and clear. Aunty Sweets stood on tiptoe to watch the rumpus, perfunctorily picking pigeon peas with tense fingers.

"See the mad bitch, how she shout and cuss up! De girl has no class and no training. She behave like that ever since she a child. If I her mother, I'd whip her sore. There again, the father jus' as bad. Always trying to sex every woman he see. De whole family useless." Just then she caught the eye of the young woman who was storming down the road. "Hello, darlin'. Lovely to see you. What a nice surprise! How you doing? How's your daddy? Long time since he call on we."

"Afternoon, Mrs Foster. You all right?"

"I fine, sweetheart!"

The girl stomped sullenly down the road.

"Meddlesome slut! See how she spy on we! The woman suffering from mucho eyetis."

"From what?"

"She always spying in other people business, and making trouble. What she should know is trouble make monkey eat pepper."

I sauntered around the garden, admiring the different fruits and vegetables which hung from the trees, pulling off here a mango, there a lime.

"Well, now you out here, pick de pigeon peas for me, chile."

"How do I do that?" My mind was still swimming from the heat, the travelling, and the culture shock. After St Lucia where people left the room when they wanted to cough, Aunty Sweets' ripe expressions came as somewhat of a jar.

"Jus' pick everything from de tree. Everything – tout bagai."

"Tout bagai! That's Creole."

"Stop your foolishness an' pick de damn ting, chile. Creole me ass."

My whole body was drenched in sweat as I picked the pigeon peas from the tree. My arms ached as I reached up to tug the more stubborn green peas from the top branches. As the merciless sun beat down upon me, I wondered what it must have been like to be a slave, working in this fashion from morn till night, with only a bowl of maize flour at noontime for sustenance. A slave's life must have been too horrific for the modern mind to imagine. After a while, with every muscle in my body racked with pain, I gathered up the peas and took them into the house.

Aunty Sweets was eating an Indian confection called barfi. The telly and the radio were still on full blast, producing an ear-splitting din. Maudy, sitting on a commode, smiled pleasantly at me.

"See how she come," she remarked to Aunty Sweets. Aunty Sweets looked me up and down and said, "Well, don' jus' stand there waiting like a damn fool. Go into the kitchen an' peel de tings."

"Yes, Aunty Sweets."

"An' when you finish peeling them, come back in here an' rub my leg with methylated spirits, then Maudy need her hair cane row."

"But Aunty Sweets, I'd like to go out and see Port of Spain."

"Is why you want to go there?"

"Just to look."

"Look at what?"

"People, shops, roads, things like that."

Aunty Sweets gaped at me as if I were a rare species of animal.

"Port of Spain much too dangerous for a young woman to go to alone. You want to go there, you go with me, you hear me, chile."

"But I —"

"I say you don' go there alone! De gate is lock up, an' only I have de key, so no one goes anywhere I don't feel they have any business to be, so if I were you, I'd go back into that kitchen, shell de peas, come back in here, rub up me leg with methylated spirits, and cane row Maudy's blasted hair before I get vex!"

"Yes, Aunty Sweets."

O-oh, I thought, as I shelled the peas in an off-hand manner. I'm a prisoner here, a bird locked in a gilded cage. My heart and temples began to throb.

For the first five days I did nothing at all save watch American series on the telly, whilst listening to the radio. Oh, how I yearned to smash that telly, so strong was my hatred for it. Every time I mentioned going out somewhere, Aunty Sweets would say, "Yes, yes, in a minute. Jus' let me fix a few ting up firs'," and she would settle down to watching that benighted television.

In the mornings, prayers would last for over an hour. After long

Bible readings, Aunty Sweets threw water into the yard to ward off any evil spirits, a West African practice often performed by my father. Another West African trait kept up by Aunty Sweets was her method of cooking very fiery food. A table-spoon of brown sugar was burnt into the fat before adding the meat, and very delicious it was too. During the long days locked into the house, I learnt to cook *rôti*, *balpawri*, pigs' tails in calalloo and myriad other Caribbean and Indian delicacies. But I was frustrated. Maybe I would never get to see Trinidad, and my trip was fast approaching its end.

Whenever I expressed a wish to go out, I would be told it was "too hot", "too dangerous", or "why do you want to go out? Just to see a lot of old niggers in a lot of old houses!" So I sat on the rocking chair in the porch, trying to ignore the telly and radio; wishing and wishing but never quite sure what it was I was wishing for.

Ambrose, the nephew came home tired and wan each evening. After washing the clothes, cleaning the kitchen, massaging Aunty Sweets' shoulders, and making everyone very sweet cups of tea, he would collapse in front of the telly and doze off. Very subtly, while all the family members slept, I would turn the telly off, but inevitably, Aunty Sweets' eyes would snap open, and, with a lot of hoo-hah she would demand that the sound was once again turned up to top volume.

Conversation with Ambrose was a difficult process, because he could hardly understand a word I said, goodness knows why, because the Trinidad accent is not too far away from standard English. While Aunty Sweets slept, I would hint very strongly to him that I would like to be taken out. Every night it was the same, and the ritualistic conversation went as follows:

ME: Er Ambrose – do you know of any night clubs?

AMBROSE: Wha'?

ME: (repeat of above.)

AMBROSE: Wha'?

ME: (Repeat of above.)

AMBROSE: I don't understand.

ME: Are there any night clubs round here that I could go to?

AMBROSE: Wha'?

And so it would continue, deep into the night, until one of us decided to go to bed.

One hot morning, when we had finished our cheese and coconut bread, I asked Aunty Sweets, as usual, if she could take me into town. It was a hollow question, asked without much meaning or feeling. In fact I had grown to ask her more from habit than anything else; but this fine morning, she belched powerfully, spat into her plate, and said,

"Lawd, chile. You jus' remine me. I got to go to bank today. Come, let's go."

"Let's go," said Maudy.

"Oh hoh no, Maudy. Not you. You too much damn trouble. Jus' me an' Miss Whaternem is going. You stay here, dear heart."

I felt dizzy with heady excitement. An excitement bred from the knowledge that you are leaving a house of a thousand noises, and exploring deep into the heart of a thronging capital city.

Aunty Sweets took an unbearably long time getting ready. Her hair needed to be unplaited and combed, her dress pressed, and Maudy's meal had to be cooked and laid out on a brass tray. Aunty Sweets may have had a tongue of fire, but her heart was of pure gold. Her life was dedicated to the upkeep of Maudy's every comfort.

The day was cloudy and muggy. Everyone who passed us in the leafy street inquired after the health of Aunty Sweets, and wished us both a civil good day. The bus took a very long time to arrive, but Aunty Sweets filled in the time by gossiping about every acquaintance who walked by, telling me who had said what to whom, and why.

When we finally reached Port of Spain we were both exhausted.

"Let's go somewhere for a drink, Aunty Sweets."

"Stop your nonsense, chile. Why waste your money on a drink when there's perfectly good water at home. We not going to be here for long, you know."

The Port of Spainians are a very mixed people, from raggedy to flashy, with many beggars trying their luck on rich Indian ladies who swanned past them, without so much as a second glance. Black Muslims, wearing long white robes and skull-caps, sold perfumed oils and jewellery in winding alleyways, and small market stalls were set up by pitifully empty shops. A sickening stench of incense curled its way around many of the stalls, where fat Indian men hawked for trade. Indian music seeped from narrow passageways. On many of the stalls, old men were selling replicas of Hanuman, the Hindu Monkey God, and on these stalls would be a red flag, flying in honour of the god. A pundit behind one stall glared malevolently at me. Wearing only a dhoti to cover his modesty, his forehead, his arms and throat displayed his caste marks.

The ugliness of Port of Spain remains indescribable. Only those who have taken a stroll underneath the Hammersmith flyover on a hot summer's day could picture in their minds the concrete squalor of the town. Only one square in the centre of the capital looked vaguely reasonable, with a Regency cathedral in gothic style overlooking a small park.

That being said, the town had much charm and vibrancy, due to the purposeful drive of the inhabitants.

Aunty Sweets headed straight towards an imposing bank, shopping bag held like a club, looking neither right nor left.

A dirty cluster of wooden huts, just in front of the bank, seemed to sell the most interesting collection of saris, jewellery and ornaments.

"Hi," said a tall, good-looking man, stepping out from behind one of the sheds.

"He-*llo*," I replied, stopping in my tracks.

A sharp slap stung my wrist.

"Keep your eyes away from the mens!" shrieked Aunty Sweets.

I turned back to the man with an embarrassed titter, and WHAM, another slap caught me square on the back of the head.

"You keep your eyes on the road straight in front of you, or you get more licks and slaps from me, chile!"

A chorus of laughter resounded from behind my back, as the world seemed to swim with humiliation.

"Dat's right, girlio! You do what your Mama tell you!"

"Yey, Mama, show your daughter some manners, heh heh!"

Had she been anybody else than Aunty Sweets, I would have given her a stern piece of my mind, but Aunty Sweets inspires naught but cowardice.

The bank was crowded with people on every level of the social scale.

Trinidad, so rich in the seventies from the oil boom, is now virtually impoverished due to the slump in oil prices. Ten years ago, I was told that peasants who had previously lived off the land, were driving cars, selling up their farms, and moving into the big city. Now, the people who struck rich on oil are all but destitute.

"You see, chile, I got to get a lotta money from de bank to pay for the mortgage of me niece and nephews in New York. Eversince I lef' off being the matron of de hospital, I getta nice lotta money, hey!" and Aunty Sweets scratched her belly and laughed. The queuers waiting to be served turned to smile and exchange pleasantries. One young woman remarked upon the striking resemblance between myself and Aunty Sweets.

"In looks, maybe, but not in temperament. This here girl's lazy and spoilt."

"Aunty Sweets, please!"

"It true, isn't it! Is why your mother pamper you so?"

The young woman smiled indulgently. I shuffled my feet and focused my eyes on the handsome young Indian bank clerk.

"See how she like de mens. What would *you* do with a niece like that?"

The young woman pondered for a while. "I tink I'd keep she lock up."

"Eh heeh! Wise woman. Dat jus' what I doing! Woooo!"

Pretending not to have heard, I cheered myself up by plotting the perfect murder. The only problem in my mind was whether to commit it this minute, or when I reached home.

On the way back to Aunty Sweets', we passed the most sumptuous houses overlooking the Savanah. Houses that made the palaces of Haiti's Pétionville look like shacks. Fabulous in their splendour, the mansions were being patrolled by armed guards, dressed in austere uniform.

"These the houses of the Indians and Chinaman. Only one Chinaman alone live in that great big one there. Terrible, isn't it? The damn Chinaman not even there half de time 'cause he away on holiday."

If the owner himself was away, the house was by no means neglected. Savage dogs, and a bevy of industrious staff milled about in the courtyard.

"Where do these people get all their money from?"

"How you spec me to know dat? Stealing I suppose."

No one who climbed onto the large bus escaped Aunty Sweets' needle sharp tongue.

"See de woman dere! Hey! Look at de wig she wear. Look like de top of a dead palm tree. An' see de Indian man face! Ha! Remin' me of de ting dat come out from your throat early in the morning. Oi yoi yoi! An' what about de girl's shoes. Look! Look! Hat like a queen but shoes like a beggar woman, wooo!"

I looked out of the window, ignoring the comments; comments made all the more pathetic because all the passengers greeted Aunty Sweets and myself after they had boarded the bus.

The radio and the telly were switched on at top blast as soon as we reached home, and there was nowhere to escape it. Holes were carved prettily into the walls, so the abysmal racket could be heard in every room. Occasionally Trinidad Bill, David Rudder, Sparrow, or another one of my favourite calypsonians would blast from the radio, but they would inevitably be drowned out by the noise of guns or screaming from the TV. So I sat in the living-room, locked inside the house, hypnotised by the violent images on the screen, unable, even, to dream.

Next morning, Aunty Sweets shook me vigorously from a sweet sleep.

"Shift you self, chile. You 'fraid of what happen las' night?"

"What happened?"

"You don't hear it?"

"What?"

"The earthquake."

"You're joking!"

"The whole house shook, cups and plates smash, all the burglar alarms went off at once, and every dog in the yard went mad barking their throats out, an' you tell me I joke. Is why it didn't wake you up?"

'Because,' I said to myself, 'whatever happened last night was probably a blinking sight quieter than the normal household din.' But I didn't say anything. Instead I asked the usual, "Can I go out today?"

"I'll take you out another day, dear heart."

So I sat inside for the whole hot day, eating *rôtis* and drinking Guinness, wondering what it was I had done so wrong in my past life.

Ambrose returned home unexpectedly early that night. As soon as his skeletal figure jangled through the door, I asked him if he could take me out in his car to buy a newspaper. Newspapers were the one English commodity I missed. In fact I *yearned* for newspapers. What was going on in England was anyone's guess. Was Margaret Thatcher still Prime Minister? Had the Queen abdicated? Were there earthquakes in London as well as in Port of Spain?

"Aunty Sweets," whispered Ambrose timidly, "she say she want to go buy a newspaper."

"Is what you want a newspaper for, dear heart?"

"To read," I said through clenched teeth.

Aunty Sweets emerged from the kitchen, her hands sticky with dough.

"How you going to get to the shop?"

"Is it all right if Ambrose drives me?"

Ambrose quivered beneath her gaze.

"What you mean, (in a high, affected voice) 'is it alright if Ambrose drives me!' Woi! Ambrose got his own mind, isn't it! Is why you don't ask Ambrose. After all, you're only going to get a paper, you won't be more than five minutes – will you?"

"No, of course not, Aunty Sweets."

"Good, then get your backsides away from my door, and buy me some dinner mints on de way back."

Ambrose and I walked sombrely from the house after Aunty Sweets had clanked open the gate, and relocked it with one of a hefty bunch of keys.

As soon as Ambrose began to drive away, I begged him to take me dancing.

"Dancing? How you mean, dancing?"

"You know, like – dancing."

"But where do you want to go?"

"To a place where people dance."

"Is it?"

"It is."

"But I don't really know of any sort of place like that – wait a minute – a friend from the hospital where I work, a nurse, she like to go out to that sort of place. Maybe you could meet her, and go somewhere together."

"Oh Ambrose, I would be your friend for life if you introduced me to her. Already I think of you as my favourite cousin. Where does she live?"

"Ooooh, a long way off. It in a town called Arima."

"Arima! What a lovely name. I vow and swear that if ever I give birth to a girl, I shall call her Arima, and I shall tell her, in years to come, that she was so named because a wonderful cousin of mine drove me there, one hot night in Trinidad."

"Wha'?"

"You're driving me to Arima to see your friend."

"Am I?"

"Of course."

"When?"

"Now."

"But Aunty Sweets said that we mustn't take a long time."

"No she didn't. She said that we can take as long as we like, all night if we want to. Don't you remember?"

"We-e-ell."

"So mek we gwaan, as they say in good old Jamaica."

"Well if you sure that Aunty Sweets say we can . . ."

On the way to the alluring Arima, we drove past shimmering white Hindu temples, wreathed with pillars and delicate lace fretwork. Like a prisoner seeing sunlight for the first time in thirty years, I could hardly contain my excitement at being let out.

"There the Mall. It's a really nice shopping centre."

"Well, what are you waiting for? Let's go in and have a look round."

"But Aunty Sweets said –"

"Aunty Sweets has gone out for the evening. She said she won't be back till five in the morning."

I threw caution to the winds. *Che sarà sarà* was the order of the night.

Inside the Mall were the costumes of last month's carnival. Looking at their exquisite loveliness was like being in Aladdin's cave. Every stitch, every sequin was sewn with perfect skill and care. They were quite unbelievable in their intricacy.

Ambrose cheered up at the sight of the costumes, and began to tell me how much he enjoyed watching the carnival on TV.

"I was working all through it, so I couldn't go."

The Trinidadian countryside is very scary in the dark. The mountains are just too huge, and the mangrove swamps, thick with mist, present a terrifying spectacle in the moonlight. Roots as high as a man twist in eerie shapes above the ground. The mangrove trees guard the water they rest by, casting uncanny shadows.

The air became unbearably dense and sticky, and even with the car windows wide open, the stuffiness was inescapable. Behind us, Port of Spain was soon reduced to a collection of glowing lights.

After we had driven a good long way, we came to a squalid collection of hovels, clumped together on the side of the street.

"See the ghettos there." Ambrose turned quickly away from them, sighing at the forlorn spectacle they presented.

All of a sudden we found ourselves in a bright, flashy town populated by very poor Indians. Rum bars, loud Hindu and calypso music, and twinkly lights made up a world of vivid decadence. The pavements were packed with people drinking coconut water from cumbersome jelly coconuts, parading up and down in gangs. Barefoot children ran in and out of the bars, screaming and playing raucous games, rolling and tumbling in the dust. Derelict old Muslim men and women squatted on their haunches, laughing over something, their blackened teeth glinting in the red and green flashing lights. El Dorado, the town was called, the romantic lost city of gold.

Our next port of call was a town called Aruka. Some would say that a town with so fanciful a name had no business to be so dull and quiet, but such is life. Only a church, set outside the town, provided some source of intrigue. Loud drummings and harmonised songs boomed from the wooden building, shattering the silence of the sultry night. This was a Shango church, a church whose ceremonies combine the rituals of many West African religions with Christianity. Worshippers jerked their bodies convulsively; maybe they were possessed by one of the twelve obas who attend the supreme god Shango. From the small glimpse I caught of the church (Ambrose refused to allow me inside), I could see that the worshippers were wearing white robes, with coloured chains around their necks and waists.

"Jus' a lot of stupidness in a place like that. We stopping in Aruka for a while, if you don' mind, cause I got a feeling that my friend will be stopping at her boyfriend's for the evening. Her boyfriend live in this house here."

That house there was a ghostly mansion set well back in a sprawling, tangly garden. Ambrose stopped his car, and marched briskly through the tendrils of tropical weeds. Over the door of the heavily built house was a sooty web measuring over two feet across where IT must live. Luckily the monster was not at home.

A dreamy Hindu man opened the door a crack, and seeing Ambrose's familiar face, welcomed us in with a yawn.

"Ambrose, you all right? Dipak in de sitting room, man, watching Americans killing one another on de blasted TV."

"Thanks, Mr Puri. Rhada here?"

The old man's eyes glinted wickedly.

"Ah yes, she here. Sitting on me son's lap. Ha ha ha!"

"This me cousin, Zenga."

"Zenga, man. Nice to meet you. You all right?"

"Fine, thank you, and you?"

"Hey, what! The girl a foreigner! Eh eh! Well, come in and make yourself at home, you like *rôti* and breadfruit?"

"Yes please."

Ambrose and I walked slowly through the old colonial house. Dusty books were everywhere: in the passageways and the kitchen, sitting in rows on makeshift shelves in every room. Many of the books were Hindu texts, but most were French, Russian, and English literature. When we finally arrived in the living room, we found a strikingly handsome couple seated on a Persian divan. The girl was sprawled half over the young man, gazing up into his face like a passion flower turning to the moon. The young man sat limply watching the telly, having unhinged his lower jaw.

When she saw us, the girl flew from her seat like a bird, and shook our hands fervently.

"Ambrose, man. How good to see you! This your cousin you were telling us about! Hello, hello. My name's Rhada, an' this is my fiancé, Dipak."

Dipak flicked his eyes away from the TV for a split second, then made an incomprehensible sound. It may have been "hello" but it sounded more like, "please go".

Rhada brushed back her long black hair, and chatted pleasantly to us, offering us sherbet water and Portugals, a very sweet form of orange.

"Here, have some ladoons as well, it's an Indian sweet, whoops! Make sure it doesn't crumble all over your frock. Well, Ambrose, let's take your cousin out tonight. First we'll go for a Chinese meal, then we'll go to a disco. I *love* discos. Dancing is my greatest pleasure in life, isn't it, Dipak?"

Dipak delicately picked his nose.

"Dipak adores dancing too. So, let's get ready. Zenga, what are you wearing? Those pants? That all right, man. I'll jus' keep on my jeans. Dipak, man, come, let's go."

"Naw."

"What? How you mean, no!" Rhada giggled flirtatiously and minced over to his seat.

"Come, darlin'. Please come along."

"Can't you see I watching TV, man."

"Oh *please* come, dear heart."

"Naw. I watching TV."

Rhada's eyes filled with tears.

"Dipak," I said sternly, "come along now."

Without dragging his eyes from the TV screen until the last moment, Dipak walked wordlessly from the room.

"Goodbye, Mr Puri!" we chorused as we left the house. Mr Puri ran from the kitchen holding a greying manuscript, and shook our hands warmly.

"Now you make sure you look after me son. Heh heeh!" Rhada's face flushed with pleasure.

"Oh, Papa, you know I always do that."

And, after running through the overgrown garden, we were in the car, and driving off into the night. Trinidad insect noises are so loud as to be positively deafening. Fireflies shone in the headlamps. Rhada kept up a ceaseless stream of chatter. I wanted to ask her why she had a Welsh accent, but somehow the question seemed too personal. If she had substituted the word "boyo" for "man" I would have readily believed her to have arrived hot foot from Holyhead.

Illuminated mosques and temples flashed past us.

"Aren't they beautiful? Isn't Trinidad a lovely place?" gushed Rhada.

We all agreed; all, that is, except Dipak, who sat bolt upright in the back of the car, looking neither right nor left.

"Zenga," asked Ambrose, "would you like some bananas?"

"No," I whispered quietly, hoping Dipak and Rhada could not hear me, "because they have spiders in the bananas here."

"They don't have spiders in the bananas in Trinidad. Why, do they have spiders in the bananas in London?"

I was laughing too loudly to be able to answer him.

"Do they, do they?" I could hear him asking, obviously very concerned about the welfare of the Londoners.

Never was my happiness more keenly felt than during that glittery night in Trinidad. The Chinese meal was cooked by expert hands, and brought a smirk even to the lips of Dipak. The night-club, although freezing cold due to an over-enthusiastic air conditioner, was as a Trinidad night-club is in one's dreams. Wild in their gaiety, dancers spun to the strains of abandoned calypso. Rhada shook her sylph-like figure, flashing her large eyes at Dipak, who turned his face away, a faint scowl passing o'er his alabaster brow. Ambrose stood by the bar drinking Coca-Cola, tapping his foot every now and then in time to the music. Myself and a dapper man of Chinese origin took the floor, and "wined" the night away.

"So, you from the UK. What is the name of the British External Affairs minister?"

"I don't know."

"Well, he is arriving in Port of Spain for a delegation tomorrow."

"Oh is he?"

"Yes, for talks on the OPEC oil crisis. He will be endeavouring to maintain external exportations at a controllable level."

"That's nice." At this point I made an excuse and left, yearning for the more comfortable conversations such as "how are you enjoying the club?" Too many Trinidadians, I came to discover that evening, have an overabundance of brain power.

The racial barriers which are supposed to exist in Trinidad were nowhere in sight that evening. The newspapers may have ranted on about the fragile racial balance, but as far as I could see, interaction between black, Chinese and Indian was a commoner sight in Trinidad than anywhere else in the world.

When it was time to leave, Ambrose offered to drop everyone home. Unfortunately, I fell asleep on the way back, missing the rumbustiousness of the town I had fallen in love with – El Dorado. We arrived home at four in the morning.

"Shhh, don' touch de dog, 'cause if it wake Aunty Sweets, we sunk!"

Slowly and carefully, Ambrose unlocked the wrought-iron gate, then tiptoed to the front door. Just as he was fumbling with his keys, the door flew open with a jolt, hitting Ambrose smack on the nose.

Standing in the doorway, arms akimbo, stood Aunty Sweets.

"Is what time you call dis?"

"Em, er – that is to say, um –"

"Four-thirty in de morning! You don' even have de decency to tell me where you going!"

"I – er –"

"Get in the house now, and prepare for a whipping!"

"Aunty Sweets," I blubbered, as she dragged Ambrose and myself into the house by our ears, "it wasn't my fault!"

"What! Aunty Sweets! It *her* fault for true! She told me to."

"No I didn't, Aunty Sweets. I *pleaded* with Ambrose to take me home, but he insisted we go to a discotheque. *I* didn't want to go. What would *I* want to go to a discotheque for?"

"She lie! She lie! Aunty Sweets, it her idea, you mus' believe me!"

From round the waist of her dressing gown, Aunty Sweets removed a knotted cord.

"You tink I wan' to hear excuses? You tink I care whose idea it was? All I know is that you went out until de Lord knows what time, an' leave me here to worry about you. Ambrose, hole out your hand."

Breaking away, I rushed into my bedroom, and pushed the bed against the door. This may not have been a wise move, for I was only delaying the torture until the next day, but it was the only possible way of escaping the knotted cord. Maybe Aunty Sweets would have a less lethal weapon on the morrow.

Early next morning, before anyone awoke, I made breakfast for the family, placed jugs of freshly squeezed orange juice on the table, and cleaned up the kitchen. Then I unpacked the rest of the souvenirs I had brought for friends in England, and laid them on the table as a peace offering.

Aunty Sweets emerged from her bedroom and eyed the contents on the table with haughty contempt.

It took over three hours of apologies before she finally retied the cord around her waist, and managed a sour:

"Jus' so long as it don't happen again." I was redeemed.

"Where is the nearest church?" I asked, as we ate our breakfast in near silence. Ambrose had not risen from his bed.

"Which church you want? Catholic, Protestant, Hindu, Muslim, or lunatic?"

Suppressing the urge to say lunatic, I asked her what church was nearest.

"Methodist."

"Well, could you tell me where it is."

"Why?"

"So I can go."

"Don't tell me you believe in God?" Aunty Sweets choked on her toast, and rocked with laughter.

"All right, I tell you. But I don't want to hear none of your nonsense when you get back. And if I fine you been going to any night-clubs instead, you don't get let off so easy as before, understand?"

"Yes, Aunty Sweets."

"Well, jus' walk up de road past de dirty ole house on de corner. Mr Baker's house. Oi! Dat man has some confused plants in his garden. I t'ought my plants were confused, but dey nothing compared to Mr Bakers. Oi yoi yoi! Anyway, at de end of de road, dere you see de church." Aunty Sweets' eyes ran up and down my dress.

"I hope you not planning on wearin' dat crease up ole ting. Take it off and let me press it, chile."

So after a long wait, while Aunty Sweets set up an ironing board and pressed my dress, I set off in search of a church.

Sunday morning in Trinidad, and the streets were jumping with music and people sitting outside bars drinking rum. And then another sound caught my ever-flapping ears, the sound of wailing prayers. I followed the noise until I came to a church set in between two shops, with a sign over the door heralding it to be a Spiritual Baptist Church.

Inside the building, a smell of incense all but knocked me into a seat, where I sat at the back of the hall. The room was filled with people wearing long white robes, the women sporting large white turbans on their heads. In the middle of the floor was a sacred pole, by which stood white candles, bowls of water, and a large basin of olive oil.

"Go wipe you hands in the oil," a plump woman muttered in an undertone. "You miss half the service already."

A woman preacher intoned Biblical texts, standing at the end of the room beneath a wooden crucifix, wreathed in incense smoke. Then, in a pure voice, trembling with passion, she began to sing the text. Wails and moans spread around the congregation, and a baby began to cry.

"Praise the Lord! Ah, praise him! Jeee-sus, oh Jeee-sus!"
"I seen the lightning flashing,
An' heard the thunder rolling
I felt sins quick as dashing
Trying to conquer my soul.
I heard the voice of Jesus, telling me to fight on.
He promised never to leave me,
Never to leave me alone."

The congregation began to sing loudly, joining in the gospel song that the deaconess had begun.

A man dressed in white and blue robes stood up and asked for anyone who had troubles, the sick, or those who had gone astray to come to the front and be blessed.

Seven women stood before him at the altar, and knelt down on a strip of blue carpet.

"Never to leave me alone! Never no never!" the swaying mass of people chanted, their voices rising steadily.

Three elders of the church placed hands on the foreheads of the kneelers, intoning prayers, softly at first, but increasing in volume minute by minute, matching the level of the noise of the singers.

Two women appeared from the side of the room with ropes, which the elders took solemnly, and tied around the waists of the women who knelt at their feet.

"Out demons! Out Satan! Leave the bodies and the minds of these sisters who lie prostrate in the wilderness. Leave the bodies and the minds of these sisters!"

The chanting had by now turned to screams. A young girl standing in front of me twisted in convulsions, her eyes rolling so far up in her head that only the whites were visible. One by one, the women who knelt before the elders fainted, gasping and twisting as they did so. The holy elders lashed them softly with the ropes, chanting, "Out, demons, out, demons."

Very soon it seemed as if the entire congregation had become possessed. Some were shrieking, others danced on the spot, their eyes rolled upwards, punching at the air, speaking in "tongues".

Gently, after about half an hour, the elders lifted the unconscious women from the ground, and poured oil on their temples. Carefully, they spun the semi-alive women round on the spot seven times, first one way, then another.

A young man with a trance-like aspect, grabbed my hands and began to dance with me, calling out to God in what sounded like a West African tongue.

And then, as if by a secret sign, everything quietened, and we were told by a deaconess to join hands and pray. The prayers were said aloud, producing a jumble of noise.

"Amen," the deaconess concluded, and like magic, the service had come to an end.

"So, how you doing. I never see you round here before, but it nice to meet you."

The young woman who spoke in so cheerful a voice, was the same woman who had, only a few minutes previously, been twisting in agonising convulsions, writhing on the floor, and fainting.

Now, the spirit in the church was one of joky *bonhomie*, and no sign of the trances and possessions was visible. After a brief chat with a few of the church members, I walked back to Aunty Sweets', slightly shaken by the intense experience.

"So you decided to go to de lunatic church, is it? How you enjoy all de Glory Halleluia? Heh heeh! Oi!"

Aunty Sweets found my descriptions of the church uproariously funny.

"When all de Shango people come to my hospital before I retire, dey sit by my patients' beds banging drums, and going 'hoo, hoo, hoo!' I just walk up to dem an' say, 'Stop your nonsense now, I got sick people in this ward, so out you go before I give each one of you a licking!' You see I got no time for stupidness," and Aunty Sweets belched with good-humoured malice.

"Anyway, no time to sit about talking, dere's dinner to be prepared, an' limes to be picked before any of us goes down to de beach."

"The beach!"

"Don' back talk me, girl. Get in de kitchen an' peel de potatoes, cook callaloo and okra, and fry de chicken. Also, cook up a few bakes. Ambrose! Am-brose! Get your backside in here dis instant."

Ambrose plodded in, looking a trifle the worse for wear.

"Get in de garden, chile, an' pick de limes, an' quick. You know you can't take blows!"

Ambrose darted into the garden as quick as a wink.

Preparing food for Aunty Sweets always took over three times as long as it should. Aunty Sweets would sit on a chair in the kitchen watching my every move, criticising between belches.

"What? You never peel potatoes so deep! Don' dey teach you noting about food value in England! You haven't put nearly enough oil in de pan, chile. Put some more in – no! Not that much! You want us all to die of heart failure! An' what you season de meat with? You never hear of Angostura Bitters? You have? Then why you don't throw some in? Watch out! See how you burn up de vegetables, nah!"

Eventually though, food was cooked, limes were picked, Maudy's costume was found by Ambrose (it had been in the drawer all along) and, after packing the dinner in the boot of the car, we were off, destination, Maracas Bay.

The beauty of the Trinidad countryside is not instant in its appeal. Rain forests are too dense, rivers too vast, and the mountains are overlarge, swamping the onlooker with their green-black, ominous aspect. One feels afraid, conscious of the fact that we are but mere specks of dust when facing up to Nature's might. After a few hours of driving through narrow streets and passing over precarious bridges across gushing torrents, a change takes place in one's heart. The impenetrable forests become awesome and soul stirring, and you fall deeply under the spell of their vivid charm. Parrots fly across the roads as you drive, and the sound of tropicana is never far off. Hot winds blow in your face through the windows of the car.

From the tin shacks erected by the roadside came tiny children, shading their eyes with a flat hand to gaze brightly at the car as it sped past. By midday the forest basked in torrential sunlight. The jungle was all very beautiful to look at from the outside, with the brilliant green and yellow birds chattering in shrill tongues, but, as Aunty Sweets so rightly said, "I wouldn't step my foot in de bush for all de money in Wall Street!"

Maracas Bay was a joy to behold. Trinidad's most famous beach was like a garden of palms, flowers and humming-birds, fluttering in the sunlight. Flitting from the waxy white flowers which drooped to the ground near the beach, they flashed and shimmered in metallic purples and blues.

When Ambrose had parked his car on the sand, I leapt into a swimsuit and dived into the cool waters. The sea was crowded with bathers and swimmers of every colour but white. Tourists are very rare in Trinidad, which, in my opinion is part of the island's unshakeable charm. Radios played forth calypso music, and families played ball, laughing in the heat and the beauty of the day.

After an hour or so's doggy paddle, I trooped back to ask Aunty Sweets and her party why they had not yet left the car. The three people were sitting in the oven-like vehicle eating the lunch packed that morning, pouring, every now and again, glasses of sweetened orange juice.

"Is what you mean 'Why we don't come into the sea to join you!' Eh? What you mean, chile! You don' care 'bout we! You jus' jump out de car like a Chinaman, leaving us behind like so many damn coolies! What blasted manners you call that?"

"B-b-but Aunty Sweets! I thought you were going to follow me into the water. How could I enjoy my swim leaving all of you behind?"

"Don' mamaguy me, now, chile. In future watch you damn troublesome self. You an' your dirty manners."

I turned to Ambrose for moral support. Ambrose looked away. He was still angry about being whipped for the escapade of the night before.

"Eat you dinner, now chile, an' make sure it gums up your damn jaw so I don't hear no more of your nonsense."

After lunch, I asked Aunty Sweets in my politest 'pupil to headmaster' voice, if I could leave the car to sunbathe.

"What? Why you ask *me* for? Am I your mother?"

On the way home, the scenery seemed even more awe-inspiring than it had done the first time, only by now I adored every palm, every creeper and even the red and green flies which danced over the mysterious pools of lilied waters.

Monday morning I told a lie.

"Aunty Sweets," I said nonchalantly, as I massaged her hard little feet with olive oil.

"Yes, heart-string."

"An old schoolteacher of mine lives in San Fernando, and I have just remembered that he said I ought to look him up when I reach Trinidad. He says he has a few facts to discuss with me concerning bio-chemistry."

"What trouble is this?"

"Schoolteacher – San Fernando – bio-chem –"

"Is how you tink you can get to San Fernando?"

"Bus."

"What bus?"

"Any bus that goes to San Fernando."

"You tink you can find your way to San Fernando alone?"

"Well, it's rather important, you see. I was thinking of taking up bio-physics as a profession, and this schoolteacher – the one who lives in San Fernando – is the only one who can help me."

"But I thought you said it was chemistry."

"What was chemistry?"

"You said chemistry first of all, and now you say physics."

"Exactly. I told you I was bad at science! I can't even tell the difference between chemistry and physics, but luckily Mr Zion-Tiffick can set me on the right track. I told him I'd see him today."

"You tink I stupid?"

"Yes – I mean no!"

"So tell me true, is why you want to go to San Fernando?"

"Seriously, I *do* have an old schoolteacher who lives there, I would just love to see him, that's all."

"All right. If you really insist. Take de bus to Port of Spain, den go to de bus station and ask for de San Fernando bus. But make sure you back by four."

"Yes, Aunty Sweets. Thank you, Aunty Sweets. Bless you Aunty Sweets!"

"Back by four, you hear me, chile!"

I walked into Port of Spain through the Botanical Gardens, through unearthly delights. When I reached Port of Spain, I asked a young Indian boy if he could tell me where the bus station was.

"If you're going to San Fernando," he replied in a Welsh accent, "then it's best you get a Maxi Taxi. I going there myself." So through the derelict streets of Port of Spain we went, past practically empty shops devoid of customers, selling ridiculously high-priced goods.

A Maxi Taxi is a smart-looking coach, which goes in its own good time after it has filled up with travellers. As far as public transport is concerned, Trinidad leads the West Indies.

"I'm just going out of the Maxi Taxi to get a drink and some doubles. Would you like some?"

"That's very kind of you," I replied to my Welsh accented companion. "What are doubles?"

"Doubles are like *rôti* with vegetables. I'll get you some and you can try it. What about a drink?"

"Thank you."

He sprang out of the coach and returned a few minutes later with piping hot "doubles", a spicy pickle and two cans of iced lemonade.

"Thank you, how much do I owe you?"

"Owe me?"

"How much were they?"

"No, no, forget about it. It all right, man, my treat."

"But I insist!"

"No, no, no."

Surely only in Trinidad could this selfless hospitality exist. Everyone who climbed aboard the bus shouted, "Morning everybody!" to which the reply was, "Morning!"

On the way to San Fernando, Trinidad's second largest city, we passed great stretches of sugar-cane fields. Just outside of the city stood tall wooden shacks on legs, high above the ground, presumably to keep the termites away. The winding dusty streets on the outskirts of San Fernando seemed full of promise. Although very poor, they were exquisitely picturesque.

When we reached the town centre, my friend showed me a crowded indoor market, and somehow or another, whilst looking at a group of old women haggling over the price of fresh thyme, I lost him, and search as I might, I could not find him.

So many Indian shops abounded, that I kept forgetting where I was, thinking I was either in India, or Southall on a summer's day. When the people in the sari shops spoke to me in a Welsh accent, I became even more confused.

After I had looked around the shops, buying beautiful Indian paintings as souvenirs, I wasn't quite sure what to do, because I had no information about San Fernando.

Walking aimlessly past a group of young black men, I heard one of them call out to me. Turning back I saw that a small, finely-boned man was hot on my trail. He wore a peaked cap, and cut-off shorts, and in his arms he carried two small guitars. Catching up with me, he asked me where I was going. He had large penetrating eyes and a smile that could make a mouse hug a cat. I could not reply to him. I suddenly felt very ashamed of my English accent, and could not bear him to hear me speak. Sometimes one feels one must hide one's face from the world, at other times it is one's light that is hidden under a bushel. Today it was my voice.

"You won't talk to me?"

I shook my head.

"My name is Petruchio, could you tell me your name in sign language?" I shook my head.

We passed a clothes stall.

"I'm going to look in here. Where are you going?"

I pointed up a hill.

"Well, well. You going up there, so, I'm going in here, so. Goodbye, Miss No-Talk."

I waved and walked up the hill, only to find a notice saying, 'No

Admittance', so I walked slowly down again, feeling most uncomfortable and sweaty. A man walked out of a shop and all but collided with me.

"Hey, No-Talk! It's you! So you finish your business early up that hill."

I nodded.

"Will you come with me to the music shop? I want to buy some strings for my guitar."

Trying to gesture the fact that I could only come with him for five minutes was very difficult, so I was forced to speak.

"You're a foreigner!"

"I am."

"Never mind. You shouldn't let it get you down. Come with me to the shop and help me buy de ting."

So we walked down a lane to a music shop owned by a very dour Indian man.

"Here, hold my guitars," said Petruchio, slamming his guitars into the shopkeeper's hands. The man looked askance, shooting Petruchio the most poisonous of glances, standing awkwardly, holding the guitars in both hands. Petruchio picked up a bright, shiny guitar from a display stand, and began to strum it, singing an improvised calypso:

"Walking through San Fernando feeling very amused,
I saw a strange sight that made me feel unenthused.
Down through the High Street who should appear
But Miss No-Talk (to Indian) the gal who standing right here.

She don't say a word.
She don't breathe a thing.
The woman can't laugh and the woman can't sing,
All she can do is keep her teeth close . . ."

The last line was too rude to repeat, but it certainly rhymed with close. Then he sang another song, a soft calypso, the words of which escape me. All the while, the dour shopkeeper stood holding the guitars, frowning solemnly.

"There, I finish!"

I clapped heartily.

"Thanks for the use of your guitar, man," said Petruchio, returning the instrument to its stand and sweeping his own guitars out of the grim shopkeeper's hands with a flourish, "I hope you sell it quick," and without another word, he left the shop.

"What about the strings?"

"Strings can wait forever, No-Talk, but walking to the beach with you can't. Come, let's take a nice long stroll."

On the way to the beach, Petruchio told me some Trinidadian jokes so blue in complexion, they were almost purple. I laughed and laughed and laughed, and laughing, it occurred to me that I had not laughed so long and so hard for a long time. Humour is the lifeblood of sanity.

"What do you do for a living?" I asked, in-between giggling at the one about the bridegroom and the corkscrew.

"I'm a professional street walker."

"I beg your pardon!"

"I walk the streets all day, that's what I do."

"Do you get paid for it?"

"Who'd pay me for walking around?"

"Then you're an amateur street walker."

"Yes! That's what I am! An amateur street walker! But I play calypso too you know. Play it all day long, wherever, whenever."

San Fernando has a far more pleasing aspect than Port of Spain. Old-fashioned streets wind down to a very charming beach. Walking to the craft market, which lies very near the sea, we chatted about the origins of calypso.

"The rhythms of calypso are African, created by the slaves, but influenced by the Hispanic music of Venezuela. To confuse things even further, the music of the English, Irish and French have also been incorporated into calypso, because, No-Talk, you must remember that only French and French patois was spoken in Trinidad during the nineteenth century."

"What does calypso mean?" I was hoping to stump him after his being such a clever clogs.

"Calypso? Now that opens a wide field of discussion. Some say it comes from the Hausa word *kaiso* meaning 'oh!' Some say it comes from the Hispanic word *caliso* meaning 'local song', and yet other scholars debate it comes from the French word *carrouseaux* meaning . . ."

"All right, all right."

"Meaning festivity. But calypsos can be about anything, love, sex, humour, work, politics."

"Politics! That's what all the calypsos were about during the Dominican 'King' competition."

"Of course they would be about politics! The world is going to hear those calypsos, and it is important for the singer to get his political opinion across."

Reaching the beach we found little boys fishing for eels in tiny rafts made from polystyrene. Catching the wretched creatures, they tied a string around their necks and dashed their heads upon the rocks. The children performed this act with breezy indifference, not with hoots of joy as English boys would, nor with squeamish fear. Killing eels was to these boys a fact of life, where emotions need not arise.

Everywhere on the beach were bobbing fishing boats and tangles of fish nets; but although the setting was idyllic, there was none of the sleepy stillness that abides in St Lucia. In Trinidad raucous laughter could be heard, perhaps interrupted by the angry shout of an old lady.

Very soon, Petruchio and I found ourselves in a pub. Petruchio ordered Puncheon rum, a drink which lifts the lid off your head, causing fire to pour from the top.

"Why do you drink this stuff?"

"Jus' to show off. I don't really like it, but I know it impresses you."

"Well, it doesn't."

Very slow fans revolved up above our heads, creating a pleasant breeze. Petruchio told me how he plays "pan" (steel band) for the carnival, and sang a few more calypsos, drawing quite a crowd. He did indeed have a very melodious voice.

"In our carnival, in Notting Hill Gate last year," I said, "a man got stabbed."

"Well, what can you expect in England? Our carnival is always peaceful, but there's too many people like you in England, so your carnival is bound to be troublesome."

"What, pray, do you mean by that?"

"People of mixed African and European descent, very blood-thirsty lot they are!"

"How dare you!" I cried, only just resisting the urge to punch him.

"Only joking. Listen, I feel so bad letting you buy all the drink. I feel you have emasculated me."

"Never mind, eh."

"But if you keep paying for me, you might try to kiss me, an' then I get frightened."

A group of eavesdropping Indians at the next table laughed raucously. One of them slammed his fist upon the table, quite weak with mirth. I looked at his watch. The time was nearly three.

"Good grief!" I sprang up and started to run out of the smoky room.

"What's up?"

"I'm late! I've got to be back by four! My aunt will skin me alive!"

"Phone her up and explain."

"You could do that to a normal aunt, but not Aunty Sweets!"

"All right, let's go. I'll show you how to get a taxi back to Port of Spain."

"Bless you, Petruchio."

We stood by the taxi, waiting for it to fill up with enough customers to make the driver's journey worthwhile.

"I'd like to see you again, No-Talk."

Petruchio's eyes shone yellow in the sun.

"I'd like to see you too, but I am afraid it can never be."

"Why?"

"I have an aunt . . ."

"Say no more. But couldn't I phone up as your father?"

"No." An idea flashed into my mind: "But you could say you're my teacher from London."

"All right, then."

I moved over in my seat to let a man into the cab. He turned to leer drunkenly at me, then squeezed his way out of the car, and stood swaying in the street.

"Is the man drunk?"

Petruchio chuckled. "Naw. That's Heidi Cock. The man mad."

"Heidi? Isn't that a girl's name?"

Heidi Cock cackled at two women who had seated themselves in the car.

"See! Very mad, isn't he. Know why he's called Heidi Cock?"

"No."

"Because the man sexed with his sister one time, an' when they heard the parents coming home, the sister yelled out to him, 'hide de cock!'"

I flushed with embarrassment, and the taxi moved away.

"I phone you soon, No-Talk!" Petruchio shouted, running by the side of the cab. I stared straight in front of me, hoping no one had heard that diabolically rude tale.

"De man shock you?" asked the driver, blowing cigar smoke into my face.

I nodded.

"That's life, though, not so? Very rude, and very funny."

'Where have I gone wrong?' I mused.

*   *   *

A few days later, the phone rang sharp and clear, penetrating the sounds of Cuban dance music and an American quiz show.

Aunty Sweets lumbered over to the phone and said, "Eeee? Who? Yes? Really? Very interesting? Never I did know dat before? Ah yes, education is a wonderful ting, eh heh, I know that. Mr who? OK, I tell her. Sweet thing," she whispered, placing her hand over the receiver, "there's a University lecturer on the phone for you, from Oxford in England call Mr Duff-Duff-Smythe."

"Really?" I said, trying to keep a straight face.

"Yes. He educating me about politics an' laws."

"Oh yes, that must be the teacher I was telling you about."

Aunty Sweets' eyes shone with profound admiration as she handed me the phone.

"Hi, No-Talk, how you feel about going liming with me tonight?"

"Yes, Mr Duff-Duff – er um –"

"Smythe. There's a pan yard just near where you live, so I thought it would make a nice evening. What do you say?"

"That would be nice, Mr Duff-Duff-Smythe."

"Is what he saying?" Aunty Sweets held her ear very near to the receiver. I pulled away slightly.

"I would love to come along to the lecture tonight, sir. Where shall we meet?"

"Is he telling you about the new laws?" asked Aunty Sweets in a loud stage whisper.

"Why don't I come round to collect you?"

"I think it's better if we meet by the zoo in the Botanical Gardens."

"What time?"

"Seven?"

"Fine. Did I tell you the one about the priest and the rosary?"

"What's he saying?"

"He's talking about philosophy, Aunty Sweets."

"Well there was this priest, right, an' he was giving confession, an –"

"Yes, Mr Duff-Duff, seven o'clock it is."

"An' he took out his rosary –"

"Goodbye, Mr Duff-Duff-Smythe."

I banged down the phone quickly.

"Now that was a very nice man. The only sort of man I'd allow you to associate with. I glad you going to see him."

And so glad was Aunty Sweets, that she let me go to the zoo on my own. After a pleasant stroll around, watching the tayras and reptiles at play, I took a stroll in the Botanical Gardens. An enormous banyan tree provided comforting shade.

At seven, long after the darkness had spread, I stood by the gates of the zoo, waiting for Petruchio. Indian men cat-called and whistled, throwing me salacious smiles, a phenomenon that could never happen in London. At last, after I had waited an hour, Petruchio turned up, slapping my shoulder, and chattering all the way to the pan yard.

The concert had already begun by the time we arrived, and the complicated rhythms of the steel band were playing a fast rumba, sounding as exhilarating and skilled as any band I have heard. A woman even played a solo passage on her tin lid, creating a rhythmic swing worthy of virtuoso jazz.

Playing of the steel band, and indeed drums of any kind, was forbidden to the labouring classes in Trinidad up until the Forties. Stiff penalties were imposed by magistrates on anyone found playing pan in their backyards. Today, steel bands are the national music of Trinidad, a music that came into being primarily because all other types of instruments were denied to the slaves. Bamboo sticks and dustbin lids were utilised as tuneful instruments for masquerade. Now, steel bands perform in churches and concert halls, evolving into one of the Caribbean's most dignified forms of art.

It was noticeable that only people of African extraction were there that evening to enjoy the music.

"That's because," pontificated Petruchio, "we blacks are the only islanders who look to Trinidad as their true home. Indians, Europeans and Chinese look to their mother countries, but Africans were so uprooted during slavery having their music, language, religion, and every other aspect of their culture stamped out by colonial imperialists, that we can only look to Trinidad as our spiritual home, so we have created a rich, indigenous culture, the envy of the world. Not through choice, but by force."

"Petruchio, you're so clever, my aunt was right. What were you talking to her about? Laws or politics or something."

"I was telling her about Einstein's law of relativity. Anyway, how about another glass of rum? Tomorrow I'll show you the Pitch Lake."

"But my aunt –"

"Tell your aunt you're going to a lecture on Asphaltivity."

I did just that, and next day, met Petruchio in San Fernando, and from there we took a bus to the Pitch Lake.

The Pitch Lake, south-west of the island, has the largest deposit of asphalt in the world. Sir Walter Raleigh was the first European to discover it, and used the asphalt to caulk his ships in 1595.

Petruchio reluctantly agreed to hire a guide, who showed us around the stinking sea of sticky black tar, which emitted an aroma very much like bad eggs.

There was nothing stimulating on offer in this smelly stretch of bitumen, the only exciting aspect being whether the gooey substance could ever be removed from one's shoes or not.

When we had finished our tour around the lake, which Petruchio cut short, complaining about the damage caused to his nostrils, we took a bus back to San Fernando.

"I know you!" said a lubberly-looking man, standing by a hospital. Petruchio caught his breath, then wrapped the stranger in his arms.

"Will! Will, man, how you doing! Good to see you! Meet my friend, No-Talk."

"All right, No-Talk. Hey, Petruchio, I going to the hospital to see my cousin. He well sick. You want to come?"

"Yeah, man, course! No-Talk, this here's my good friend Will. We used to fish together in Point Fortin when we were kids."

As we cantered up the steps of the grim hospital, Will asked me earnestly whether guns could be bought in London.

"No. Why do you ask?"

"Because I want a gun, and I want one right now, but you can't buy dem here."

"Why do you want a gun?"

"So I can kill plenty people."

I reeled back in horror.

The wards of the hospital in San Fernando were horribly cheerless. Men wired up with drips lay on ragged beds, wearing torn shorts and tee shirts. A group of nurses sat in an antechamber, laughing and joking, and the only people who appeared to be taking any notice of the patients were Pentecostal women, who moved from bed to bed, preaching in harsh voices. The poor men rolled over and over, trying to escape the sound of the bedside sermons, some going so far as to put pillows over their heads, but the women blathered on regardless.

A grey-faced man writhing with his eyes closed, cried out in torment as he saw one of the Pentecostal sisters approach.

"Leave him be, now, sister. This me cousin, you know."

The sister nodded knowingly and moved on to the next bed.

"Hello, cuz. You all right? This Petruchio, remember him?"

The cousin, without opening his eyes, gave a twitch-like nod.

"An' this is No-Talk, my future wife. See how I love she!"

I gurgled a murmur of protestation, but was quickly silenced by Petruchio's nudge.

"Let he dream, sister," he said softly.

Will and his cousin spoke in broken French for a while, and I sat in silence. Petruchio had slunk off somewhere. When Petruchio returned, Will slapped a mosquito from his fat arm, and said:

"OK, Petruchio an' No-Talk, let we go now. I got a car, so we can take a tour of the island. How about seeing Carnage and Diego Martin?"

Petruchio nodded, and we galloped out of the sordid hospital and into Will's waiting car.

Every new island I had been to seemed more beautiful than the last. Trinidad, however, claims the title "Empress of the West Indies", so fair is its isle. Hills, harbours and little fishing villages remain unmatched in beauty.

"You should come to one of these villages on a Friday night for a bacchanal! The fishermen drink rum and go with oopsie women. They're all very sexy, you know."

"How can you say that! Me father a fisherman! He don't go with the type of woman you talk of!" Will's eyes swam with tears.

"All right, Will, calm down! Only a joke I tell."

"I don't like that kinda joke."

I was going to ask him if his plea for a gun was a joke, but felt it best to leave it until another time.

"Let's go to see a very dear friend of mine who live in Diego Martin. A very nice lady. My mother used to cook for she, an' she always welcomes me into her home like a son. I tell you the woman sweeter than syrup."

The lady lived in a posh little suburb of modern bungalows, with wide streets lined with palms and breadfruit trees. As we walked up her chi-chi driveway, a slavering Alsatian leapt from the jaws of hell, and pushed Will to the ground. Petruchio and I tried to rescue the poor man, who screamed and tussled as the Alsatian pinned him down and snarled in his face.

"What going on! Who out there!"

An Indian woman stood in the doorway holding a flat pan in her hand, a horrified gaze on her voluptuous features.

"Lady! Come an' help my friend. You dog attacking him!"

"What! Oh you poor thing! You'll be all right, don't worry, let me rescue you. Don't cry!"

Lovingly she pulled the hound of Satan away from Will, and steered it away into the house.

"There, there, you poor thing, never mind, come in and have some milk."

Will puffed out his plump cheeks in relief, and neither Petruchio nor I had the heart to tell him that the words of sympathy were directed to the dog.

"Now, what do you people want?" asked the lady sharply, returning from her bungalow.

"Mrs Khadda! You don't remember me? Will! Vita's son."

"Who?"

"Will. My mother used to cook for you."

"I have no idea what you're talking about, but if I were you, I'd leave my door before I let out the other dogs."

"But Mrs Khadda!"

"Is this some kinda joke?"

Petruchio and I headed towards the car, and after a few more desperate words from Will, he followed us, rubbing his stout thigh painfully.

"That woman is an apocalypse," he muttered, starting up the car. "She bad an' rude. Where to?"

"Back to Port of Spain. My aunt –"

"Don't worry 'bout she, No-Talk. I phone her up, and explain everything," chuckled Petruchio.

"You did what?"

"Phone her an' explain why you won't be back till late."

"When? How?"

"While you sitting in the hospital speaking you broken French I couldn't understand, I take the time and the liberty to phone up your aunt. We had a nice long chat."

"Petruchio! What did you say to her!"

"Don' worry you inquisitive self about it."

"You got an aunt as well, is it? So have I," remarked Will, glumly. "My aunt full up with superstition. She only walks through a door backwards in case she draws in the evil spirits after her. If you walk in the right way, she says that they'll follow you in. She crazy."

The sky was darkening as we drove back to Port of Spain, but the horizon was lit up by the myriad sparkles of open fires.

Before we entered the large art deco cinema in Port of Spain, I felt I had to ask The Question. It was now or never. Finding the right time to obtain the vital information proved a bit of a problem, so the deed had to be done over the buying of popcorn whilst waiting in the foyer.

"Er – Petruchio?"

"Yes, No-Talk?"

"Before I step foot in the cinema, I have a vital question to ask."

"Well, spit it out before it scalds you."

"Do you have – how can I put it? Do you have vampire bats in cinemas here?"

Petruchio munched on a piece of toffee coated popcorn in a ponderous manner.

"Vampire bats? No, why, do you?"

"Do I what?"

"Have vampire bats."

"No."

"Ah," said Petruchio, which just about summed everything up.

The film was most enjoyable, vastly improved by Petruchio being the type of person who doesn't mind an obtuse person asking, "What's happening?" every five seconds. Most people say, "Can't you watch the blasted thing and shut up!" but dear Petruchio diligently explained why the girl was having another fit, and that the Thing in her bedroom was merely a dream sequence. A fine, upstanding bastion of society, Petruchio, and one of my few companions who can stomach watching a whole film me without storming out in the middle.

Will's claim to fame was that he could eat three bags of roasted nuts, four ice-creams, and hot dogs measureless to man, whilst snoring loudly. We left that cinema a satisfied threesome.

"Where you bin?" asked Aunty Sweets when I returned home.

"Didn't my – tutor phone to explain?"

"Tutor me backside!"

"But I thought he said that –"

"A policeman phone to say dat you were found drunk and disorderly in San Fernando market, an' that you in court waiting to go to prison!"

I clutched at the wrought-iron railings, the heart pounding about sixteen times faster than it should have done. The beautiful Indian dancer on the telly began to resemble Kali the Destroyer, so great was my confusion.

"A policeman . . ." was all I could muster. I clung to my crucifix and began to pray.

"So is why you not lock up?"

The only thing I could think to do at this dramatic juncture in the narrative, was to pretend to die. Clutching my throat, I threw myself to the ground, and writhed in agony, muttering, "The tablets! The tablets!"

"Get up off the floor, you yam-faced baboon! Is only a joke I tell! Oi yoi yoi! Heh heeeeh! Wooo! See how de chile frighten up and roll 'pon the floor like a mongoose at a snake. Woi! What! You got something so bad to hide! You tink if policeman phone I ever let you step one of your size nine foot in my house again! Aye yi yi!"

I sat up, trying to pass off the whole episode as a breezy joke, and simpered in what I hoped to be a gay and amused manner. The world, previously inside out, slowly turned outside in, and Kali the Destroyer, who before had been indulging in a spot of human sacrifice on the TV once more became the beautiful Indian dancer.

"Have some food, dear heart, and rest you self up. You tutor say you attend an all day deligation this afternoon about Iranigate, an' I expect it take a lot out of you. What," she asked, serving me a dish of cold stewed goat, "exactly was that Iranigate business all about?"

"Well, Reagan said that he had sold something to the Contra rebels."

"But that's Nicaragua. What that got to do with Iran?"

"The Contra rebels in Iran."

"Don' act the ass, or people will ride you! Explain de ting seriously, nah."

"Another time, Aunty Sweets, I'm tired now, if you don't mind."

"All right, all right, darlin'. With all dat sittin' in stuffy rooms listening to professors, I expect you brain feel ready to bust out its shell."

"Yes, Aunty Sweets, and thank you very much for the meal, it's lovely. Tomorrow is my last day, and as a thank you present, I'd like to take you on a treat."

"What trouble is this?"

"I'd like to take a tour to the bird sanctuary and the mangrove swamps."

"Who taking you?"

"A tour agency."

"Indian or Negro?"

"What does it matter?"

"Indian or Negro?"

"What difference does it make? Whatever they are, if you prick them, do they not bleed? Are they not men and brothers?"

"Indian or Negro?"

"Indian."

"Eh eh! Trouble! They'll cheat you, you know!"

"Please come. You and Maudy."

"You wastin' good money, but I come anyway jus' to give them Indian crooks a full size helpin' of my mind! Cheating ignorant tourists like you poor damn self. Heh!"

All night long I tossed and turned. Would Petruchio, who was accompanying us on this tour, behave with the dry, stultifying manner befitting a man who is supposed to be steeped in the stagnant waters of academe? Demonic thoughts floated in my mind: thoughts of Petruchio telling Aunty Sweets some of his more spicy brands of joke. When sleep finally stole silently upon me, I dreamt of Aunty Sweets untying her belt, and after administering twelve lashes on Petruchio's back, pushing him into the swamp.

Sunlight streamed through the window, and the day had begun. Although I had been in the Caribbean for many weeks, I still thought, 'what a lovely day!' every morning. Old habits die hard.

"What time de professor coming, heart-string?"

"Twelve."

"Better get the house fix up nice for de man! Go to de market an' buy some flowers and cakes and ting."

"He says he doesn't mind a bit of mess."

"Well tidy yourself up at least, chile! Come. Let me plait your hair."

"I've got a headache!"

"Stop your nonsense!" and before I could say "comb" my head was being squelched between two fat knees, and gnarled fingers picked and twisted the crowning glory. As an adult, however, I could appreciate the effect the hours of torture produced. My head became an intricate lace filigree, worthy of the things which made people go blind in days of yore.

At twelve precisely, a knock at the door resounded through the house. The hairs on my back began to bristle. Aunty Sweets sat watching an Australian soap opera, looking neither right nor left. The rapping continued. At last, after Aunty Sweets had shouted, "Open de damn door, chile! You know it for you!" I leapt out of the easy chair, and swung open the door.

In front of me stood a pompous little man wearing a corduroy suit and a bowler hat. The expression on his face was so outrageously self-important, that if it were not for the sly wink, I would never have recognised him to be Petruchio.

"Miss Longmore. Good day to you."

"Mr Duff-Duff-Smythe! *Do* come in, meet my aunt."

Petruchio walked into the living room, raising his knees most oddly.

If he were auditioning for the role of Spiderman, he would have landed the part in a thrice.

"Mrs Foster! This is indeed a pleasure! I deemed it necessary to make your acquaintance. I *say*! What a charming little homestead you have here! What was it that Wittgenstein said about the home? 'The home will allow one to think – but never to be thoughtful.' Ha, ha, ha. How true, how charmingly true." Petruchio jerked his spiky knees over to Aunty Sweets, and kissed her hand.

I was so busy making faces at him to stop overdoing it, that I neglected to notice how Aunty Sweets was taking this mind-boggling display of braggadocio. When I finally plucked up courage to look at her, I saw that a great change had overtaken her countenance. The old Aunty Sweets, the Aunty Sweets who causes strong men to quail, had vanished, and in her place was an Aunty Sweets who could be booed by any wayside goose. Her eyes had removed themselves from their home base, and she gaped at Petruchio, her lips forming one of the most idiotic grins of the season. Picking at the side of her skirts, she bowed her head and focused her gaze upon the carpet, utterly lost for words, like a country lass in the presence of her courting swain. Aunty Sweets had been reduced to blancmange. Petruchio had succeeded where all others had failed.

"Well, Mr Duff-Duff-Smythe," I said, to break the eternal moments of silence, "my aunt and I would like to thank you for your company. The tour agents should be here in a moment, and when my other aunty is dressed, we can set off."

Petruchio's finely shaped eyebrows shot upwards contemptuously.

"My dear young lady. I find such senseless prattle most displeasing to the tutored ear. Why," he asked Aunty Sweets, "should a woman's tongue find endless gratification in the facile? The trite? The state of silence is a treasure to be preserved, not desecrated!"

Aunty Sweets quickly found her previously tied tongue.

"Hush up, now, chile, or I whip you into nex' Sunday!"

"Yes, Aunty Sweets!"

"Ah, hah! That's what I like to see! Stern reprimand of foolish youth! Capital, capital. Screw the dagger to the sticky place, as the Bard used to say, what! Was it Plato who spoke of the benefit of beating one's nieces?"

"Petru – er, Mr Duff-Duff-Smythe, may I have a private word, about um – the conference yesterday."

Petruchio must have sensed something dangerous in my eyes because for a second his brash self-assurance wavered.

"Certainly, Miss Longmore."

I led him onto the patio, and jabbed a sharp nail into the fleshy part of his arm.

"Now listen here, mush. You're supposed to be on my side in this."

"Cool off the juice, No-Talk! I being what I was tole to be, a educated university man, an' that's how they all are! One bag of no-goodery, the lot of them. I start being *nice* and the whole ting's blown sky high. What professors are nice? You ever met one? Well then, clap your leather lips, an' leave the blasted ting to me."

"You want to see blood? Give my aunt another inch and you will. So lie a bit lower. And by the way, what's that walk in aid of?"

"Isn't it how they all walk?"

"No, but it's too late now. Now go back in and be a bit more pleasant, especially to me. On a lighter note, though, the Wittgenstein bit was very good."

"Slow your rolls, No-Talk, an' let me do de ting how it should be done."

We rejoined Aunty Sweets and Maudy, who sat at the table wearing her Sunday best, topped by a large white hat so covered in flowers it was as if Kew Gardens had, by a means as yet unknown to science, been beamed onto the top of her head.

"This is a university professor!" explained Aunty Sweets. These were, if I am not mistaken, the only words that were spoken before the tour guide picked us up in his shiny red car.

After Petruchio had run out of the names of philosophers he knew we settled back to listen to the driver, who told us he had a girlfriend who wrote for the Trinidad newspaper, *The Bomb*, a scandal paper mainly attacking the government. He was an excessively charming man, inviting our whole party on a boat trip in a week's time.

"My girlfriend will cook for you all! Come along!"

I waited for Aunty Sweets to give him a piece of her mind as she had promised to do, but, quite naturally, I waited in vain.

When we arrived at the bird sanctuary, a few miles out of town, the driver led us onto the bank of a river, where we sat and waited for a boat to pick us up and take us through the mangrove swamps.

A group of Indian boys sitting at a wooden table, engaged in a noisy game of cards, grew quite wild at the sight of Petruchio's bowler hat.

"My Liege!" one of them shouted, and soon the small company of boys set up a mocking masquerade, laughing and posturing, calling their friends over to join in the cavalcade of amusement.

Petruchio enjoyed every second, bellowing to them that he would "horsewhip them on the steps of their own club!"

The boys shrieked back, slapping their thighs and bawling lewd comments in Hindi.

"Don't take no notice of them, they're ruffians, you know. How do they know any better?" Aunty Sweets pursed her lips, and shot them so fiery a look that the boys backed away, and behaved themselves. No one can withstand the terror of a look from Aunty Sweets.

Only three tourists came with us on the boat. Two giggling French girls, and a large American man in a peaked cap, hailing from Georgia. Going out with other tourists on the same trip is a bit like going to evening classes. You always feel as if you are supposed to chat and become bosom pals in a very short stretch of time, but in actual fact, no one speaks to each other. The American looked rather sad, as if nurturing a secret sorrow.

We sailed up the creek in a long wooden boat, a silent Indian man skilfully handling the oars.

I look upon that excursion with ecstasy, as if it were a jewel whose light will never fade. Eerie mists surrounded the mangrove swamps, as they stood magnificent in their beauty, their roots twisting high above the shore. Fiddler crabs scurried up and down the gnarled trees, and mud skippers darted here and there. Fish was apparently plentiful in these waters, because up a shallow creek, there occasionally lurked fishermen and women, sitting in dug-out coracles. The trees formed a rabbit warren-like avenue, as we floated down the mystic green waters. The liquid light shimmered on the trees, a purple light, casting diamond sparkles on the forest around us. The human mind can only comprehend paradise, once the eye has seen Trinidad.

All of a sudden we floated towards a glimmering pool, and there we saw the scarlet ibis in flight. The ibis is a long-legged wading bird, with a black arching bill. Their fantastic colouring is impossible to describe: a brilliant blur of fiery crimson. Across the sky they sailed, landing far away in the muddy banks of the swamp, looking, no doubt, for their meal of fiddler crabs. Behind them, snowy white egrets laboriously flapped their wings, following the never-ending trail of the ibis.

Our guide sat in the back of the boat reading a book, impervious to the majestic spectacle.

We rode back through the now orange-tinted swamp, and our journey through heaven was done.

Just as Petruchio was climbing from the boat, holding his bowler hat with a slender finger, a man walking past the shore caught sight of him, and burst into peels of laughter.

"Heh! Petruchio! Is why you dress up like a clown, man!"

My heart stood still.

Petruchio observed the stranger with a cold eye.

"I *beg* your pardon, young man."

"Don't put that stupidness on me, man! You going to a fancy dress ball, or what?"

I ran on ahead, pulling Aunty Sweets and Maudy by the arm, hoping they hadn't noticed.

"Petruchio, man! It me! Ivan."

"I'm afraid I have no idea *what* you are talking about," and so saying, Petruchio caught us up, and began a long speech about the lack of discipline so commonly to be found in idle youth.

"Goodbye, Mr Duff-Duff-Smythe," simpered Aunty Sweets, as we stood by a St James Taxi stand. "Please call on me again. It was such a pleasure to meet you. I only wish I could persuade Zenga to marry a man as worthy as your good self."

"Indeed, it would be an admirable thing for your niece to wed a man as worthy as myself, the problem, however, would arise from persuading so worthy a man to marry your niece."

"True, ah, true. I so glad I not her mother."

"So, Mrs Foster, am I. Good day to you, I shall keep in touch. Good day to you too, Zenga. Would it be possible for us to meet tonight for talks on the 'nationalist marginality of dimensional factors'?"

"I'd love to, Mr Duff-Duff-Smythe!" I thought of the party that Petruchio probably had in mind. My last night in Trinidad would be spent in a whirlwind of rum, heady music, and undiluted pleasure.

"No, Mr Professor man, de girl got to be up early tomorrow, an' she got to get a good night's sleep. Don't put too much brain in she head lest you run she mad."

Petruchio and I eyed one another tragically. Two victims of a brutal aunt-dominated society.

We parted in a state of unsweetened sorrow. With an elegant tip of the bowler, Petruchio walked jerkily towards a taxi, then, with a final flourish of the lace cravat around his neck, he climbed into the car, and sailed away. Two men sitting in the back of the cab caught their breath at the sight of him, then I could see them guffawing, taking turns in trying on Petruchio's hat. Fortunately Aunty Sweets had not witnessed this uproarious masquerade.

"You see de nice man! Always willing to educate an underworked brain like yours."

"Yes, Aunty Sweets."

"Underworked brain like yours."

"Yes, Aunty Maud."

Unless she repeated the last line that had been spoken, it was all too easy to forget the existence of dear Aunty Maud.

When we arrived home, I insisted I buy Aunty Sweets some Guinness, her favourite tipple. Walking out into the sultry street, I decided to take a brisk trot to the Botanical Gardens, so I could savour their beauty for the last time. When I reached the overpoweringly lovely stretch of overblown vegetation, I felt a deep stab in my heart. A ceaseless gnawing that usually says I've had too much to eat, but today said that I could not bear to leave the West Indies, these vivid isles that had begun to feel so much like home, so much more like home than the cheerless English terraces where people sneer with heart-breaking monotony. And now I was returning to a land which I knew would seem so foreign to me. I clung to a fern-like palm with both arms, and prayed that time would stand still; that I would hold this tree in the tropical evening for ever, and never grow old, and never feel another drop of icy sleet upon my face again. It was a crystal moment suspended in infinite poetry, rudely broken by the high-pitched tones of an Indian man shouting, "You wan' hole onto somet'ing nice an' big, lady? Den leave go de tree, man, an' let me give you somet'ing plenty more sweet!"

Too affronted for words, I untwined from the noble palm, and wended my way back to Aunty Sweets'. That irreverent man had crashed in upon one of the most spiritual moments of our time; a grotesque imitation of the man from Porlock interrupting Coleridge's immortal session.

Aunty Sweets was sitting on the porch when I arrived home, looking most strange. She sat hunched in a wicker chair, her palms facing upwards upon her lap. Salt in great quantities lay in her hands, spilling onto her frock. "Something," I told myself, "is afoot."

"Cup of tea, Aunty Sweets?"

"Later, later, sugar dumpling."

"Are you all right?"

"I expecting a man who owes me a lot of money, an' when he comes, he'll try to obeah me, but wid de salt in me hand, dere's no obeah dat can touch me. Now stand out me way."

I thought of reminding Aunty Sweets that she had laughed at me for what she termed my superstitious ways, but I didn't, because obeah is not a superstition, it is a fact. Instead, I hurried into the kitchen and poured a liberal helping of salt into my own hands (making sure that I threw some of it over my left shoulder); after all, it's best to be on the safe side.

As far as I know, the debtor did not show up. I fell asleep very early, wondering vaguely how I would be able to manage in life with no Aunty Sweets to tell me what to do.

Ambrose was to drive me to the airport next day at the unearthly hour of four in the morning. He was still not on speaking terms with me, and was only communicating through Aunty Sweets.

"She pack up yet, Aunty?"

Sad to say, Aunty Sweets was not on speaking terms with Ambrose because he had stayed out until half-past ten the night before.

"You pack up yet, dear heart? If you are, tell Ambrose you ready to go" (muttering under breath). "Half-past ten me backside! You tink it decent to stay out all night? You call dat training!"

Much as I was yearning to tell Ambrose that at the age of thirty-three he should have learned to know his place and respect his elders and betters, I kept my tongue; after all, it was four in the morning, and the hapless man was giving me a lift.

Saying goodbye to Aunty Sweets was no easy task. When it was finally time to leave her, perhaps for ever, I found myself shedding an unchecked spate of tears.

"Stop you stupidness, chile, before I whip you backside clean off. Take de sandwiches I make for you, and remember to bring de cake to eat for you journey home. Say hello to you mudda, and tell her not to sen' you back in too much of a hurry. You troublesome ways give me too much damn headache. Behave yourself on de way home, you hear me, chile!"

"Yes, Aunty Sweets."

"Now get going, an' remember not to come back too damn soon."

We hugged warmly, then she stood on the porch, keeping a sharp eye on Ambrose and me as we packed up the car and drove away.

The last words I heard Aunty Sweets scream were, "An' remember to keep away from de snake hip nigger bwai!"

We were off, sailing away from the land that I had begun to claim as my own.

"Ambrose," I said when we reached the airport. Ambrose turned his face away, and was just about to leave without saying goodbye when I lured him back with a small parcel.

"What this?"

"A present for you."

Shooting me a highly suspicious glance, Ambrose unwrapped the parcel, and found inside the Indian paintings I had bought in San Fernando.

"What do I want these for?"

"A sorry present and a thank you present combined."

"But that's Indian stuff. I'm a Negro, so what would I want with Indian pictures? You tink I ashamed of me own race?"

"Ambrose! Do us a favour! You're beginning to sound like Aunty Sweets."

"An' what wrong wid dat! Aunty Sweets is a very good person, always helping people and working and working."

"You're right there. That woman doesn't know the meaning of the word fatigue."

"Nor do I, but there again, I only know a few long words."

"Goodbye again, Ambrose, and thanks."

"Bye, cousin. See you sometime – maybe."

Ambrose turned tail, and wove his way through a posse of hearty German tourists.

The final curtain had been drawn over my Caribbean adventures. I would love to say that something exciting happened to me at the airport, but I am afraid nothing did.

"Why did you come to the Caribbean?" asked an old English man on the plane, "to find yourself?"

Find myself! I got totally lost. In every island I was a different person. "High" in Jamaica, "Mestizo" in the Dominican Republic, "Mulatto" in Haiti, "Black" in Dominica and St Lucia, "Mulâtre" in Martinique and Guadeloupe, and in Trinidad I was none other than a "red skin nigger". Such is life, and such is the unhealthy obsession with race, a colonial legacy that brutalises the Caribbean from top to toe.

No, I certainly did not find myself, but I learnt so much, mainly, that I can laugh at those who talk of Caribbean culture, as though there is but one culture practised throughout the West Indies. Each island has a religion, language and lifestyle all of its own, evolving from Europe, Asia and Africa.

I only visited nine islands, about one-sixth of the Caribbean countries, and each island was totally different from the last. The only thing all the islands have in common is a perfect, natural beauty, and maybe the words "no problem", which are endlessly repeated in Spanish, French or English, depending on where you are.

But from Little Mannie's Jamaica, to Lionel's sweet St Lucia, from tap-taps to Trinidad there abides a joy and a robust zest for living.
As the poet sayeth:

> There's no place I would rather be
> Than in the jewelled Caribbee.

Caribbean Chronology

500 BC *approx* – Siboneys, nomadic hunters, moved in from the mainland.

AD 400 *approx* – Arawaks, peaceful farmers, arrived from the mainland.

1000 – Caribs, warlike hunters, arrived from the mainland.

1492–1504 – Columbus landed on each of the major islands.

1506 – Pope allocated West Indies to Spain, and Brazil and West Africa to Portugal.

Spain divided land into large estates: Arawaks included as if livestock; all dead within thirty years from massacres, starvation, overwork or illness.

The small islands were inhabited by Caribs, hence no Spanish settlement.

Large islands were used by Spain as harbours and as a source for provisions for ships on the way to fetch gold and silver from South America. Cattle were introduced to provide salt beef in Jamaica, Cuba and Haiti.

1505 – First African slaves were brought to the West Indies.

by 1517 – Steady supply of slaves was organised by Portugal from West Africa. The Pope gave Portugal monopoly.

1562 – First British slaver (Hawkins).

by 1560 – Fleets of treasure ships moved in well-organised convoys from South America, visiting a port on each island, then on to Spain. They returned from Spain with supplies to the colonies.

British, Dutch and French pirates preyed on Spanish treasure ships and forts. There were smugglers and pirates' forts on most of the islands. After 1600 the power of the Spanish Main declined.

1622–28 – Small islands, Lesser Antilles, were settled by French, English and Dutch. Caribs were massacred, usually when sleeping in hammocks. Large islands all had pirate towns. Most settlers were pirates, but some grew tobacco for export on small farms. Throughout sixteenth, seventeenth and eighteenth centuries

European wars were fought over possession of islands; ruling powers took over settlers of French, Dutch, English, etc origins, who were little affected by changes in rule. Dutch, French, English, Danes engaged in slave trade.

1650 – Dutch traders encouraged sugar plantations in Barbados.

1655 – Cromwell sent British fleet against Spain and captured Jamaica.

by 1680 – Barbados and Jamaica were parcelled out among large absentee estate owners, managed by white overseers: sugar replaced gold and piracy.

1680 – Barbados became chief sugar producer. Islands ruled from Europe. Local assemblies of white managers instituted local slave codes. Their one wish was to get rich and return to Europe. Children of overseers and slaves were often freed and educated in Europe; caste of light-skinned freemen created.

1692 – Port Royal in Jamaica, chief British pirate stronghold, sank in sea after earthquake. Kingston built.

1697 – Spain ceded Haiti to France.

1713 – Treaty of Utrecht: Britain to discourage instead of encourage pirates. Britain to have monopoly of supplying slaves to Spanish colonies.

by 1720 – Jamaica had become chief sugar producer.

by 1737 – Galleon convoy system abolished.

by 1730 – Liverpool had replaced Bristol and London as centre of slave trade.

by 1780 – 30,000 slaves annually carried to West Indies in ships built in Liverpool. Triangular trade: to West Africa with cotton goods, guns, gin, etc: to West Indies with slaves: to Liverpool with sugar.

from 1500–1807 – Four-and-a-half million slaves had been sold in the West Indies. One-and-a-half million were alive at the end of period.

by 1780 – Haiti had become chief sugar producer.

1791 – Haitian revolution followed French Revolution.

1797 – Spain gave Trinidad to England.

1807 – British parliament ended slave trade.

1838 – British parliament ended slavery in colonies.

1848 – French ended slavery in colonies.

1876 – Puerto Rico ended slavery.

1886 – Cuba ended slavery.

1838–65 – Jamaica ruled locally by white assembly. Many slaves became self-supporting small farmers and traders. Sugar declined due to competition from Cuba and sugar beet.

1844 – Crown recruited indentured labour from Calcutta and Madras for Trinidad sugar estates. Workers housed in barracks and paid five shillings weekly.

Ex-slaves moved into towns: gradually East Indians bought land.

1865 – Islands became crown colonies. Bananas, aluminium, bauxite encouraged in Jamaica. Oil asphalt in Trinidad.

1915–34 – Haiti occupied by United States.

1946 – Guadeloupe and Martinique become *départements* of France.

1958 – British parliament gave self-rule to West Indian Federation.

1959 – Cuban revolution.

1962 – West Indian Federation gave self-rule to Jamaica, Trinidad, etc.